British Government: The Triumph of Elitism

To Alex

British Government: The Triumph of Elitism

A study of the British political tradition and its major challenges

A P Tant
University of Plymouth

Dartmouth

Aldershot · Brookfield USA · Hong Kong · Singapore · Sydney

Published by
Dartmouth Publishing Company Limited
Gower House
Croft Road
Aldershot
Hants GU11 3HR
England

Dartmouth Publishing Company
Old Post Road
Brookfield
Vermont 05036
USA

A CIP catalogue record for this book is available from the British Library

Library of Congress Cataloging-in-Publication Data
Tant, A.P.
   British government : the triumph of elitism : a study of the
British political tradition and its major challenges / A.P. Tant.
       p.   cm.
   ISBN 1-85521-209-9 : $59.95
   1. Government information—Great Britain.   2. Official secrets—
Great Britain.   3. Freedom of information—Great Britain.   4. Great
Britain—Politics and government.   5. Political culture—Great
Britain.   I. Title.
JN329.S4T36   1993
306.2′0941—dc 20   92-36093
                                                                          CIP

ISBN 1 85521 209 9

Printed in Great Britain by
Ipswich Book Co. Ltd., Ipswich, Suffolk

Contents

Acknowledgements

My thanks must first go to my wife Jackie, for putting up with my paranoia, obsessive behaviour and absences during the completion of this work. I would also like to record my thanks to Andrew Currey, social sciences subject librarian at the University of Plymouth, for good humoured and comprehensive help, and to Elly Sample, who read and commented helpfully upon various parts of the work. Lastly, thanks are due to Carole Sutton in the Computer Centre, for much appreciated help regarding formatting and layout. Whatever faults remain are of course my own responsibility.

Introduction

In substance this work unites three major concerns. It attempts to establish firstly the narrow and elitist nature of the British political system, and secondly, the historical processes from which it derived its specific character. The third concern is with the historical and contemporary consequences of the first two points; in the system's capacity for self-perpetuation and self-defence against challenges from a contrary, participatory direction. In general, or at what we might term the 'macro' level, in examining these concerns the analytical value of the relationship between three distinct contexts is highlighted. These contexts are: the institutional framework; its underlying theory and philosophy; and actual political practice. The macro analysis also informs a more specific or 'micro' level of analysis. Historically, this is related to the failure of the challenges of nineteenth century Radicalism and the early twentieth century Labour Party. In the contemporary period, it relates to the durability of official secrecy in the face of the Campaign for Freedom of Information, and to the way in which 'Thatcherism' was aided by favourable rather than hostile ideological and institutional norms and practices.

In the case of neither macro nor micro analysis do I claim that the relationship between the three analytical contexts provides the only important explanatory factor. I do consider such to be crucial however, and certainly more important than is acknowledged within much of the established work on the British political tradition. Nevertheless, there is a third, intermediary level of analysis which, I believe, also contributes significant explanatory value. I refer to the need to take full account of the rôle of contingent and conjunctural factors in the relationship between macro and micro levels (see Figure 1.1).

Figure 1.1

Analytical Focus   Substantive Concerns

Macro : institutional framework ;
            underlying ideas ;
            actual political practice.

Intermediary : contingent and conjunctural
                     factors in relationship
                     between macro and micro.

Micro : failure of Radicalism ;
           failure of Socialism ;
           failure of FOI.

Elitism of British
political tradition ;
historical processes
accounting for it ;
its consequences.

Related concern :
critical assessment of
'orthodox' analysis of
both the evolution of
the British constitution
& official secrecy / FOI

The proponents of freedom of information (FOI), and those contributing to the debate surrounding the relative merits of FOI and official secrecy, quite often seem unaware of the importance of these relationships. Neither, in my view, are such relationships fully explored in much of the existing work on the British political tradition. Thus, in addition to the three major concerns identified at the outset, another will be to assess critically the traditional approach to the analysis of both British political and constitutional history, and to the matter of official secrecy. Though I would not describe such as a 'minor' concern, it is something of a byproduct of the three major ones.

The general approach taken here thus relates historical and contemporary concerns to each other, hopefully in a lucid and complimentary manner. I believe that the nature of British government is best analysed and explained via the above relationships, as are the problems of those campaigning for FOI best explained and understood via such an appreciation of the elitist nature of British government. The basic argument upheld here is that traditional British governmental practices are underpinned by (pre-democratic) elitist concepts of representation, and the notion of 'responsible' (rather than responsive) government. But the reforms advocated by supporters of FOI in the contemporary period - as with the earlier challenges to the British political tradition represented by Radicals and the early Labour Party - are underpinned by popular participatory and accountable concepts of democratic government. There is therefore a fundamental conflict between the two, which is seen in the severe practical difficulties encountered by the would-be reformers.

The importance of the relationship between the three analytical contexts is seen in the uneven struggle between on the one hand the status quo, with mutually supportive institutions, underlying theory and the political and governmental conventions derived from these, and on the other, the participatory challenge necessarily made within such a hostile environment. The progress of any policy proposal or constitutional reform at odds with the representational and governmental theories underpinning the traditional operation of British govenment, is thereby inhibited at best. Any proposed new practice which conflicts fundamentally with the status quo must either supersede the existing theory and practice, and in so doing create a new, appropriate, institutional framework, or be itself defeated. The latter is the norm, but such a defeat is not necessarily either total or an immediate consequence of the challenge. Often it is accomplished through a subtle and protracted process of incorporation/assimilation. Nevertheless, such a process of 'constitutionalization' does see the challenge effectively disarmed.

This hypothesis is examined against a consideration of the major constitutional developments from Absolute Monarchy to the present. As will be shown, the norm throughout the British political tradition is one of continuities between Old Tory, Old Whig, Liberal and Liberal-Democratic constitutional forms, with the institutional framework of modern British government coming to be underpinned by a synthesis of Liberal/Conservative perspectives. On the other hand, nineteenth century Radicalism, the Labour Party of the 1920s and '30s, and the contemporary Campaign for Freedom of Information, have each represented a challenge to such continuities, and to the established theory, institutions and practices of British government which uphold them. In each of these cases however, the challenge was first undermined and then disarmed through just the kind of 'constitutionalization' process outlined above. In studying these cases, it further becomes apparent that not only does the relationship between the traditional concepts of representation and government influence crucially the outcome of proposed reforms, but the very awareness of this can also shape the nature of the demands of the would-be reformers. Hence 'the triumph of elitism'.

The layout of the book

Chapter One introduces the issue of official secrecy, and demonstrates the inadequacy of seeing the debate around official secrecy and FOI through a contemporary perspective only. The chapter begins by identifying and summarizing a general stance apparent in many publications of recent years, and goes on to undertake a critique of one of the best, namely

K.G. Robertson's *Public Secrets*. Looking at Robertson's work provides a stark example of how things have changed from the early 1980s to the early '90s. But also, Robertson goes beyond the typical (condemnatory) description of official secrecy and the demands of its critics, to offer a very creditable explanatory comparative analysis of the variations in the levels of governmental secrecy between Britain, Sweden and the USA. Robertson's mode of analysis and explanatory framework are interesting and useful. His argument that the level of government secrecy is related to the nature of the structure of political power and authority is broadly correct in my view. But in its specifics, I think Robertson's position is faulted by his concentration upon the formal, structural/institutional conditions obtaining in each country. I am also critical of the 'top-down' perspective in relation to concepts of representation and government, through which his consideration of British political history is undertaken. Nevertheless (and despite his conclusions proving far wide of the mark), Robertson bridges the gap between the purely contemporary and the historical perspective which I consider to be necessary to provide an adequate means of analysis.

The chapter considers the inherent difficulties involved in any attempt to gain a proper understanding and explanation of such matters of interest to both Robertson and myself. Indeed, I believe that any such attempt must take full account of both the theoretical complexities within a particular, micro issue, such as the challenge of FOI, and those within the macro nature of the British political tradition. The first point is therefore taken up in the remainder of Chapter One, and the second in Chapters Two and Three. As has already been indicated, the importance to the analysis of the relationships between the two forms the general analytical approach throughout, but Chapter Four demonstrates its relevance in regard to the constitutionalization of the Labour Party, and Chapter Five in regard to the modern practice of the Campaign for Freedom of Information, and also in relation to the 'Thatcherite' period. In this sense, Chapter Five shows that differential outcomes follow from whether a political project conflicts with, or corresponds to, the basic nature of the British political tradition; the Campaign for Freedom of Information being 'constitutionalized', 'Thatcherism' representing the reassertion of the British political tradition.

The second part of Chapter One thus builds upon the chapter's initial considerations, with close analysis of some of the parliamentary debates around official secrecy and FOI. In relation to the question as to why, despite the discrediting of official secrecy and vigourous campaigning for FOI, such bills have at best only reached the statutes in a form very different to that originally put forward by FOI Campaigners themselves, I make a significant analytical distinction between two qualitatively different aspects of the demands within FOI bills. These I define as 'freedom of information', and 'open government' demands. The former mainly concerns non-political 'citizen interest' related material nevertheless held by government departments and public authorities. The latter refers to overtly political/governmental matters of policy, policy making and implementation. The early FOI bills included 'open government' as well as 'freedom of information' demands, the two being intertwined within the bills' clauses. This meant that although 'freedom of information' is substantively constitutionally acceptable, its non-differentiation from 'open government' demands - themselves in conflict with the very nature of British government - led to government hostility and defeat. The chapter concludes that either the Campaign for Freedom of Information must transform the elitist nature of British government or be itself transformed by it.

The conflicting views of democratic government upheld by each side are by now quite clear; supporters of FOI stressing popular participation and accountability, and defenders of the status quo the need for strong, decisive and 'responsible' rather than responsive government. The seemingly self-perpetuating 'Executive dominance', through which the participatory challenge of FOI was seen in Chapter One to have been held at bay, provides the incentive for deeper analysis of the British political tradition; not least to investigate whether such challenges - and defeats - have occurred before. Thus Chapters Two and Three take up these tasks. A great many works were utilized here, among them the two classics of the 1960s and '70s, Anthony Birch's *Representative and Responsible Government* (1979), and Samuel Beer's *Modern British Politics* (1982). The more recent and greatly impressive three volume *The British Political Tradition* (1983) from W H Greenleaf, is also utilized. Unlike many British government texts, which tend to be descriptive rather than analytical, and to concentrate upon institutions rather than ideas, these offer some valuable insights into how ideas about the concept of political representation and the role of government underpin concrete political institutions and practices. Better still in this respect (though still not without criticism), is what can probably be described as having become the standard work on British government over the last five years or so, namely John Dearlove and Peter Saunders' *Introduction to British Politics* (1984).

As I have indicated, the historical consistencies in the theory of representation and government, and their institutional forms, are, in many important senses, more significant than the extent of their having changed. In fact, the role of governmental office, whether performed by the Monarch alone, shared by Monarch and unreformed parliament, or exercised by an Executive drawn from the reformed parliament, has shown a remarkable consistency despite the deep changes in the nature of British society itself over the period. It was government's task to weigh the 'particular interests' in the search for policy in the interest of the whole nation: government and only government was arbiter of the 'national interest'. This consistency saw the tradition of strong, centralized, independent and initiatory government sustained. Indeed, British political and governmental conventions, including the nature of the Executive's accountability to parliament, the nature of parliamentary representation, and that of the electoral system, all reflect and support the elitist tradition.

Although Birch, Beer and Greenleaf provide excellent raw material from which to analyze the British political tradition and its consequences, in each case I feel the analysis is to some extent limited by the generally apparent pluralist/liberal underlying assumptions. Dearlove and Saunders are particularly critical of other works' almost total concentration on the 'democratic' aspects of British politics and government. They are therefore less limited in the range of matters theoretical and empirical that they find worthy of close scrutiny, and include a critical dimension absent (most particularly) in the earlier works. On the other hand, like Greenleaf, they more or less begin from the point of the Whig 'balanced constitution', and the general approach is still one seeing the depth of continuities and strength of traditionalism throughout the evolution of the British constitution as something quite natural and virtually inevitable. Similarly, all this is still seen predominantly from a 'government-down' (to the people) position.

With the exception of the last point, there is in fact an interesting parallel here in some Marxist work, notably Ralph Miliband's *Parliamentary Socialism* (1973). Also emphasizing the elitism and traditionalism (as well as the class content) of the British political tradition, the constitutionalization of the Labour Party is thereby seen as a virtually inevitable consequence of the party's initial decision to work 'within' the capitialist system. In my view these two approaches are less distinctly separated by the nature of the analysis than by their attitude to the outcome; they are two variants of a similarly inadequate approach strongly coloured by hindsight. To properly understand and explain these developments requires that we forgo such hindsight, 'reproblematizing' instead. The analytical approach already outlined, taking account of the relationship between the three analytical contexts at the macro level, as well as the particulars of the micro level and the intermediation between these provided by contingent and conjunctural factors, is, I believe, completely appropriate to such a task.

My critique of the 'orthodox' approach to the analysis of British government and the British political tradition is therefore from the 'bottom-up' (radical democratic) perspective. Thus, I am most interested in the challenges to the status quo from this direction. For example, Chapter Three deals with political and constitutional developments from Absolute Monarchy to the Liberal era and the beginnings of parliamentary democracy.

Here I am greatly concerned with the question as to why nineteenth century Radicalism failed, in contrast to the established works which, to the extent that there is a question implicit, see that question as being 'why and how did Liberalism succeed?'. As a consequence of pondering such matters as the failure of Radicalism, a much broader concept of political culture emerges than is in evidence in most other works. It becomes more important as an explanatory factor. More specifically, a concept of political culture which stresses an 'active-inhibitive' role and function emerges, in contrast to the 'passive-continuous' conceptualization employed by those seeking explanations via continuities. The inhibiting force of institutionalized political culture - the mutually supportive environment of theory and practice expressed in contemporary institutions and conventions of politics and government - becomes crucial in explaining the failure of a challenge to the existing order.

This concept of the role of institutionalized political culture as inhibiting other than marginal change, is developed further in Chapter Three, which considers the growth of Collectivism. The chapter begins by assessing the nature of the British constitution at the turn of the century, and the analytical importance of the fact that Collectivism emerged within the context of a Liberal/Conservative political consensus, and grew without transcending that basic institutional framework. The implications of this are crucial, both in terms of future developments within the Labour Party, and in turn, in relation to the current 'free-market backlash'.

In the former case, as taken up in Chapter Four, the Labour Party's confusion and conflation of 'labourism' and 'Socialism' is important in the emergence of key assumptions regarding the role and purpose of a Labour Government. The Labour Party's theoretical weaknesses and the strength of the hostile institutionalized political culture are clearly related, and each is very important in terms of both the party's constitutionalization and (partially thereby), in Collectivism's failure to transform the Liberal/Conservative institutional context.

Thus a detailed analysis of the history and development of the Labour Party is undertaken, with particular attention paid to the process whereby the party's political and economic orthodoxies - initially representing another threat to the nature of British politics and government - came to be made compatible with traditional norms. Again the relationship between the three analytical contexts, and the 'active-inhibitive' concept of institutionalized political culture, is employed within this explanation of the Labour Party's constitutionalization. But in problematizing the emasculation of the Socialist challenge, as indeed was the case in relation to nineteenth century Radicalism, a number of contingent/conjunctural analytical factors are also identified. Radical theory for example, is shown to have been distinctly 'grey' in certain areas, lacking integration and internal consistency. Likewise, as indicated, similar flaws are apparent within the Labour Party's political orthodoxy and conception of Socialism. These matters are related to the consequent survival of the traditional institutional framework of British government, which is in turn also important in regard to both the failure of Collectivism, and the subsequent return to a laissez-faire approach under Mrs Thatcher.

Having closely examined the FOI issue in Chapter One, and undertaken a thoroughgoing analysis of the British political tradition in Chapters Two and Three, and its effects on the Labour Party in Chapter Four, Chapter Five initially examines the successes and failures of the Campaign for Freedom of Information. In similar fashion to the cases of Radicialism and Socialism, the Campaign can be clearly seen as another example of how a participatory challenge to the elitist British political system has been constitutionalized. The 'open government' demands in conflict with the underlying assumptions and actual political practice of British government were progressively 'filtered out' from later bills sponsored by the Campaign. This happens partly through the Campaign's 'self-censorship' and partly through government insistence upon such as the price for parliamentary time. In fact it can be seen that the whole strategy of the Campaign becomes dependent upon government's willingness to adopt and support its now much more limited bills. Thus, although it is clear to me that a number of important gains have thereby been made by the Campaign on our behalf, the price of such government support has been the abandonment by the Campaign of its more radical aims.

The remainder of Chapter Five is taken up with a consideration of the 'Thatcherite' era in regard to the foregoing. It is shown that in many important respects Mrs Thatcher's style of leadership as well as her philosophical orientation, represented a reassertion of the British political tradition; emphasizing strong decisive leadership, rejecting consultation and 'responsiveness', stressing instead the independent authority of 'responsible' initiatory government. Thus Mrs Thatcher was able to bring about radical change (from post-war norms) with a minimum of institutional innovation. She was simply willing to utilize fully the opportunities presented within the basic framework of British government to achieve her policy goals. The willingness to do this, as much as the policies themselves, marks 'Thatcherism' as a break with the post-war consensus.

In contrast to the participatory challenges analysed earlier (nineteenth century Radicalism, early twentieth century Socialism and the contemporary Campaign for Freedom of Information), the institutional and conventional 'environment' of British government can be seen to be favourable to the 'Thatcherite' project. Thus here we turn to the other side of the extent to which that same environment was inappropriate and unfavourable to the concerns and needs of the post-war consensus. The consensus was therefore another challenge to the British political tradition, which was more successful than Radicalism or Socialism, and which certainly marked a break from previous norms. Nevertheless, it amounted to only a partial departure from the norms of the British political tradition; the Collectivist challenge failed to transform the institutional framework - which therefore remained appropriate to a laissez-faire economic and political individualist approach. Mrs Thatcher's determination to overturn it has therefore been aided by the struggle being fought out on terrain favourable to such a project.

The analysis of Thatcherism as the reassertion of the British political tradition therefore aids the understanding of both the failure of Collectivism and Thatcherism's 'success' (to the extent that such could be claimed). Given that the first chapter established that official secrecy fits happily with the underlying assumptions and established conventions of British government, this approach also aids the understanding of the significant tightening of official secrecy, as well as the further extention of Executive dominance, which have been features of the Thatcherite era.

The brief 'Conclusion' to the work draws together the themes and strands of argument running through it as a whole. It summarizes what has been shown in regard to the nature of British government and the problems encountered in the attempts at radical reform, as well as the relationship of each aspect of the work to the others. Executive dominance today, given the (lack of) effectiveness of parliament's means of holding the Executive to account (ministerial and cabinet responsibility, 'question time', and the Parliamentary Select Committee system), has if anything been shown to be more pronounced. Given these shortcomings in British governmental norms and practices, and the desirability of rectifying them, the impact of proposed constitutional reforms is considered. The implementation of a Freedom of Information Act, proportional representation and a written constitution with a bill of rights would alter profoundly the nature of British government. Given that these things constitute European norms, with the increasing importance and impact of the European dimension, the task for proponents of these constitutional reforms here might well become a little easier. I for one sincerely hope so.

PART I
A Contemporary View

1 Official secrecy and freedom of information: contemporary issues ?

Introduction

From the 1960s and '70s, but particularly over the last decade, the use of official secrecy has been greatly criticized, with progressively greater support being gained for its polar opposite, freedom of information (FOI). A wealth of publications on these matters attest to this [1]. Some of these works take a largely comparative format, some focus mainly upon particular issues, case histories, or certain legal absurdities. A few combine several of these approaches. What they have in common is the view that there is an iniquitous imbalance between secrecy and disclosure within the British governmental, administrative and legal apparatuses, with an overwhelming dominance of secrecy in government and public administration [2]. It is thus clear that in Britain 'the government's privilege to conceal ... (is) valued above the public's right to know' (Michael, 1982, p. 18). Indeed it would seem that:

> the desire for secrecy is an automatic reflex in the executive. Britain's extensive secrecy laws ... were introduced to reinforce an already well-established doctrine and practice of executive secrecy (Ponting, 1989, p. 43).

Robertson (1982), is still amongst the best of these publications. In attempting to explain the development of, and variation in the levels of government secrecy in democratic political systems, his scope is far broader and his orientation more rewarding than most. In his comparison of three countries, Britain, the USA and Sweden, Robertson puts forward a hypothesis as to how such variations might be explained and understood, which provides a good starting point for the present work. However, Robertson procedes with an attention to detail unnecessary to repeat here. In summarizing his 'main argument' I will therefore enter into detail about the respective political systems only to illustrate clearly the thrust of Robertson's argument. Figures 2.1 and 2.2 similarly aid in illustrating the argument clearly but relatively briefly.

Following this summary, a more substantial section will be mainly, though not exclusively concerned with Robertson's position in relation to Britain. I will assess critically the internal logic of Robertson's argument, and also develop a more damaging criticism of his general position. In regard to the latter, although critical of what he calls the 'traditional' approach to governmental secrecy, Robertson's own focus is directly and almost exclusively upon the 'formal' constitutional conditions obtaining within each country. For example, following his definition of official secrecy as 'secrecy in government', and therefore related to the notion of 'office' and the duties thereof, the concentration upon the formal can be seen in the way Robertson operationalizes this definition. The extent to which a government achieves its aims via covert means, and/or activity by proxy rather than via direct public policy, must surely be an important aspect in any 'measurement' of secrecy in government. Moreover, the political philosophy underlying 'Liberal-Democratic' systems precludes such quite specifically. Yet Robertson does not take up such points, and his hypothesis certainly does not take account of such factors.

This is not to say that 'informal' political and governmental processes are ignored totally by Robertson. On the contrary, there are many instances whereby non-constitutional and extra legislative practices (e.g. Britain's 'D Notice' system), are shown to influence levels of secrecy. But where such an awareness is demonstrated in the text, Robertson's actual hypothesis takes no account of such 'informal' variables. This detracts from the explanatory value of his work. In a nutshell, he is critical of what he implicitly regards as a too theoretical approach, only to err himself on the side of a too formal empirical approach.

Having thus undertaken some important groundwork via Robertson, a more adequate consideration of the emergence of the FOI issue in this country, and the manner by which the early FOI campaign developed, will be facilitated. This historical chronicle will be supplemented by study of the parliamentary debates around the issue. These expose contrasting views of democracy held by proponents of FOI and 'traditionalists'. Given that, as will be shown in the chapters on the British political tradition, the nature of the British political system is markedly traditionalist, this provides the key to understanding the relative lack of success for the Campaign for FOI in this country; the FOI demand is contrary to the very nature of British government itself.

Secrecy and political systems

Robertson begins by pondering whether the variation among democracies in the amount of government information which is available to the public and to legislatures, requires us to doubt the democratic credentials of the less open political systems. This, says Robertson, is the 'traditional' approach; secrecy is related to alternative definitions of democracy and to 'rights', the 'right to know' for example. However, his departure from this tradition is acknowledged at the outset (p. 1), after all 'There will never be a democracy with all of the virtues and none of the flaws'. The boundary between 'reason' and 'politics', says Robertson, determines the point at which disclosure ends and secrecy begins.

Robertson therefore proceeds on the basis that it is both perfectly understandable and acceptable for democracies to vary in this respect. But he also seems to begin from the position that secrecy is 'political', whereas 'reason' is not. The former proposition should raise few eyebrows; of course the ability to 'withhold information and to judge the timing of its publication is part of political power' (Hennessy, 1988, p. 5.). But to treat as quite uncontroversial the idea that 'reason' and 'politics' are unconnected, if consistent with Robertson's concentration upon the formal, is nevertheless to display some political naivety. However, if secrecy is political, then study of the secrecy issue should tell us much about particular political systems. Thus we reach Robertson's general standpoint: via the specifics of particular political and governmental structures, the variation in levels of secrecy between countries sharing democratic characteristics may be explained.

The main argument

Robertson's 'main argument' is therefore that the degree of government information available to the public depends largely upon the structure of political authority. More specifically, firstly it is the type of authority that elected representatives have over officials -

particularly where officials are directly subordinate to a unified political authority - and secondly, the extent and clarity of government responsibility for state activity, which determines a given political system's level of secrecy. For example, the polar 'ideal types' forming the basic hypothesis of this mode of analysis would be:

System 'A':
a clearly identifiable group of elected representatives ('the government') are responsible for all state actions. A strong incentive therefore exists for this group to control the dissemination of information, because 'no actions will be neutral politically' (Robertson, p. 2). They would therefore consider FOI damaging to their interests. Their authority and consequently their (electoral) political future might thereby be undermined, both by the failure to exercise the control their position 'should' ensure, and by details of the factors influencing 'their' decisions becoming public and therefore the decisions themselves becoming open to question.

System 'B':
more than a single group of elected representatives with divided and limited responsibilities for state actions. Disclosure of government information will therefore not necessarily undermine the political authority of government nor threaten political futures in general.

To this general picture Robertson adds that where administration is seen as government's responsibility and is therefore related to a government's survival, then information bearing upon this relationship between government, state and citizen, will be likely to be subject to secrecy. There are therefore two key variables in Robertson's scheme of things; the motive to exercise control of information, and the ability to do so to the extent desired (see Figures 2.1 and 2.2).

In Figure 2.2 each of the three countries dealt with by Robertson is assigned a place on what we might call the 'Robertson scale', with brief details as to why they should be so located. From this it would seem that Robertson's hypothesis is broadly correct. However, whilst this is an important contribution, in my view what is identified here is only the *basis* for an explanation, rather than the explanation itself.

Put Robertson's way, variations between countries in their extent of governmental responsibility, and in the nature and structure of their political authority, account for the differential levels of government secrecy. But isn't this just another way of saying that different types of *democracy* support higher or lower levels of government secrecy ?

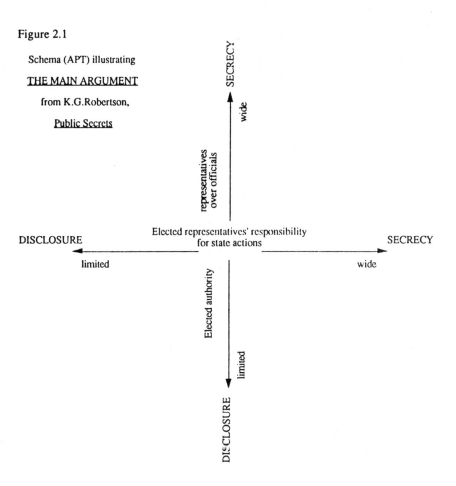

Figure 2.1

Schema (APT) illustrating

THE MAIN ARGUMENT

from K.G.Robertson,

Public Secrets

Robertson's insistence that a high level of secrecy does not necessarily detract from a country's democratic credentials does in fact carry a number of analytical consequences. It accounts for his prioritizing of the 'micro' (secrecy) over the 'macro' (democracy) for example. More importantly, it sees a similar neglect of the macro as with that of the informal (in favour of the formal) already mentioned. Thus Robertson provides only the most cursory definition of a 'democratic' political system - one 'under which certain inalienable rights are preserved' (p. 17) - and simply states that the level of government secrecy varies among countries 'generally acknowledged to be democratic' (p. 1). Further, since Robertson's 'case studies', Britain, Sweden and the USA, vary as greatly in the (macro) nature of their Liberal-Democratic forms as in their (micro) levels of government

Figure 2.2

THE TWO VARIABLES - and the three countries
(Best read in the order 'Britain', 'USA' and 'Sweden')

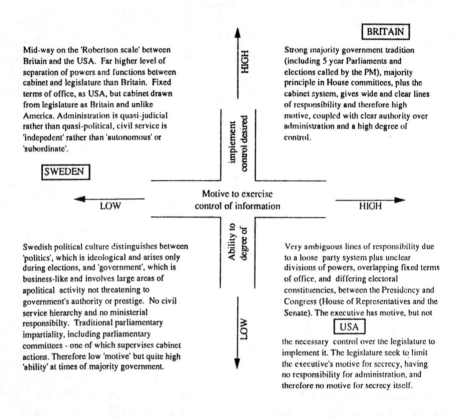

Mid-way on the 'Robertson scale' between Britain and the USA. Far higher level of separation of powers and functions between cabinet and legislature than Britain. Fixed terms of office, as USA, but cabinet drawn from legislature as Britain and unlike America. Administration is quasi-judicial rather than quasi-political, civil service is 'indepedent' rather than 'autonomous' or 'subordinate'.

SWEDEN

BRITAIN

Strong majority government tradition (including 5 year Parliaments and elections called by the PM), majority principle in House committees, plus the cabinet system, gives wide and clear lines of responsibility and therefore high motive, coupled with clear authority over administration and a high degree of control.

HIGH

implement control desired

Motive to exercise control of information

LOW   HIGH

Ability to degree of

Swedish political culture distinguishes between 'politics', which is ideological and arises only during elections, and 'government', which is business-like and involves large areas of apolitical activity not threatening to government's authority or prestige. No civil service hierarchy and no ministerial responsibilty. Traditional parliamentary impartiality, including parliamentary committees - one of which supervises cabinet actions. Therefore low 'motive' but quite high 'ability' at times of majority government.

LOW

Very ambiguous lines of responsibility due to a loose party system plus unclear divisions of powers, overlapping fixed terms of office, and differing electoral constituencies, between the Presidency and Congress (House of Representatives and the Senate). The executive has motive, but not

USA

the necessary control over the legislature to implement it. The legislature seek to limit the executive's motive for secrecy, having no responsibility for administration, and therefore no motive for secrecy itself.

secrecy, some firm justification for prioritizing the micro - beyond that the reverse constitutes the traditional method of analysis - would seem to be required. It therefore seems that rather than his conclusions deriving from his analysis, Robertson's analysis derives from his pre-stated and seemingly prejudicial conclusions about the relationship between democracy and secrecy. This is a point to which we will shortly return.

However, another example of the neglect of macro concerns is in that Robertson does not concern himself greatly with *why* the institutions, conventions and practices in a given country have come to take their particular form. Description rather than analysis characterizes Robertson's consideration of how such things occurred, and in general it lacks a questioning or critical edge in regard to the macro level. He thus does not really **explain** the development of such structures and practices adequately. A similar point can be made in relation to something already indicated. That is, in the text, Robertson shows an awareness of some (if not others) of the ways by which non-formal methods can be employed to extend secrecy beyond that which can be explained via the formal political and governmental structures. That such mechanisms do not figure in his actual hypothesis is one criticism. Another is that at the same time, Robertson speaks of the 'extent of government responsibility for state actions', and the nature of government 'authority over officials', when it would seem that the *public perceptions* of these things would more accurately describe his variables.

Finally, and bringing the points about covert activity and public perceptions together, Robertson seems not to appreciate that any type of government must to some extent be open to the use of informal 'illegitimate' means by which the formal and legitimate structures and practices are able to be circumvented. This is true even in relation to those structures and practices supposedly most prohibitive of secrecy.

The criticisms introduced here will be elaborated as each of these matters is taken up in more detail. But before moving to Robertson's work on Britain, let us first examine further the argument that democracy and secrecy are not incompatible.

Democracy, secrecy and Robertson

The argument that democracy and secrecy in government are not incompatible is in fact completely contrary to what proponents of FOI tend to argue; that government secrecy such as is maintained in Britain is severely detrimental to democracy. Robertson first takes up the argument in (limited) theoretical terms, and later seeks to substantiate it by examining the relationship between the emergence of official secrecy and democratic reforms in Britain, arguing that since 'official secrecy arose when democratic reforms were being introduced', this must seriously question 'the truth of the propositon that secrecy and democracy are in opposition to one another' (p. 41). To this end, Robertson also points out that in Sweden, FOI in the form of the right of access to government documents, came with the Liberal (i.e. before the democratic) state. As can be seen from Figure. 2.2, Britain on the other hand, is something of a classic example of secrecy tendencies on the 'Robertson scale'.

Robertson begins his consideration of the compatibility of democracy and government secrecy by asserting (in Chapter Two) that the dominant view of proponents of FOI is one seeing disclosure as a means. That is: if democratic government rests upon citizens' representation, then citizens have a clear interest in disclosure of official information. Government secrecy would therefore indicate government's inability to justify (at least some of) its actions, whereas a high level of disclosure provides a means to check, for instance, that those making decisions are actually those with the proper responsibility for such decision making. In this manner Robertson holds that disclosure provides a solution to a particular kind of problem, to be judged by how effectively it deals with it. This is again to prioritize the micro (disclosure levels) over the macro (nature of democracy) [3], and Robertson continues by examining this orientation against four ideological positions: the 'left'; the 'anti- statist'; the 'rationalist'; and, again as he puts it, the dominant ideology of proponents of disclosure, the 'liberal' view.

These four ideological traditions are in one sense united; within each lies a fear of conspiracy. For the left the premise is that all major centres of power in the capitalist state are determined to prevent the implementation of a socialist programme. Disclosure is therefore necessary in order to prevent a leftist government from capitulating to such pressures, and to ensure the protection of working class interests. The anti-statist fears the constant growth of government power. Vigilance is therefore necessary in order to prevent this, whilst checking and continuing to limit existing state power. The rationalist fear is that 'political' rather than 'rational' decision making may come to characterise government. Disclosure is seen as a means by which such ideologically motivated decision making would be made more difficult and therefore less likely. Each of these positions could be debated at length, but, as the dominant and most relevant one to our concerns here, I will take up the liberal view.

In this view, freedom is seen in terms of individual rights against collective authority, whilst democracy is regarded as the best system by which such individual freedom may be preserved. The ideal ('liberal-democracy'), is therefore a system which provides for both a form of popular sovereignty/majority rule, and the protection of individual and/or 'civil' rights. In this context government secrecy raises the suspicion that government is overstepping the boundary between its proper and legitimate role, and the private domain of the individual; disclosure is therefore necessary for individual self development. But it is important to remember that democracy is seen not in terms of social justice, but rather as the means of freedom from unwarranted political power and restraint.

By this route - that disclosure is not directly related to democracy - Robertson opens the argument that secrecy in not necessarily opposed to democracy. But examination of this argument shows it to rest on an assumption, and also to involve a paradox. The assumption is that if disclosure is the solution to particular problems, then the absence of disclosure signifies that these problems - suspicions that government is overstepping properly drawn boundaries for example - have not arisen. Although Robertson does not explicity connect his theoretical discussion in Chapter Two with his empirical study of Britain in Chapters Three and Four, it is clear that he does adhere to this assumption. His argument is that until relatively recently, such problems as would require disclosure were not widely believed to exist in Britain, and as they have come to prominence, so have calls for FOI. So in terms of the rest of Robertson's work, this assumption is consistent. Yet Robertson's own work actually demonstates that even though FOI is a comparatively recent demand, official secrecy has been abused by governments almost from its inception. So rather than that such problems have not existed in Britain, here is another example of the importance of public perceptions rather than realities. My own argument is moreover that the elitist nature of the British political system supports official secrecy and is opposed to FOI. Robertson's reluctance to take up the macro argument - that there are greater and lesser democratic forms of government - obscures this.

This is in fact related to the paradox referred to, which is in that if we see disclosure as the solution to government 'stepping over the boundaries', this, as outlined, is very much the liberal view of democracy and disclosure. But what is absent from Roberson's account is that the view of democracy which is compatible with secrecy is also a liberal view. The former is the liberal view from the standpoint of the individual under government; the suspicion that secrecy evidences the assertion of collective authority over individual rights and freedoms. The latter sees the picture from the standpoint of the representative *in* government: 'parliamentarism'. In this view both MP and government must be free to take decisions 'on behalf' of those said to be represented, in what they consider - through superior position/knowledge/expertise/judgement - to be their best interests. Thus the ordinary person need not know, indeed would probably misunderstand the relevance and importance of, sophisticated details of policy. In fact FOI could be seen as a positive hindrance to 'democracy' in this view of 'responsible' government.

These points will be taken up at greater length in the consideration of the British political tradition (see Chapters Two and Three), but we can already see their significance in relation to Robertson's argument about democracy and secrecy in Britain and Sweden. That is, since Sweden had FOI before democracy, it can be said to have been a consequence of the liberal rather than the democratic state. Similarly, since official secrecy arose in Britain alongside democracy, for Robertson, FOI is not necessarily related to democracy. But surely all this really shows is that FOI is underpinned by liberal views, and, though in different ways, so too are the forms of democratic government existing in Sweden, the USA and Britain. What begs exposure however, is why different aspects of these liberal views, and therefore different types of institutions, structures and political practices arising from them, came to be emphasized in each country. Hence, the concern, in the present work, with such an explanation in relation to Britain.

However, to return to Robertson, having introduced the argument as to the parallel developments of official secrecy and democratic reforms in Britain, he subsequently undertakes a closer analysis of these. Indeed Robertson provides an excellent exposition of how what I will argue is a particularly narrow and elitist concept of democracy and the role of governmental office (not that Robertson acknowledges such), came to be enshrined within the traditional constitutional norms of British government. I will attempt here to briefly but faithfully reproduce this exposition, as well as to assess its validity, and to also point out where clear contrasts arise in relation to the Swedish and US systems. First however, the context within which these developments emerged must be considered.

Traditionalism in British politics and government

Robertson's theme in Chapter Three is that there are certain central planks of British politics and government which have, until recently, gone virtually unquestioned. These are: the sovereignty of parliament; the oppositional nature of politics; and ministerial responsibility. Throughout the chapter Robertson holds, correctly in my view, that the level of secrecy in Britain is a consequence of these definitive characteristics of British government. To this end he also points out that the attack upon secrecy comes at the very time when these features of the British sysem are themselves increasingly criticized. The chapters on the British political tradition will explore fully the nature and context of these conventions, but each will first be considerd briefly here.

The sovereignty of the British parliament is evidenced in that there is no matter upon which parliament cannot legislate, and no parliament can be bound by a predecessor. This is quite unlike the situation in Sweden and the USA, where the scope of legislation is limited by written constitutions which cannot be changed by simple legislative majority. Also unlike Sweden and the USA, British courts have no right to review legislation or to declare it unlawful or unconstitutional. In the traditional and still dominant view, the British parliament must not be subservient to any other body, as neither must any of its members. Thus each parliament is sovereign, and open only to influence, and even this is true to a lesser degree than in either the Swedish or US legislatures.

All of the above evidences the characteristic hostility, in the British tradition, to extra parliamentary bodies. In this country the definition of democracy came to be seen in terms of the elimination of outside interference in the deliberations and activities of parliament: parliamentary democracy. As Robertson indicates and as will be elaborated in Chapter Two, this is traditionally and historically associated with the limitation and then removal of the political and governmental powers of the Crown. So in the British context, parliament has come to be seen as virtually the sole representative institution of democracy. Only the government, which, as in Sweden but unlike the USA, is drawn from the legislature, is said to represent the 'national interest' and the 'public good'. Thus no other interest can legitimately oppose the government, and politics is focused upon the task of winning the legitimate authority of government to determine the national interest and act upon it in making and implementing public policy. 'Democracy' has thus not traditionally been defined as implying the participation of extra parliamentary functional or interest groups, which would thereby acquire rights, statutory or conventional, to government information. The release of official information is therefore a matter of governmental discretion, as determined 'by the government's perception of its rights and duties as the sovereign authority and not by consideration of the rights of extra parliamentary interests in a pluralist democracy' (Robertson, p. 23).

With regard to the oppositional nature of politics, Robertson first emphasizes the fact that the electorate's ability to influence the actions of (a prospective/incoming) government depends upon their being offered a clear choice between contrasting and opposing political programmes. He then points out that, as with the USA but unlike Sweden with its system of proportional representation, elections in Britain are undertaken using the 'first past the post' system, whereby 'winner takes all'. That is, the candidate with the highest vote, though not necessarily a *majority* of the votes cast, is elected the single member for each constituency. The limited co-operation between Government and Opposition is a further consequence of oppositional politics, and these things together mean that in Britain responsibility for government actions lies clearly with the government in office. This is also the case in Sweden, but not so in the USA. Finally, Robertson reminds us that in Britain the survival of the government depends upon its party's support in the House of Commons. A high degree of party discipline is therefore necessary, unlike in the case of the US legislature. Party loyalty (among MPs) is also important in terms of an individual's chances of achieving a position in the government.

The above results in any information possessed by a British government being seen as potentially an aid to the Opposition's efforts to criticize and undermine the government, in their attempt to replace it and substitute their own chosen programme. Government therefore has a very strong predisposition to release only such information as will aid the achievement of its programme. This is perhaps also the case in the USA, but (even if it would like to) the government there does not have such control of information. In Sweden, since there is not the same connection between government and administration, this would not be seen in the same light, except perhaps at election times.

British norms, unlike those in the USA or Sweden, also see back-bench MPs largely unwilling to 'embarrass' a government of their own party when sitting on House committees. Thus the issues of greatest importance are often those least likely to see crucial information yielded. British oppositional politics therefore results in a lack of independent critics of government within the legislature, and a lower incidence of the release of information which the government would prefer kept secret. As Robertson points out, all attempts to broaden the base of information available from government, through for example, reforming the Select Committee system, have failed to revitalise the role of the back-bench MP, because they have failed to break the realities of party loyalty and discipline.

In Britain the civil service must also serve a House divided over even the basic objectives of government, as well as the means of their achievement. Thus civil servants must not be identified with party politics and particular policies; their required anonymity means that their advice to government must be secret. This is simply not relevant to the Swedish context, and in the USA it is more complicated. American civil servants must not be 'political' in that they are identified with a party or its success, and as in Britain, their neutrality requires their advice to be secret. On the other hand, the US constitution guarantees them the right to express 'opinions', so they are *able* to be identified with policies (and such often leads to their being selected by a President for political office). By comparison to the USA it can be seen that very clear lines of responsibility are the essence of Britain's elitist tradition of government and representative democracy.

In regard to ministerial responsibility, a concept absent from Swedish convention, Robertson cites its emergence out of the fact that state activities are carried out via both elected representatives and non-elected officials. Democracy is thus assumed to require a mechanism by which such activity is a consequence of the system of representation; 'officials' must be seen to be subordinate to 'representatives'. In Britain this has taken the form of a minister sitting atop the administrative hierarchy within each government department. Since the minister is an elected member of the government, the legitimacy of the actions of subordinates derives from their being under the minister's authority. The same is assumed in the USA, except that there ministerial authority is derived from appointment by the Presidency. Since the actions of all those in a department are said to be the responsibility of the minister, in the case of politically damaging errors the minister may feel compelled to resign. In practice this rarely happens these days, but the 'myth' of ministerial responsibility remains, and, as another Robertson puts it:

> It is constitutional fictions like ministerial accountability and parliamentary sovereignty that are invariably paraded in opposition to proposals to increase citizens' legal freedoms (G Robertson, 1989, p. 130).

However, the secrecy surrounding civil servants' activities is said to be necessary to preserve their 'anonymity', signifying their subordination to the minister, which in turn is said to be evidence of democratic control. The democratic process would therefore be at question if civil servants were able to undermine the authority of ministers [4]. If civil servants' views became public knowledge and therefore a part of the public debate, says Robertson, in the event of a minister rejecting civil service advice, the way would be open for a civil servant to appeal for public support for his or her views over those of the minister. The clearly subordinate position (in theory at least) of the British civil service to the political authority, a particularly powerful governmental office, is thereby justified via the best democratic credentials.

The role of the courts

Robertson points out that in the USA and Sweden the courts played an important role in the introduction of FOI Acts. However, another aspect of British traditionalism, largely derived from the absence of a written constitution, can be seen in that British courts lack both comparable powers and traditions to those of Sweden and the USA. Robertson illustrates this well, whilst showing that an examination of this aspect of the British context is nevertheless valuable.

In Britain, the doctrine of 'Crown Privilege' has weighed heavily upon the activities of the courts when called upon to intervene in a dispute between government and members of the public. Crown Privilege means that courts have, in general, no authority to disclose the workings of government if a minister considers such to be against the 'public interest'. The extent to which ministerial opinion is final, as against the right of court review, has of course been questioned. For example, the Duncan V Cammell Laird case in 1939 established two tests as to whether non-disclosure serves the public interest: with regard to the *content*, or the *class* of a document. The ruling held that the minister's decision was final where a signed statement held that the public interest was served by non-disclosure of a document falling into one of these catagories. However, with the 1968 Conway V Rimmer case two new principles were introduced; first that courts did have the right to inspect documents for which Crown Privilege was being claimed, and secondly, that claims of Crown Privilege based upon the class of a document were more likely to be questioned than those based upon content. Therefore some narrowing of the scope of Crown Privilege as a means of ensuring secrecy was achieved, despite the government's claim that uninhibited freedom of communication between public servants - which required secrecy - was necessary.

Such a narrowing of Crown Privilege was also evident in that government had, to some extent, complied with the pressure it had also been under to restrict the number of occasions upon which Privilege was claimed. One of the courts' arguments was that Crown Privilege '... is a more serious matter the more the activities of the state increase... unbridled claims ... (should not be allowed) to prevail when the state was the subject of so much activity' (Robertson, 1982, p. 32). The breadth and depth of areas of state involvement in the lives of the people, and the consequent need for government to be properly accountable, is a point often taken up by FOI campaigners. It would seem therefore, that the courts' self image as protectors of the public against the Executive evidences the liberal belief that the public do require such protection.

'Ultra vires', the doctrine of an action being beyond due authority, has also been the basis of court attempts to limit the power of the Executive. Such cases have mainly taken the form of questions as to whether: (a) a decision or action is within the powers of a particular authority; or (b) the basis for such a decision of action, judged by the reasons given, can be said to be reasonable. However, an action under ultra vires does not necessitate access to all information arguably relevant to the particular decision or action. Also, British courts have tended to consider only the law, rather than question the accuracy of the 'facts' upon which decisions are said to rest. Further, as most government actions have not been characterised as 'judicial', even the requirements of 'natural justice', that is, the right to be heard and to an impartial judgement, need not be upheld. In conclusion:

> The courts in this country have not sought to use principles such as ... natural justice to argue that participants in a dispute with government have the right to see all the documents held by the authority; they are, however, taking a more active role in 'protecting' the citizen from the actions of government by making the conditions

which are necessary for the lawful use of state authority more stringent (Robertson, 1982, p. 34).

The general non intervention of courts until recently is, according to Robertson, a reflection of the belief that British civil servants and ministers were not only incorruptible, but rational and responsible in their actions. This being the case, the best interests of the citizen were thought to be served by allowing the administration significant autonomy from popular accountability. However, echoing his stated position in regard to the other traditionalist aspects of British politics mentioned, Robertson argues that the extent to which an increase in judicial intervention can be identified, represents:

> a reflection of the belief that ministerial responsibility has ceased to be effective ... the civil service has become too large for its decisions to be overseen by the minister or parliament, and that therefore some outside body is necessary if the civil service is to be 'brought under control' (Robertson, 1982, p. 34).

Robertson's 'main argument' reassessed

The above lends support to Robertson's initial argument that the attack upon secrecy arose at a time when long unquestioned central aspects of the British political system had come to be challenged and undermined. Certainly, the civil service, in all its aspects, has attracted great criticism for some thirty years now. Similarly, the viability of ministerial responsibility has, over an even longer period, become the subject of much scepticism. Indeed the Fulton Report of 1966 virtually pronounced it dead in all but name. Parallel to these developments the critique of official secrecy undoubtably strengthened. But Robertson actually goes so far as to suggest that these trends would result in official secrecy being greatly liberalised, a conclusion now shown to be optimistic in the extreme, and in my view one more indication of his overemphasis upon the micro rather than the macro condition. That is, although the trends he identifies in relation to the secrecy issue are correct, he underestimated the integration of official secrecy into the very nature of the British political system; official secrecy is defended very largely in terms of its necessity for the maintenance of strong, effective and efficient government. The 'Thatcherite' period, during which Section Two of the Official Secrets Act was significantly tightened, bears this out particularly well, as is shown in Chapter Five.

It is certainly true that modern realities make ministerial responsibility impractical, although the public perception of its operation lives on. Thus, again, Robertson's 'main argument' can be said to rest more upon the public perception of the extent of government responsibility, than its actuality. Such a view is lent support by the fact that the supposed subordinate position of the civil service has been much challenged in more recent years, something particularly associated with ex-minister Tony Benn. Benn has argued (see eg Benn, 1980, and 1981), that through various administrative methods, top civil servants have actually subverted government policy intentions. His purpose in publicizing such charges has clearly been to change the public perception of the realities surrounding ministerial responsibility and the civil service. These same realities have been taken up, very entertainingly, in the BBC comedy series' 'Yes Minister' and 'Yes Prime Minister', which illustrate the ample opportunities open to civil servants to 'turn the tables' on their political 'masters'.

It was also an early ideological priority of Mrs Thatcher and her cabinet colleagues to change the public perception of the other main Robertson variable, namely the extent of government responsibility. They argued that the government cannot 'control' the level of employment ('governments cannot create "real" jobs, only employers can do that'). Similarly, it was argued that public sector pay is the business of public sector managers, and not government. Indeed government should not 'meddle' in such business and commercial matters. Further, unemployment and recession were argued to be largely consequences of 'international economic factors beyond the control of government'. Such arguments represent clear attempts to narrow, in the public perception, the scope of government reponsibility. Whether or not the popular perception and the reality are actually the same in a given instance, and whether the extent of government responsibility *should* be reduced, are irrelevant for our purposes here. The point is that it is the public perception of these things which determines electoral fortunes, which suggests that this is the true basis for Robertson's variables.

Secrecy and the nature of British democracy

In looking closely at 'The development of official secrecy in Britain' (Chapter Four), Robertson develops further the argument that since official secrecy in Britain arose with democratic reforms, the proposition that secrecy and democracy are antagonistic is effectively countered. As he puts it, in Britain secrecy became 'one of the mechanisms used to enhance the control of elected representatives over unelected administrators' (p. 34). By contrast, autonomy of administration is a major factor in explaining the openness of Swedish government, says Robertson. It is therefore quite significant that in the British case the period from 1830 to the 1870s saw the loss of civil service autonomy. The same period also saw government control of state papers established, indicating the loss of autonomy by individual members of present or past governments, and acceptance that such individuals only hold official papers in trust; they belong to government office. The 'unauthorised' release, and publication in the press of official information had caused nineteenth century British governments much concern. Such 'leaks' had been supplemented by the publication of correspondence to and from ministers and diplomats, and public statements from civil servants:

> The government response to these events was related to the doctrine of ministerial responsibility, the development of a permanent civil service staffed by 'officials', and the rise of political parties as the main instrument of parliamentary authority. By the 1870s the government had established that civil servants were not individually responsible for what they said or did, and that the House could not hold civil servants directly responsible for their actions (Robertson, 1982, p. 51).

A Treasury minute of 1873 is significant in relation to these developments. It relates to the 'premature disclosure of official documents', and although it does not refer to espionage but instead specifically mentions the press, it warns that dismissal of a culprit would result wherever possible. As Robertson points out it thus appeals to the ethics of officials as anonymous bureaucrats, and is clear evidence of the move in this direction. The trend is continued with another minute published in 1875. This points out that in the event of leaks, those with known links with the press may be under suspicion, and if found to be responsible, will be dismissed. A further minute, published in 1884, spells out clearly for the first time the nature of the offence which will be grounds for dismissal, namely, 'publication, without authority, of official information'. The generally broad and ambiguous wording of this minute - with for example no distinctions made regarding the degree of danger or harm which an unauthorised disclosure may entail - anticipates the nature of subsequent Official Secrets Acts.

Robertson gives a wealth of detail about the background to both the 1889 and the 1911 Official Secrets Acts, all of which supports his contention that a government campaign was waged to stop leaks and generally restrict access to official information. Rather than being anti-democratic, says Robertson, this campaign signifies that the view of democracy held by government required that the 'traditional' civil service view of itself as part of government must be ended. The civil service's role thus 'became that of adviser, not participant' (p. 44). It must be separate from, and brought under the control of, the elected government. Official secrecy was part of that control, part of a given structure of authority: ministerial responsibility.

This is significant both in regard to our contemporary and historical concerns here. As will be shown subsequently, a large part of the parliamentary discussion as to how official secrecy could be liberalised is concerned with the need to ensure that such would not undermine ministerial responsibility. Robertson here indicates something seemingly unappreciated by speakers in these debates, in that the wholehearted defence of the one convention inevitably thwarts the attempt to reform the other. The second point deserving of mention here (even if Robertson seems uninterested), is the limited conceptualization of democracy implied by such a structure of authority, and requiring such mechanisms of control. This point will be taken up in the consideration of the British political tradition. I will say here only that it is clear that it is a view of democracy which legitimates the concentration of nearly all of the power in the Executive, very little in the legislature, and practically none at all with the people; a kind of 'retrospective' democracy at best.

However, it is also noteworthy that Robertson takes up the point that official secrecy deals with the *unauthorised* release of official information; it can therefore neither explain why those authorised to release information choose not to do so, nor would its abolition necessarily increase the volume of information available. The question 'why do governments choose not to release information' therefore has to be answered separately. But here Robertson is more than a little disappointing in my view. He says:

> the arguments which any government uses to justify a law   which prohibits   the   release of certain information by subordinates ... (are) likely to be regarded as convincing reasons as to why it should not release such information itself. If a major reason for the Official Secrets Act is that civil servants and ministers are so closely intertwined that it is impossible to have civil servants release certain official   information without this   leading to an involvement in politics, then it is also impossible for ministers ... (to do so) without this also leading the civil servant into politics (Robertson, 1982, p. 51).

This argument needs to be looked at very closely. First, Robertson sets up the Official Secrets Act as part of democratic control, part of a system establishing the authority of ministers over unelected administrators. Then, rightly, he says that this does not explain why ministers do not release more information. To explain this, Robertson moves to the position that if a government minister considers that information should not be released by subordinates, that minister is also likely to consider such information unsuitable for release at all. But this is surreptitiously to move from a view of legitimate authority within a democratic context, to one about particular categories of information itself.

In fact, as will shortly be shown, and will be elaborated in Chapter Five, many attempts have been made to define and differentiate between categories of information and their relative suitability for release to the public, as a means by which official secrecy might be liberalised in this country. Such has certainly been the direction taken elsewhere (Canada, Australia and New Zealand e.g.), in the adoption of a FOI Act. But British governments have resisted such a move, preferring (in the defence of ministerial responsibility) to leave such decision making in the hands of ministers. Yet this crucial distinction between whether official secrecy is to be seen as justified via a view of legitimate authority and political practice, or to protect particular categories of information from causing harm by their release, is lost in the above shift undertaken by Robertson. Also lost thereby is the relationship between specific information and political consequences. This is explicit in the 'particular categories' rationale but **hidden** in that of 'legitimate authority'.

The argument that ministers could not release information without civil servants being drawn into politics ignores this distinction between the two possible rationales of official secrecy, and the many attempts - successful abroad, unsuccessful in this country - to categorise information appropriately. I therefore find it entirely spurious. Again however, what is apparent is the narrowness of a view of democracy which would find the above acceptable and adequate; many would find this so elitist as to be contrary to any real sense of democracy at all. Section Two after all helped 'to maintain the convention that no-one outside the executive branch of government has a right to know anything' (J Cornford, in May and Rowan [eds], 1982, p. 37). Clearly this view of representative democracy merits the further study to be undertaken subsequently.

In terms of Robertson's approach, again a major problem seems to be that although explaining official secrecy in terms of the 'structure of political authority' fits well for his purpose (and avoids dealing too closely with the macro nature of British democracy), in order to sustain this position he has to avoid attributing to ministers anything other than such formal (and honourable) motives for their attitude to the release of official information. He therefore 'muddies the waters' by conflating the two separate issues identified above. However, having noted that this whole issue requires the deeper examination to be undertaken subsequently, let us continue with the assessment of Robertson's arguments in relation to the British case.

Robertson doubts whether 'spy fever', the usual reason given for the introduction of the 1911 Official Secrets Act, was the real reason. Nevertheless, Section One of the Act is of course 'clearly concerned with spies and not simply with the unauthorised disclosure of information by civil servants' (Robertson, p. 67). Also, most of the early prosecutions were under Section One and of German nationals. However, the position of 1911 represents the success of government efforts:

> to have a comprehensive Act on official secrecy which attached
> criminal sanctions to civil servants' leaking information, and which
> brought the press under the Act by making the receipt of such leaked
> information an offence, as was its further publication (Robertson,
> 1982, p. 68).

In this respect therefore, whatever the real motivation, government had now achieved a long coveted goal.

In 1912 the Services, Press and Broadcasting Committee was formed, in order to institute voluntary co-operation between media and government regarding the publicity of defence matters. The government was concerned that all information finding its way into journalistic hands, whether 'authorised' or not, should be subject to a specific government interpretation as to whether publication would be against the public interest. This is consistent with what we will see to be the traditional view that it is government's role - and only that of the government - to determine the national interest. Thus 'D' notices (issued by the SPBC), although not formally obligatory, and of themselves carrying no penalty for non-observance, do widen the potential for government control of information even beyond that of the Official Secrets Act. The government 'has a method of influencing the press in secret and without having to pass a censorship law whose use would then be subject to scrutiny in the courts' (Robertson, p. 76). Indeed, some have described the intimidatory situation arising from the above considerably more strongly, Leigh for example saying:

> Unpublicised bullying beforehand is always a more effective
> censorship tactic than efforts at revenge after the event. Those
> inevitably have to be conducted more or less in the open, in a

courtroom, and be unsympathetically reported by the professional colleagues of the people in the dock (Leigh, 1980, p. 26).

Such covert and indirect governmental means of achieving desired ends do not figure in Robertson's analytical scheme, a criticism already mentioned. However, Robertson does point out that neither in the USA nor Sweden would the press be willing to accept such restrictions, indeed they would be unconstitutional. But this only takes us back to the nature of British democracy, or, as Robertson prefers, to the structure of political authority. It is within this context that the broad scope and loose definition of the Official Secrets Act, with the uncertainty in a given instance as to whether the government would undertake a prosecution, provided the press with the 'incentive' to co-operate.

In 1914 a Treasury memorandum relating to the production of official documents before Parliamentary Select Committees was issued, as an attempt to establish certain principles to be followed. Documents were to be refused on grounds that they related to war arrangements, as were some departmental internal memoranda, since they 'did not necessarily reflect the views of the department', but were only 'advice' or 'suggestions'. The argument that access would inhibit necessary communication was (and is still) used, and also, that revealing memoranda would put ministers in the 'intolerable' position of having to justify acceptance or refusal of such advice. Again, is it not a very narrow, elitist view of democracy which would regard such a situation as 'intolerable'? Likewise, the refusal of access to advice and suggestions circulating within a government department, to the proper parliamentary organ of governmental scrutiny, seems equally difficult to justify in any democratic terms.

In 1920 the Official Secrets Act was amended to include most of the provisions of the wartime Defence of the Realm Act, whose powers the government did not want to see terminated with the end of the War. The new Act was very broad and ambiguously defined. Its powers were 'potentially devastating in their impact upon civil liberties and political activity' (Robertson, p. 70). For example, the definition of a foreign agent under the amended Act was 'someone who is *reasonably suspected* (my emphasis) of being employed directly or *indirectly*, by a foreign power, to undertake acts *prejudicial* to the *safety* or *interests* of the state'. The interpretation of all the words in italics above is left to the state itself, with the courts not challenging government's views on these issues.

The government presented the amendments to the House as being a necessary defence against spying, to counter the more modern and sophisticated methods of espionage; 'the opposition proved bitter but ineffective' (Hewitt, 1982, p. 82). Despite the protestations as to 'the incursions upon ordinary rights ... which were thought to be inappropriate to a peacetime society' (Robertson, 1982 p. 71), by concentrating on spying and Section One, the government got the amendments through. Section Two was thereby broadened without the government having to justify such at all. This could therefore be cited as another example of covert action by government in order to achieve its purpose; in the face of real concern in the legislature about the infringement of civil rights, the government at best avoids the issue and at worst deliberately misleads parliament. There are of course many other examples of major decisions being taken without the issue being debated in any form in parliament. The original decision for Britain to maintain an independent nuclear weapons capacity, and the 'Chevaline' update of that capacity in the 1970s, are examples of such under Labour Governments. The decisions as to the siting of cruise missiles, and as to what parliament would be told in relation to the 'Belgrano' affair (covered in more detail in Chapter Five) are examples from contemporary Conservative Governments. That legislation can be passed which is of such great import without proper debate in the institution which, as has been indicated but will subsequently be far more fully substantiated, represents virtually the totality of British democracy, again shows the narrow and elitist concept of representative democracy in operation.

Robertson has some interesting things to say in relation to the civil service 'loyalty campaign' (which as always he details impeccably) between 1948 and the early 1960s. This campaign was quite different to that which took place in the USA, says Robertson, because in Britain it never became much of a public issue. This was because British politicians always claimed to be, and for the most part were popularly **perceived** to be (my emphasis rather than Robertson's), in control of the situation. That is, democracy in Britain was assured because there was no problem over the relationship of elected ministers to their civil servants. Also, by contrast to the USA, British governments were mainly concerned with actual damage to the state, and with potential damage only in a few specific instances. Robertson's view seems to be that this was because of the predominant and constitutional view of the British civil service as neutral, whereas in the USA loyalty to a certain 'way of life' within the civil service was seen as the means of ensuring that political decisions were 'representative' or in the interests of the people. In turn, although Robertson does not put it quite like this (see pp. 78-99), such evidences the belief that political authority there has passed to the civil service.

Robertson continues the chronology of events up to the end of the 1974-79 Labour Government, a time scale which includes, among many other things, the already mentioned Fulton Enquiry, the Franks Report (on Section Two of the Official Secrets Act), and the 'ABC' Trial (see following chapter). We are reminded of the book's publication in 1982 when he makes the point, clearly and quite forcibly, that both the Official Secrets Act and ministerial responsibility were (then) apparently sorely discredited. Indeed the former was so thoroughly 'blackened' that it seemed it must be scrapped (p. 74). His conclusion points to the (at that time) successive government reports and statements on the secrecy issue each more liberal than previously, and he considers that such trends would continue; the view that ministerial responsibility is a myth was growing, and the proponents of FOI were:

> following the pattern of argument to be found in America and Sweden; that open government is a necessary part of the system by which the citizen can challenge and scrutinise the actions of government, and that the legislature and the courts can no longer be relied upon to perform this function adequately (Robertson, 1982, p. 91).

Robertson's conclusions have proved defective of course; not only has the 'thoroughly blackened' Section Two of the Official Secrets Act survived, but the 1989 reform represents its tightening (see Chapter Five). Hence at a time when FOI 'is becoming almost a defining characteristic of accountable democratic government elsewhere in the world ... it is implacably opposed by the British goverment and its senior bureaucrats' (G. Robertson, 1989, p. 145). No progress at all has been made since 1979 towards the kind of Freedom of Information Act envisaged by FOI supporters in the 1970s. As regards Robertson's approach, although he acknowledges official secrecy as a consequence of the structure of British political authority (and therefore concentrates upon the discrediting of both as evidence that change is on the way), he seems to have failed to appreciate the extent to which that (micro) structure of authority is intrinsic to wider (macro) notions of the nature and purpose of British government. Again then, the durability of British 'responsible' rather than responsive government - the nature of British democracy - has to be the focus for such an explanation. The structure of political authority is very important to the understanding of a given political system and its specifics, but Robertson concentrates too much on the former and not enough on the latter. The relationship between a given structure and its theoretical underpinnings, as well as the historical developments stressing and maintaining certain aspects of the relationship, are also important.

We will therefore now turn to examine official secrecy and FOI in relation to these factors, beginning with a thorough examination of the FOI issue as it emerged in the 1970s. The two chapters which follow will provide an understanding of the British political tradition, necessary in order to expose the manner whereby the traditional concepts of government and democracy - and their institutional framework - arose. Only after such contemporary and historical considerations will the durability of official secrecy be properly appreciable.

Countdown to a campaign

The movement for FOI emerged in the middle 1970s, but can be said to have had its origins considerably earlier. The Radcliffe Committee Inquiry of 1961, instigated in order to review security after the Portland spy case, might be considered among its origins. Such spy cases and inquiries have, on the one hand, aided the maintenance of official secrecy, through its legitimation in relation to national security interests. In turn this has made secrecy easier to maintain in those areas not legitimately related to security requirements. But the questionable relationship between the two has also been a source of great criticism of official secrecy, which has aided the proponents of FOI.

In 1962 six members of the (CND) Committee of 100 were convicted under *Section One* of the Official Secrets Act, even though they had not been charged with anything relating to espionage. This was taken to the Court of Criminal Appeal and to the House of Lords, where the ruling was that espoinage was **not** a necessary part of an offence under the Act. This meant that evidence that the accused's purpose was not one prejudicial to the state was **inadmissible**; it was for government to decide what was prejudicial. This shows both the strength of the system at that time and the beginnings of its undermining, since the convictions prompted great criticism and outrage.

In 1966 the Fulton Inquiry into the civil service was critical of its outmoded structures and its failure to modernise. The Report also recommended a Committee of Inquiry to investigate the eradication of unnecessary administrative secrecy, including the possibility of revising the Official Secrets Act. The 'Biafra case', in 1968, intensified this pressure. A multilink chain of information passing had led to The Sunday Times' publication of extracts from a confidential Report from the British High Commission in Lagos. These refered to the extent of British military aid to the Federal Nigerian Government during the Biafran War, and they contradicted public ministerial statements on the matter. The government was stung into action, but prosecutions were undertaken only against some of the links in the chain. Again a public outcry ensued, and the case ended with the aquittal of all four defendants and the trial judge, Mr Justice Caulfield, concluding that it was perhaps time that Section Two was 'pensioned off'.

In 1971 the Franks Committee was set up specifically to investigate Section Two of the Official Secrets Act. A very critical Report was published in 1972. It recommended Section

Two's replacement with an Official Information Act, but more significant still was that no 'protection' was proposed for internal working papers, minutes, or advice offered to ministers. cabinet documents were to be covered however, because of the need to arrive at collective decisions. Thus, implicitly the Committee accepted the reality of cabinet responsibility whilst rejecting that of ministerial responsibility (more will be said of these subsequently).

Probably the biggest impetus to the emergence of the FOI movement however, was the 'ABC case', so called because of the names of the defendants, Aubrey, Berry and Campbell. Charges had been brought originally against these under Section One, but they were dropped and replaced by charges under Section Two. Though all three men were found guilty of the lesser charges, the judge gave only token sentences. The defence had stressed that the information collated by the defendants for publication was in fact already available elsewhere. This, plus the vigorous public campaign in defence of the three and the token sentences denoting a 'moral victory' for the defendants, served to badly discredit the Act to the point where it seemed it must be scrapped. Thus, from 1977 the FOI movement was well under way.

An Official Information Bill was introduced in February 1977, and another in July, though both fell through lack of time. Also in July 1977 came the 'Croham Directive' on the 'Disclosure of Official Information' (mentioned in more detail subsequently). In July 1978 a generally disappointing White Paper on Section Two was published. This was followed by the introduction of Clement Freud's Freedom of Information Bill in January 1979, with two government publications on 'Open Government' following in March; a Green Paper, and a report on disclosure of information in other countries. Both put what will be shown to be the orthodox view; that more disclosure could only be a gradual process in accord with traditional constitutional practice. Other 'general' FOI bills continued to be submitted to parliament, but none made any headway. Nevertheless FOI had been very much a live issue up until Margaret Thatcher's 1979 General Election victory, which seemed initially to virtually extinguish what had been a persistent and growing movement. Indeed in Mrs Thatcher's early years the likelihood of FOI bills even reaching the Commons' debating chamber looked very remote. This faltering was however partially reversed with the launch of the 1984 Campaign for Freedom of Information, the progress of which is followed in Chapter Five.

From the perspective of the present work, the early lack of success for the Campaign for FOI is unsurprizing. That is, it is my contention that official secrecy is completely consistent with the underlying emphases within the British political tradition, and that Mrs Thatcher's governments represented a reassertion of that tradition. These points will be elaborated and substantiated subsequently. What does quickly become quite apparent however, is that the concepts of democracy, representation and the nature of governmental office implied by FOI demands are opposed to those upheld within the institutions and processes of British government, something the remainder of this chapter will show. Since the traditional concepts are dealt with at length in the chapters on the British political tradition, the main emphasis here will be upon FOI. There is little doubt that the majority of parliamentarians do adhere to the traditional assumptions underlying this country's governmental conventions, which itself aids in explaining the difficulties encountered by the proponents of FOI. What also needs to be fully appreciated however, is that even where the traditional concepts are not accepted wholeheartedly by politicians, they are nevertheless implicit in the whole of parliamentary procedure.

'Freedom of information' and 'open government'

Within publications dealing with the FOI issue, as well as within parliamentary debates, there is some ambiguity in the use of terminology; the terms 'freedom of information' and 'open government' are often used synonymously, as with references to 'access' and 'disclosure' legislation. This may not seem immediately to be of much significance, but in fact a differentiation between two 'ideal types' of legislation, each appropriate to different sets of terminology, can be helpful for our puposes here. To illustrate this, let us first consider the generally favourable stance towards FOI apparent in most of the publications on the issue and (at first glance at least), in many contributions to parliamentary debates. This general stance might be summarized as follows:

1. Britain is a highly secretive state by comparison to other liberal democracies;

2. This is largely because of the operation of official secrecy;

3. Such a high level of secrecy is unjustifiable, because people have a right to know what their government does in their name. It is also a requirement in order that people are able to make a rational assessment of the competing merits of an encumbent government or a potential future government: a high level of secrecy is thus undemocratic;

4. The movement for FOI is an attempt to overturn unnecessary secrecy and thus right current wrongs.

Beyond the first, all of the above points can be questioned, indeed the second and third have already been questioned here via Robertson, and the fourth will shortly be shown to be more complex than is initially apparent. The 'orthodox' orientation thus implies a 'heros' and 'villains' situation at odds with the far more complex reality; finding clearly identifiable 'pros' and 'antis' is in fact far more difficult than would be imagined [5]. Indeed most speakers in relevant parliamentary debates have been at best ambiguous and often ambivalent. The following statement, which is actually from the late 1970s and the then Attorney General, Sir Michael Havers, provides a not untypical example of many such, particularly ministerial, statements even today:

> The area where secrecy and confidentiality should be protected must be clearly defined and limited to the extent where it is generally acceptable and compatible with open government ... the public interest requires that matters of defence, international security and cabinet minutes, to take just a few examples, may need to be safeguarded against public disclosure. But the public interest also requires that there is no misuse of secrecy to cover up errors or bungling or to avoid criticism (Hansard 1977-78, HC Vol. 951, Col. 1258).

Initially this seems a reasonable and measured contribution to a debate on the reform of the Official Secrets Act. But closer scrutiny of what is actually said leaves the reader with little if any idea of what course of **action** the speaker favours; neither is this at all clarified by Havers' subsequent statements in the debate. The level of generality employed also makes it difficult even to identify a clear attitude on the part of the speaker. For example, what would constitute 'general acceptability' ? To whom should the level of secrecy be generally acceptable ? If the 'public interest' may require cabinet minutes to be 'safeguarded', **when** might this be the case, and **why** ? How many other examples might there be of information needing to be safe from public disclosure, since those mentioned are 'just a few examples' ?

The first and last sentences in Havers' statement seem to suggest his support for increased public access to official information, but he then continues:

> The phrase 'freedom of information' is misleading when compared with, for example, freedom of speech or freedom of choice. Freedom of information means the extent to which the public should have the right of access to official information - that is the balance of public interest.

So as far as public access to official information goes, freedom means something different to that generally understood by the word, and has to be balanced with the public interest. This is still reasonable. But when the question of how and by whom such a balance should be struck implicitly arises, Havers' seemingly favourable initial attitude changes. He says for example, 'The first Freedom of Information Act in the United States became known' - he does not say by whom - 'as the Denial of Freedom Act', and for the remainder of his speech he denigrates the FOI systems of the USA and Sweden (see Hansard 1977-78, HC Vol. 951, Col. 1259).

This is no worse an example of the ambiguity and ambivalence than can be found in very many parliamentary statements regarding the competing claims of official secrecy and FOI over very many years. In turn, this indicates some difficulty arising in the attempt to identify clear underlying philosophies within these statements. It is nevertheless possible to identify such underlying attitudes by examining the terminology employed by speakers. For example, 'protected', 'safeguarded', and 'disclosure' are words which signify a legitimate right of ownership. If information is so owned by those in authority (or 'office'), it is therefore their prerogative to 'authorise' its 'release' to those under their authority, or not, as they see fit. We have already noted that official secrecy is directly related to such a view of authority, the use of such terms can therefore be said to indicate (at least implicit) acceptance of its legitimacy.

The importance of value-laden terminology is therefore clear, and it is in this respect that the importance of differentiating between 'freedom of information' and 'open government' terminology first arises. To make this more explicit, let us return to the early parliamentary campaign to replace Section Two of the Official Secrets Act with a Freedom of Information Act.

A great deal of the passionate and powerful argument employed in favour of the early campaign (as indeed is still the case to day), emphasized the injustice whereby personal files of one kind or another were found to contain irrelevant, incorrect or spurious information about their subject, who, not having access to such a file, was unaware of its contents and unable to challenge it or have it amended. An example of this kind is provided in a parliamentary debate by Jo Richardson:

> I read of a case where a single mother on Social Security happened to
> see her DHSS file ... It said that she was neurotic and that she
> needed father figures. It also criticised her political views. I dispute
> the right of a DHSS official to make such comments on the record.
> But at least such a woman should have the opportunity to see her

file, to challenge it and to have anything which is incorrect put right
(Hansard 1977-78, HC Vol. 951, Col. 1298).

There does seem to be a gross injustice represented in the above example [6], but Merlyn
Rees, recalling when he was the minister responsible for the Air Force, provides a counter
argument (see Hansard 1978-79, Vol. 960, Col. 2176). Rees told the House of a certain
RAF man who could not stand to live with his wife. So, at his own request he was
constantly posted abroad. He told his wife however, that the responsibility for this situation
lay with the RAF, which eventually led to the exasperated woman writing to the RAF and
subsequently to her MP. The MP investigated the case, saw the file, and therefore knew the
truth. Rees considers this an example where secrecy is justified ('The records of that man
should be protected'), and certainly some would agree that there is a case for withholding
this information from the woman concerned. On the other hand, should this man expect to
be so aided in his deception of his wife ? Does she not have the right to know the truth even
if it would be hurtful? In any case, we have two examples regarding the justice and
correctness of public access to official information; one used in favour, the other against.
But the rights and wrongs of these particular cases are beside the point for our purposes
here, which should be evident from another example.
Brynmor John, Minister of State for the Home Office in the last Labour Government, has
this to say (using both terms together) on 'the question of open government and freedom of
information':

> the aim of government should be to make available ... the reasons
> for decisions which affect members of the democracy in their
> everyday lives... we are moving towards making more information
> available, for example, at a highway inquiry, which will in itself
> inform members of the public when they make their objections or
> weigh up why a particular decision has been made (Hansard
> 1977-78, HC Vol. 951, Col. 1267).

Clearly such an attitude is favourable to FOI, but what is lost here is that differential
attitudes will exist regarding the release of official information dependent upon the nature
and substance of that information. Some information, for example that related to genuine
national defence and security interests, is legitimately kept secret, whereas information
related to things like the above highway inquiry need not be. The oft-stated criticism of the
old Section Two was that it failed to distinguish between these qualitatively different types

of information, but instead made secrecy the rule open to 'authorised' exceptions. Traditionally British government has maintained a distinction between 'High Politics' and 'Low Politics'. The former relates to central government prerogatives over such things as defence, foreign policy, balance of payments, public expenditure and monetary and fiscal policy. The latter relates to the administration and management of local affairs and interests; the organization and pursuit of the 'particular' rather than the 'national' interest. This distinction itself can be said to provide a basis for understanding government's differential attitudes to the release of official information.

A broad consensus was discernable during the 1970s debates, and still can be seen today, in regard to what sort of information government should release - either on demand or after a reasonably short time lapse - and what should not be generally available. No constitutional problems are posed for example, by public access to: the safety records of various motor vehicles; which factories have had health or safety related certificates withdrawn; a person's own school, medical or service records; or the reasons for the refusal of parole for a prisoner. These are Low Politics matters, whose release would be of great value to the consumer and the civil interests of individuals, without disturbing the basic nature of British government. This is official information with the emphasis on the 'information' rather than the 'official'. 'Freedom of information' is therefore an appropriate term to refer to the demand for this kind of information because it is primarily about individuals having access to information necessary to their civil and/or personal freedom.

Information pertaining to the processes of government itself, particularly in regard to policy and decision making, is quite another thing; the 'concensus' holds that this is sensitive and problematical, particularly in regard to central government's High Politics prerogatives. Yet such information is valuable in relation to the citizens' ability to make rational political judgements; its absence must therefore limit the ability of citizens to make such judgements. The availability of this sort of information would thus seem to be at least as important as that of the former category, but here we are referring to official information with the emphasis on the 'official': relating to governmental office. The demand for this type of information would therefore seem more appropriately termed 'open government', because it is about government and governmental processes, and requires the willingness of government to be open - as far as possible - about these.

Thus a broad and long-standing consensus can be identified which accepts that there is too much secrecy in British government, and that people should be able to obtain information which it is in their own best interests to have and which does not conflict with the requirements of national security or other High Politics concerns. But this consensus also holds that the proposed means by which this should be achieved should not conflict with present constitutional practice [7].

There is a certain irony in this position. That is, as was shown earlier, official secrecy arose out of the democratization of British government, and in particular, out of the convention of ministerial responsibility. Thus the consensus seeks to combat secrecy without disturbing the system which spawned it. This irony seems nevertheless to be lost upon speakers putting the case that proposed changes must be compatible with two traditional governmental conventions: ministerial (or individual) responsibility, that is, the doctrine of the minister being answerable to parliament for his or her department's activities (thus implying civil service anonymity); and cabinet (or collective) responsibility, whereby a member of the government, whether personally a party to a policy decision or not, is bound to support all such decisions.

To illustrate the implications of this attitude, let us consider the following exchange between the sponsor of a then current FOI Bill, Clement Freud, and Merlyn Rees, at the time a minister in a government committed by their election manifesto to repeal Section Two and replace it with a Freedom of Information Act. Rees argues:

> Ministers can and do take advice from a great number of people inside and outside departments [8]. I believe that to grant right of access to such advice - even after the advice - in the short run could alter fundamentally and for the worst the entire working of government... People ought to be able to give advice in confidence, in certain circumstances at least I telephoned a person for example, and asked him what he thought ... The person concerned knew full well that I would not put down what he said on paper and that I would not reveal his advice. But I regard his advice as important, because he operates in a subject of which I know little. If it had been known that his advice ... would appear a month later, I certainly would not have had at least his words of wisdom on this occasion (Rees, Hansard 1978-79, HC Vol. 960, Col. 2184).

In his reply Freud does not refer to the contradiction between this example and an earlier statement by Rees. Nor does he challenge the significant difference between weighing alternative 'views and attitudes' (see note 8) in order to make a decision, and the above example whereby one piece of advice is simply taken. This surely is not insignificant, given that it was advice from an anonymous (but probably non-elected) individual not accountable for the decision, and whom Rees admits has an expertise which, against Rees' ignorance of the subject, leaves open the possibility of bias being accepted as 'words of wisdom'. The questionable relationship of such a practice to democracy is also left unstated by Freud. Instead, in his reply to Rees, Freud simply says 'This is the sort of thing that we would look at in committee', which is implicitly to agree that legitimate problems for FOI legislation in this country are posed by such examples, and that proposed legislation must be tailored to suit the continuation of such practices outlined by Rees.

FOI and the British constitution

The irony of the 'orthodox' position that the proposed means of change must not conflict with traditional constitutional practice is therefore clear; the rationale of FOI is subordinated to its proponents' desire to show themselves and their demands as reasonable and 'responsible'. In fact the idea that British government can operate on principles of FOI instead of official secrecy without significant constitutional change rests upon reliance on a 'change of heart' by ministers. More importantly, the crucial relationship between official secrecy and the very concept of legitimate authority enshrined within the traditional conventions is ignored.

The FOI/official secrecy issue encapsulates a conflict over the nature of democratic government itself. On the one hand the arguments of the FOI lobby presuppose that the people can expect their (majority) will to be carried into public policy by government, which acts in the people's name and by their authority. The people therefore have a right to know what government does in their name, and why. It follows that government does not have the right to avoid the people's scrutiny, and does not have the right to withhold from the people information gathered at their expense and valuable not least in order to be able to properly assess the government's performance. Such is then a participatory and popular accountable view of democracy. Yet, as will be seen in the following two chapters, such views have had little impact within the British political tradition, with less influence still on the workings of the British governmental system.

The arguments used against FOI stress the need for strong, decisive, initiatory government. This requires the people's representatives to have a large measure of discretion and autonomy in decision making 'on behalf' of the people, and in their ultimate interests. In this view government is a specialized vocation; government must therefore be unfettered, free and independent, in order to make sometimes difficult and unpopular decisions in the national interest. Accountability to the people is retrospective; the government having to face periodic General Elections. Between elections government is accountable to the people's representatives rather than to the people themselves; government is accountable to parliament via written or oral questions and the Select Committee system. This is of course the traditional view, central to the operation of the British political system.

The constitutional location of this conflict raises the possibility of a compromise, providing for some of the demands of FOI whilst defending most of the traditional views and conventions. It is in this context that the differentiation between 'freedom of information' and 'open government', and the relationship of each to High Politics and Low Politics, become most important. That is, although some provisions and principles contained in FOI bills considered by parliament in the 1970s and early '80s were in conflict with the traditional institutions and processes of British government, a basis for compromize seemed apparent even then.

As said earlier, much of the criticism of official secrecy has been directed at the injustice and needless, sometimes ridiculous pettiness, of a situation whereby taxpayers finance the collection of information to which they are then denied access. Quite apart from this being seen as wrong in principle, the potentially great benefits of public access are also thereby denied [9]. Consumer interests as well as those of social justice are clearly enhanced by the sort of FOI legislation compatible with present constitutional arrangements, and all of the early FOI bills would have allowed access by individuals to this kind of information. They also recognised that for this to be a meaningful reality, a system of 'information offices', with an index or subject register of information held, would have to be established and maintained. This itself has been used against the implementation of FOI, being seen as 'formidibly burdensome' [10]. However, this argument ignores the fact that government currently employs hundreds of 'information officers' in order that the (selective) information that it wishes the public to know is transmitted [11]. Information officers can thus be seen as the positive side of existing official information policy (government 'selling' its policies to the public), as official secrecy can be seen as the negative side (inhibiting criticism of government policy). Together these represent a managed information system arguably detrimental to the interests of democracy.

Of course no government could instigate the publication of everything relevant to everyone, so beyond the setting up of information offices etc., the obtaining of information would be at the instigation of the individual; a system of access relating to 'freedom of information' rather than 'open government' is therefore implied. I should however reiterate that the basis for the differentiation is one of 'ideal types' of legislation. Not all information regarding governmental processes need be excluded under the 'freedom of information' characterization, after all, some such information is available even under the official secrecy regime (even if usually only after 30 years). More of this type of information could be released without undermining present constitutional practice, but unnecessary caution on the part of government and civil service currently prevents it.

However, I have said that early FOI bills would have allowed access to much valuable personal and other non-political information held by government departments. But these bills also attempted to go beyond 'freedom of information' and into the realm of 'open government'. If we take the 1979 Freud bill for example, in introducing it to the Commons, Freud made clear that he sought access to the advice and information available to the minister. His bill also distinguished between 'policy advice' and 'factual advice', 'the latter to be available without delay' (Hansard 1978-79, HC Vol. 960, Col. 2140). This distinction indicates recognition of the constitutional conflict posed by access to policy advice, in that it would break the cornerstone of ministerial responsibility, civil service anonymity, as well as undermining ministerial initiative and discretion in policy making. Such a distinction therefore represents an attempt - as with numerous exceptions and limitations to access in similar areas - to compromise between 'open government' and the traditional nature of British government.

So there were attempts to establish compatibility between legislative proposals such as Freud's and present constitutional practice even before the 1984 Campaign for Freedom of Information. Increasingly however, such attempts at compatibility have been characterized, not by a two sided compromize, but rather the filtering out of elements of 'open government' from the Campaign's demands. Ministers are clearly opposed to the participatory and popular accountable principles underlying FOI being allowed to challenge their High Politics prerogatives. In this respect, even the 'Freud compromise' represents a virtual capitulation.

To illustrate this, we need only remember that at present government 'manages' the public information system in support of its policy. Under a FOI Act such as the 'consensus' would permit, documents would inevitably be prepared with their publication in mind. The same potential for justification of policy would thereby open up as is the case presently, particularly since: we would be unlikely to know **anything** (officially) before key decisions are taken; afterwards, we would not know what the **alternatives** to such a decision had been; we would not know **who** had been in favour of an alternative, or for **what** reasons; we would not know **whose advice** had been influential, or **what** the nature of that advice had been; we would not know **what contrary advice** had been given, or **by whom**. Further, and perhaps most importantly, it is well known within social science that the concept of 'factual' information (likely to be available) is problematic. It is quite possible, by the manner and the order of the presentation of 'facts', for a decision to be made to appear eminently 'rational' (as opposed to 'political').

In fact, Mrs Thatcher's hostility to FOI soon led to the Campaign abandoning the whole aim of access to ministerial advice and information; the model bill published by the Campaign included these among the exclusions. Indeed the idea of a single broad FOI Act was itself dropped, in favour of a piecemeal strategy aimed at gaining a 'toehold' by which future and cumulative extentions of the FOI principle might be achieved. The outcome of this strategy will be considered in Chapter Five.

Conclusions

This chapter has examined both the location of official secrecy within the nature of the British political system, and the complexities within the examination of official secrecy and FOI. Both macro and micro levels of analysis have therefore been introduced. The macro level is taken up in detail in the following chapters on the British political tradition. Even from the initial, micro consideration however, the explanation for the relative failure of the Campaign for FOI in this country is better appreciable. In this respect the distinction made between 'freedom of information' and 'open government', and the relationship of each to High and Low Politics concerns, is particularly instructive. In short, 'freedom of information', relating substantively to Low Politics, is compatible with the traditional norms of British government whereas 'open government', particulary in relation to High Politics concerns, is not. The early Campaign failed to recognize the importance of separating these two qualitatively different sets of demands, with the result that government was hostile to the whole FOI package. The beginnings of a process of 'constitutionalization' can however be traced back to Freud's 1979 FOI Bill. Further, as will be shown in Chapter Five, the continuation, indeed intensification, of that process, has resulted in several 'limited' legislative successes for the Campaign.

This chapter has also shown that the philosophical underpinnings to official secrecy and FOI represent polar opposite views of democratic government; elitist and participatory. Thus, having taken up the micro issue here, in order to understand the deep entrenchment of central aspects of traditional governmental practice in Britain, and to better illustrate the nature and development of such elitist concepts of representation and governmental office, a detailed analysis of the British political tradition is required. The following two chapters therefore switch the level of analysis to the macro, in providing just such an analysis.

Notes

1. See for example:

Chapman, R. and Hunt, M. (eds) (1987) *Open Government*, Croom Helm, London.

Delbridge, R. and Smith, M. (eds) (1982), *Consuming Secrets: how official secrecy affects everyday life in Britain,* Burnett Books, London.

Hewitt, P. (1982), *The Abuse of Power*, Martin Robertson, Oxford

Leigh, D. (1980), *The Frontiers of Secrecy*, Junction Books, London.

May, A. and Rowan, K. (eds) (1982), *Inside Information*, Constable, London.

Michael, J. (1982), *The Politics of Secrecy*, NCCL, London..

Ponting, C. (1985), *The Right To Know*, Sphere, London.

Ponting, C.(1986), *Whitehall: Tragedy and Farce*, Hamilton, London.

Ponting, C. (1989), *Secrecy in Britain*, Basil Blackwell Ltd, Oxford.

Robertson,G.(1989), *Freedom,the Individual and the Law*, Penguin Books, Harmondsworth.

Robertson, K.G. (1982), *Public Secrets*, Macmillan, London.

2. This is however still by no means the full extent of the influence of secrecy in British society. Most of the professions have a tradition of, and still adhere to, conventions enshrining secrecy. Indeed membership of many professional bodies used to involve the swearing of an oath of secrecy. Secret societies go back centuries of course, but another example is seen in the well known commercial convention of the secrecy of the boardroom. To a large degree secrecy can be said to provide a consistent function; it is the psychological and sociological 'glue' which solidaristically binds together those 'in the know' whilst separating them from the rest of society. The extent to which secrecy in government is related to secrecy in other areas of life is an interesting, if not strictly relevant issue here.

3. Robertson is relatively uncritical of this view (particularly by comparison to the others that he considers, namely disclosure as a 'right' and as a 'value'),

4. Robertson stresses the necessity for this to be prevented in order that democracy be protected, yet there is evidence that such has failed to be upheld. For example, Mrs Thatcher's press officer, Bernard Ingham - a civil servant - seems often to have been engaged in just such undermining of certain ministers' positions via 'unattributable' statements to lobby correspondents (see e.g. Harris, R. (1990) *Good and Faithful Servant: the Unauthorised Biography of Bernard Ingham*, Faber, London). Further:

Thatcher, through Ingham, had turned the doctrine of collective responsibility inside out. In the past the rule which prime ministers had insisted upon was that the cabinet could argue strenuously in private, but that in public a united front must be presented. Thatcher used the lobby system in precisely the opposite way: cabinet discussions were kept to a minimum, while she reserved the right to make public her disagreements with her own ministers (R. Harris, 'Hard Man At No.10', *The Sunday Times News Review*, 2 December 1990)

5. This is not to say that such do not exist, only that they are less common than might be supposed. Enoch Powell provides one of the rarest of such, a clear statement in favour of the status quo:

> secrecy of deliberation and internal communication is always of the essence of all government, and therefore the attempt to invade it is uniformly self-defeating and results only in government erecting new barriers to defend its necessary privacy (Hansard, 1977-78, HC Vol. 954, Col. 539).

A good example of the contrary view is put by Eric Heffer:

> It is vital that the people as a whole, but particularly Members of Parliament, should know how governments reach decisions. I chaired a working party on the Industry Bill when I was a minister. We issued a White Paper. I see no reason why the papers presented to that working party, and the conclusions that it reached should not have been publicly available... (Yet) I could never say how we reached decisions, because one is not allowed to ... Why should not the general public know what is happening and how policy is formed? That is what democracy is all about. If the public are more informed of course they will challenge decisions, but what is wrong with that? (Hansard, 1978-79, HC Vol. 960, Col. 2170).

Such clear examples of statements against and in favour of FOI can therefore be found, but, particularly in regard to the former, rather than being the norm they tend to be the exceptions within parliamentary debates.

6. Since the DHSS was broken up and separated into the Department of Health and the Department of Social Security (in 1988), medical records have become available (see Chapter Five) but social security records are still unavailable to individuals for inspection.
7. This consensus emerged after many years and many debates on the reform of Section Two and the potential for FOI. The Franks Report may be seen as the starting point, and by 1977 it was 'the working assumption' that:

> once ministers have reached their conclusion on a particular major policy study, the associated factual and analytical material will be published, unless ministers have good reason for deciding otherwise (Brynmor John, Hansard, 1977-78, HC Vol. 951, Col. 1266).

Here then we see (1), the division of factual and analytical information from advice, with the former to be published and the latter not, (2), that what will be released will only be so after the decision is made, and (3), ministers' discretion in regard to release would be defended. Only the last point was contentious at the close of the 1970s, and it is debatable how seriously this was disputed. Although Mrs Thatcher's election in 1979 put such a consensus 'on hold', her departure from the Premiership and the wide agreement among Opposition parties in support of FOI, mean that the consensus survives. The other aspect of the consensus, that change must be compatible with present constitutional arrangements, is illustrated in the following statements:

> With regard to legislation to put the government under a statutory duty to disclose information on demand, we have not yet examined in depth how overseas experience might be applied to our own constitutional system (Merlyn Rees, Hansard 1977-78, HC Vol. 954, Col. 537).

> we need to see exactly how such a bill, if enacted, would fit into our constitutional pattern...I can imagine nothing more calculated to be destructive of the idea of freedom of information than a bill culled from other experience which does not mesh in well with our own pattern (Brynmor John, Hansard, 1977-78, HC Vol. 951, Col. 1266).

In my view we should seek to lay down freedom of information legislation whose provisions are particular to this country (Eric Heffer, Hansard, 1977-78, HC Vol. 951, Col. 1289).

before we go too far in this direction we should realise that any new methods for obtaining the disclosure of information must be dovetailed into (the) concept of ministerial responsibility. If it is not dovetailed into it, it will replace it. It would be a bad thing for democracy and the working of this House if the concept of ministerial responsibility for the decisions of a department were even lessened, let alone done away with (Ian Percival, Hansard, 1978-79, HC Vol. 960, Col. 2195).

Mrs Thatcher and her goverments if anything intensified the view that traditional arrangements must be defended. Indeed in Mrs Thatcher's response to the founding of the 1984 Campaign for Freedom of Information, in a letter to Des Wilson's, she argues:

I'm afraid I cannot offer any encouragement to your proposal for a Freedom of Information Act ... Under our constitution, ministers are accountable to parliament for the work of their departments, and that includes the provision of information. A statutory right of public access would remove this enormously important area of decision-making from ministers and parliament and transfer ultimate decisions to the courts. ... Ministers' accountability to parliament would (therefore) be reduced, and parliament itself diminished. ... In our view the right place for ministers to answer for their decisions in the essentially 'political' area of information is in parliament... I firmly believe that major constitutional changes such as your campaign is proposing are inappropriate and unnecessary (copy of letter sent from Campaign to author).

Such an 'everything is fine as it is' stance, seems quite typical of Mrs Thatcher, elsewhere eg. she says, '... the policies and discussions of the executive are under constant vigilant scrutiny by parliament, and ministers are directly answerable to parliament' (M. Cockerell, P. Hennessy, D. Walker, *Sources Close to the Prime Minister*, Macmillan Press, 1984, p. 25).

8. Yet earlier in the same debate Rees, in reply to Freud, had said:

> It is wrong to think that there is a battery of civil servants lined up to
> give me advice, and then I say that I shall not take one piece of advice
> but another (Hansard, 1978-79, HC Vol. 969, p. 2174).

The two statements seem contradictoty. But (ibid) Rees also says:

> I have the highest regard for the small group of civil servants with
> whom I talk a great deal. It is not right to say they give me formal
> advice or try to persuade me to do what I do not want to do. But I
> expect them to put to me all the views and attitudes which I need to
> know in order to make up my mind.

Again this is very different to the situation described in the 'phone call' example, and surely
we might ask why should we not know what are all the views and attitudes put to him in
order that he make up his mind? In fact it was in response to (or in order to avoid) just such
a question - 'we want to find out about the anonymous advice that ministers are given ...
(and) to have the information that he is given which causes him to make certain decisions'
(Freud to Rees, Hansard, 1978-79, HC Vol. 960, Col. 2173) - that Rees moved swiftly to
his story about the phone call.

9. Three examples will suffice to illustrate this point. The first came to light in 1974 and
concerned asbestos workers who were crippled and dying as a result of years of working
with the substance. The Factory Inspector had known of the danger, but had not warned
the workers because she felt that the the Official Secrets Act prevented her from doing so.
In fact this is not the only inhibition to people in such a position, they could also be subject
to penalties under laws such as The Factories Act 1961 for disclosing hazards to the
workers. A second example, from 1979, relates to motor manufacturer BL (now Austin-
Rover). Despite being aware of a defective hub assembly in one of their models they gave
no warning to owners. Following the disintegration of one such assembly, a passenger
was permanently disabled. Information about all such manufacturers' parts defects was and
is available in the USA, but not here. Indeed, BL appealed to patriotism in their attempt to
dissuade the BBC from running a documentary publicizing this particular defect (which
seemingly was successful in preventing a repeat showing). A third, 1990 example, can be
cited in relation to the case of Haemophiliacs infected with the HIV virus through
contaminated stocks of 'Factor H' (the blood clotting agent). The solicitors representing the

Haemophiliacs felt that, in pursuing their compensation claim they were unreasonably hindered by the government's refusal to allow access to certain Department of Health documents. Countless less dramatic cases could be cited, but the point is I think well made by just these three.

10. This refers to the stated view of the then Head of the Civil Service, Sir Douglas Allen, now Lord Croham. Extracts from the 'Croham Directive' to Heads of Departments will suffice to bring out the 'flavour' of the directive:

> During the debate on the Address ... the Prime Minister announced that it would be the government's policy in future to publish as much as possible of the factual and analytical material used as background to major policy studies.
>
> This change may seem simply to be one of degree and timing. But it is intended to mark a real change of policy, even if the initial step is modest...
>
> There are many who would have wanted the government to go much further (on the lines of the formidibly burdensome Freedom of Information Act in the USA). Our prospects of being able to avoid such an expensive development here could well depend upon whether we can show that the Prime Minister's statement had reality and results.

11. 'Information officers' are of course only one means for government to pursue this aim. There is much evidence of a positive policy of information management. Sir William Armstrong for example, as Head of the Home Civil Sevice, said in evidence to the Franks Committee:

> in order to have a positive policy of providing information, you have to have control. If the thing is uncontrolled you cannot create a policy, if an orchestra has no score you cannot get a melodic line through. So that led us to wish to control what was being said in order that we should in fact be able to say what we wanted to be said.

As cabinet secretary, Armstrong also became well known for his role in the Peter Wright 'Spycatcher' case, and particularly in regard to the view that rather than telling lies the government were merely being 'economical with the truth'. But perhaps the clearest example of the potential for information management within the British political system is to be seen in the position of the Prime Minister's Press Secretary. Always a key position in contemporary times, in the Thatcher era the holder of this post, Bernard Ingham, demonstrated an awesome potential to manipulate the media in ways favourable to the government and its policies:

> First, he was Thatcher's personal media adviser. Second, he was the non-attributable spokesman for the entire government, briefing the parliamentary lobby journalists twice a day. Third, he chaired the weekly 'meetings of information officers' (known as MIO), attended by all the heads of information in Whitehall, which co-ordinated government presentation. Through MIO, Ingham also had oversight of the government's burgeoning advertising budget, which by 1989 was running at £168m per annum. fourth, . Ingham had been placed in charge of the 'recruitment, training and career development' of every professional information officer in Whitehall. Joe Haines, who had been a highly influential Press Secretary to Harold Wilson, later said that Ingham wielded more power than all his predecessors put together. In any other country, he would surely have been given his proper , title: Minister of Information (R. Harris, 'Whispers', *The Sunday Times*, 9 December 1990, extracted from *Good and Faithful Servant* (1990), Faber, London).

PART II
The British Political Tradition

2 From the Divine Right of Kings to the rise of Collectivism

Introduction

Many writers on the British political tradition have noted the extent to which continuity rather than radical change marks the evolution of the British constitution: Britain is set apart 'from most other modern countries ... (by) the slowness and gradualness of the evolutionary process by which she has achieved her modernisation' (Hanson and Walles, 1984, p. 3). Indeed Rose (1989) emphasizes the extent to which Britain has managed to settle domestic problems and upheavals without the incidence of extremes and revolution seen elsewhere, and that this does in fact make Britain a deviant case by European norms. It is therefore clear that:

> In the past 300 years changes have never been such as to be described as revolutionary. They have been built upon and have adapted that which already existed. The body politic may have undergone radical surgery and it may have aged considerably, but it has continued to endure (Norton, 1984, p. 37).

Similarly, 'of the 150 or more nations that .. are members of the United Nations Organisation [1], all but one have written constitutions' (Birch, 1980, p. 21). Whether this absence of a written constitution is a strength or a weakness of the British system of government is a moot point, but it is certainly another definitive characteristic.

However, few seem to feel the need to analyze, far less problematize these realities.Instead, they are, by and large, seen as 'naturally' British characteristics. British government textbooks do tend to be descriptive rather than analytical, and to concentrate on institutions rather than ideas. Indeed there is rarely any discussion about the implications for the nature of British democracy which derive from the manner in which traditionalist ideas underpin British political institutions and practices. In part at least, I will attempt to rectify this omission here. To this end I will utilize some important works which, although lacking the desired focus, do draw on the notion that the British political tradition has favoured certain ideas about politics, the state and government, and that these have shaped the institutions and structures of modern British government. They do therefore offer valuable insights into the specific character of British parliamentary democracy.

The historical analysis undertaken here will be divided into two sections. The present chapter will be concerned with this country's political development up to the nineteenth century Liberal era, and the following chapter will take us up to the present. Throughout, the focus will be upon the neglected element of the *nature* of British politics and government. Specifically, I will be seeking to establish and substantiate the idea that the institutions and practices of modern British government are underpinned by a narrow and limited 'elitist' concept of democracy.

I will identify a relationship between historical continuities which produced the contemporary British political system, and the manner of the defeat of nineteenth century Radicalism. The analytical approach utilized in the present chapter will be continued in that following, and particularly in regard to the changed orthodoxy in the theory and practice of the Labour Party. In each case parallels will be clear between these and the substantive failure of the modern Campaign for Freedom of Information. I will attempt to show that the answers given by the British political tradition to a central question of political philosophy: 'how ought we to be governed?', have both ' ... substantially shaped the way men (sic) concerted and directed their attempts to win and influence power' (Beer, 1982, p. xiv), and been remarkably consistent. That is, the contemporary power relations and internal dynamics of modern British government are inherited from a past within which political disputes had been very largely limited to the claims of competing elites; the role of the people has been essentially a passive, legitimizing one. This is not to say that such 'top - down' views of government have never been challenged, only that they have never been successfully challenged. Significantly, in the works of most writers on the British political tradition a similar top-down view is adopted; the tradition of strong, centralized, decisive government is seen as quite natural and appropriate, the view from the bottom-up - the minimal influence of ordinary people - is correspondingly neglected.

Old Tories and Old Whigs

The extent to which continuity rather than change marks succeeding dominant ideologies has been mentioned; Britain's 'political system has evolved slowly, and constitutional developments have tended to come only gradually' (Punnett, 1976, pp. 159-60). Even right back to the 'Divine Right of Kings' and the Old Tory justification of government, a number of underlying assumptions have remained consistent. Truly, the democratic characteristics of British government are 'still very much wine of recent vintage poured into an ancient Royal flask' (Michael, 1976, p. 20).

In the days when the King was accepted to be at the pinnacle of earthly existence, but in a 'chain of being' stretching up to God in Heaven, the Old Tory theory justified political arrangements. Given that the King was at the head of a Divinely ordered earthly hierarchy, he symbolized the nation and was therefore said to represent the community as a whole. As such the Monarch was to hold the initiative in policy making. The House of Commons, representing the community's constituent parts, aided the King's deliberations via its members' expressing the particular interests and grievances of their constituents. Similarly, although ultimately the King was responsible for decision making, the role of the Lords was to provide council to the King; he would have available close and trusted advisors among the nobility. There was of course no role for the ordinary people, their place in the order of things was markedly lowly. They were as children within a traditional patriarchal family, under the clear authority of the father, with the equally clear obligation to obey. Undoubtably the actual practice of politics and government differed from this somewhat idealized constitutional picture, but for our purposes what is most interesting is that even here we can identify familiar principles: an emphasis on hierarchical social and political organization; the initiation of policy by the head of government; and harmonious society and good government requiring 'order'.

The Old Tory view was overthrown with the English Civil War, which threw into question - or itself resulted from the prior questioning - of the relationship between Monarch and parliament, and indeed paved the way for a radically new balance of power between the two. Thus seventeenth century Britain was riven by divided loyalties. Following his defeat in 1646, protracted negotiations saw Charles I apparently willing to come to an accommodation with Cromwell. However, in 1648 the King launched a second war against the parliamentary forces. This led to the purging of the House of Commons of all those who favoured a constitutional compromize, and the decision that the King must stand trial for his life for his crimes against his subjects.

Charles went to his death still proclaiming his Divine Right. A period of revolutionary politics and radical new forms of organization followed a third civil war, during which the dead King's son, Charles II, had tried to wrest back his father's crown. This failure to restore the Monarchy by force of arms confirmed parliamentary government under Cromwell, who became 'Lord Protector'. But the execution of the King, the overthrow of the traditional basis of political authority and the concomitant separation of Church and state, had created something of a political vacuum; a period of ideology in flux. There was no generally accepted justification for all these events, let alone agreement about what should follow.

In these circumstances there was a revival of reactionary ideas as well as an upsurge of revolutionary thought and demands. In 1649-50 for example, a group calling themselves 'The Diggers' occupied and cultivated collectively common land in Surrey. The Diggers believed that the cause of most human suffering was private property, and that common ownership was therefore the means to salvation. Similarly, originating largely from the left wing of Cromwell's army (but including civilians) the 'Levellers' represented not just a more egalitarian society, but popular sovereignty through radical participatory and accountable democracy:

> Lilburne, who may be regarded as the leader of the Levellers, wrote in
> a pamphlet published in 1645 that the upholders of Parliamentary,
> rather than popular, sovereignty were claiming, in effect, that 'an
> ambassador had more power than the prince by whom he was sent'
> (Birch, 1979, p. 36).

Birch says that these ideas were 'the product of the peculiar conditions of the revolutionary period', and were the subject of widespread debate for only 'a short period', indeed 'after the Restoration ... they lost currency except among a small minority of people in clerical and academic circles' (Birch, 1979, pp. 37-8). All of this is quite true, but for Birch the former statement seemingly represents an explanation of the latter ones. That is, nothing needs be said in order to explain the demise of these ideas beyond their being exceptions to the general 'rule' in British political culture, of stability and continuity. Yet this understates very considerably both the depth of influence of these ideas and the violence required to suppress them. Indeed, 'After Cromwell's death in 1658 ... fears of a new Leveller Party was doubtless one of the main reasons why all the men of property resolved so quickly on a restoration of the Monarchy' (Morton, 1975, p. 70). We will shortly return to this point, but it needs to be emphasized that Cromwell did ruthlessly suppress these groups, whilst still having to deal with Royalists and squabbling factions among the parliamentarians (see eg Eccleshall et al, 1984, pp. 50-53).

So this was certainly an unstable period, with no clearly dominant positive (as opposed to 'oppositional') ideology, no settled answers to questions of the nature of political authority and the basis of its legitimacy. The shifting and changing situation increasingly led Cromwell to more dictatorial and authoritarian solutions, with parliament too being repressed eventually.

Cromwellian Puritanism, which preached the simple life of duty and abstinance and opposed any form of ostentatious behaviour as sinful, had therefore made for a somewhat harsh and austere England. But with Cromwell's death in 1658:

> anarchy broke loose. His son Richard was an ineffective Protector
> while the leading generals ... quarrelled among themselves. So the
> realists throughout the country came to the conclusion that a return to
> monarchy was the only sure way to secure domestic peace (Ashley,
> 1990, p. 192).

Thus Charles II, soon to be dubbed 'The Merry Monarch', was invited back from exile in France to accept (if not enthusiastically embrace) the limited form of Monarchy that his father had scorned even to his death. Theatres were opened again, dancing and bright - even gaudy - clothes were back in fashion. A new, happier and more stable era thus emerges (if somewhat marred by the Great Plague and the Great Fire of London, both of which broke out during these times).

Charles II died in 1685, and the throne passed to his brother, James II. This event seemed to the majority of the parliamentary elite to represent a threat to their freedom and the new found peace and security. That is, as a Catholic, James represented the threat of the return of the idea and practice of 'Divine Right'; Old Tory Absolutism. Indeed there had been a threat of a further civil war during the 'exclusionist crisis' of the 1670s, which had seen the attempt by parliament to prevent James from succeeding to the throne for this very reason. It was thus in mobilizing against this perceived threat that the Whigs properly emerged as the dominant political force of the time.

The 'Glorious Revolution' of 1688 saw James overthrown by his nephew and son-in-law, William of Orange:

> At the invitation of Parliament, the throne was taken by William and
> Mary. The new occupants of the throne owed their position to

Parliament, and the new relationship between them was asserted in statute in the Bill of Rights.The raising of taxes or the dispensing of laws without the assent of Parliament was declared to be illegal (Norton, 1984, p. 39).

Thus, the doctrine of parliamentary sovereignty 'became established as a judicial rule' (Norton, 1982, p. 11), and indeed following the 1689 Bill of Rights it was accepted that parliament had 'the right to make or unmake any law whatsoever', with 'no person or body ... recognised by the law of England as having the right to override or set aside the legislation of Parliament' (Dicey, in Hood Phillips and Jackson, 1987, p. 49). In this manner the Whigs, upholding limited, constitutional government and 'traditional' freedoms, ushered in an era of constitutional monarchy surviving to this day.

British government (as opposed to history) textbooks tend not to dwell upon, nor seek to analyze such historical events. Beer gives them more space than Birch (and Greenleaf does not cover them at all), but beyond mentioning that following the English Civil War was an unstable period within which new forms of political organization did not last, even Beer is unconcerned with any of this. Neither does he take up any discussion about the failure of the new forms of political organization. I will just mention here that these represented a complete break with the past, unlike those forms which came to be accepted in the next 'stable pattern of thought and behaviour', which, as we have indicated, 'only emerges in the eighteenth century' (Beer, 1982, p. 9). However, let us look more closely at Old Whig thought.

Eighteenth century England was a time of aristocratic pre-eminence within which the theory of the 'balanced constitution' was dominant. The idea of a hierarchical order was again very powerful. It may therefore seem at first that only the clear overthrow of Monarchical prerogative in initiating policy sets this period apart from that of Old Tory dominance. But this is not so. A shift from cosmological to sociological emphasis in the justification for aristocratic eminence in society marks the transition from Old Tory to Old Whig thought. Beer cites Edmund Burke, probably the foremost Whig and certainly a leading and most articulate figure of his time, to illustrate this transition. Burke's defence of an hereditary Monarch for example, is not based upon 'foolish' or even 'impious' notions of Divine sanction, but rather upon good societal practicalities and political pragmatism. Likewise, hierarchy, whether Divinely ordered or not, was functional, and was to be supported on that basis. Beer quotes Burke to signify the nature of the aristocrat's position in society as seen in Old Whig terms:

To be bred in a place of estimation to see nothing low and sordid from one's infancy; to stand upon such elevated ground as to be enabled to take a large view of the widespread and infinitely diversified combinations of men and affairs in a large society; to have leisure to read, to reflect, to converse; ... these are the circumstances of men, that form what I should call a natural aristocracy, without which there is no nation (from Beer, 1982, p. 12).

Clearly here then, we can see it to be their social environment which nurtures aristocratic virtues and 'fits' the aristocracy for government, rather than such qualities being inherent and God-given, and governing being their birthright. There is perhaps too the beginnings of a role for ordinary people (if still a minimal one to be sure), in that 'it is through such natural leaders, themselves hierarchically ordered, that "the people" act'. Hence 'the "little platoons", the ancient communities, the estates, ranks, orders and interests of realm and empire enter the political arena through this system of natural hierarchy' (Beer, 1982, p. 10).

The Whig balanced constitution therefore maintained modified ideas of harmony and order based on hierarchy, and the emphasis upon government independence and initiative in policy making. But replacing the Old Tory view of the Monarch representing the nation as a whole, and therefore being charged with deliberating as to the common good, was the sharing of these tasks and duties between King, Lords and Commons; Monarchical prerogative was lost; 'the Monarch, from being on a plane different from the estates of the realm, had now become one of them' (Beer, 1982, p. 13). Beer goes on to show that this meant in effect, most governmental power being transferred from King to ministry, but it was most important that the idea of a centralized, controlling governmental 'office' survived.

Of course behind this theory of checks and balances between Monarchy and parliament 'the precise practice of eighteenth century politics was ... very much more basic... Through their power of patronage, the King and the Lords were able to exert "influence" over the ... lower chamber'. Indeed, '... corruption was of the political essence, and was the practical counterpart to the constitutional theory of balance' (Dearlove and Saunders, 1984, pp. 16-17). Thus despite the ideas of checks and balances and the safeguards to limited, constitutional government, clearly 'political power was in the hands of the few' (Rose, 1985, p. 47). Nevertheless, during the reigns of the 'crassly stupid' Hanoverian Kings George I and George II, the leading ministers of the crown (the embryonic cabinet), began meeting without the King. Indeed, in practice a 'prime' minister emerged during this period (see eg Plumb, 1950, p. 50, Macintosh, 1962, pp. 50-51). We should neither lose sight of these realities, nor of the idea of government as 'a central initiating, directing, energizing body' (Beer, 1982, p. 14), enduring from Absolute Monarchy. Yet more important still, in my view, is that the 'balanced constitution' saw the change in the role of the Commons from being predominantly a 'representative' to a 'deliberative' chamber. In Burke's words, parliament was:

> a deliberative assembly of one nation with one interest, that of the whole - where not local prejudice ought to guide but the general good resulting from the general reason of the whole (from Beer, 1982, p.15).

In common with most writers on the British political tradition, Beer stresses the importance of the transfer of previously Monarchical power to the ministry as an important development both in terms of the shift from Old Tory to Old Whig thought and practice, and in establishing the strong, decisive 'responsible' (rather than 'responsive') governmental tradition surviving to this day. However, since the change in the role of the Commons from representative to deliberative assembly was particularly favourable to the further development of responsible government, and brought with it the narrow and elitist concept of representation - 'parliamentarism' - to be carried into the democratic era, surely this is more important still:

> This assertion that Members should be more or less independent of their constituencies, once they were elected, was essential to the Whig view of government. Only on this basis could they claim that Parliament was a deliberative as well as a representative body, and that the results of its deliberations were, or could be, something more than a mere aggregate of sectional demands (Birch, 1979, p. 29).

This fundamental shift in the theoretical underpinnings of the Commons and the role of its members in fact sustained the idea and practice of strong, decisive government. Had the Old Tory view of the Commons and its members representing 'particular' ('constituents') interests survived, it would have been far more susceptible to being radicalized with the nineteenth century's extensions of the franchise; the early tradition of strong government may have proved nothing more. I think this is generally unappreciated in the common tendency to read historical developments through a modern interpretive framework coloured by hindsight, rather than gaining analytical insights through problematizing them.

However, let us briefly recap before moving on. We have seen that the Whig view maintained, in modified form, the ideas of harmony and order out of hierarchy, and government independence and initiative in policy making. The fundamental break with Old Toryism was with 'parliamentarism'; parliamentarians now had the task of representing the community as a whole, expressing the various interests within society, and, in order to reconcile these, deliberating as to the common interest as the basis for public policy. But if the 'how' of representation had changed, the 'who' had not; another element carried over from Old Tory thought was the idea that society was constituted not as an aggregate of individuals, as later liberals and radicals would have it (thus forming the next major ideological conflict), but rather out of what Beer calls 'corporate bodies'. Thus it is these constituent parts of society which the Whig view holds should be represented in parliament. Other interests, particularly if they sought to bring pressure to bear on parliament or individual Members, were therefore 'illegitimate', and even 'anti-parliament' (See eg Beer, 1982, p. 16, Dearlove and Saunders, 1984 p. 17).

The corporate bodies that Beer speaks of here, the legitimate 'fixed' interests to be represented in parliament under Whig theory, consisted of: 'the local communities, united by ancient ties of interest', and 'the broad social groupings not confined to a particular place - the various "estates", "ranks", "orders", and, to use the term most commonly employed, "interests" - of which the nation and empire were composed' (Beer, 1982, p. 18). But other interests and expressions of opinion - propounded through the proper channels - such as 'municipal corporations, the universities, deans and chapters of cathedrals, magistrates in petty sessions, and grand juries at quarter sessions and assizes' (Beer, 1982, p. 17), should also be taken into account by Members. Access to these channels of representation and communication was therefore crucial, but restricted. In any case any idea of 'instructions' to Members, or of a popular 'mandate' was ruled out in favour of 'functional representation', but 'virtual representation' was also a feature of Whig thought:

> This could be applied to citizens who did not enjoy the franchise, but were said to be virtually represented by the Member for the area in which they lived. It could also be applied to communities and interests which were not directly represented in Parliament, but were said to be virtually represented by Members for other parts of the country which shared similar interests. The first aspect, the idea of

representation through the land, was mainly emphasized by the Tories; the second aspect was mainly emphasized by the Whigs (Birch, 1979, p. 28).

The stability of the Whig ascendancy and the eighteenth century constitution was however to be severely shaken by momentous events occurring towards its close (under George III). The 1776 American War of Independence and the 1789 French Revolution were each underpinned by far more radical ideas than those of the Whigs: democratic ideas, upholding the sovereignty of the people. The Whigs were of course implacably opposed to democracy, as they were to the individualism upon which it rested. Their upholding of the special place and role of the enlightened and educated 'governing class', the aristocracy, made them hostile to any greater role for the 'ignorant' (uneducated) propertyless majority. Democracy to the Whigs (and Tories) was therefore equated with 'mob-rule' (see eg Eccleshall et al, 1984, p. 58, Beer, p. 10). Burke, eloquent as ever, wrote a stirring defence of the existing order, *Reflections on the Revolution in France* (1790). For Burke, the freedom and justice represented by limited, constitutional government is rooted in the traditional way of life, its customs and institutions. Existing society is the result, the aggregate, of present and all past generations, tradition being the link between them. No single generation can possibly know better than all previous generations. To destroy an existing order's religious, social and property relations, and the political hierarchy which holds it all together, in the attempt to construct a new order based upon nothing but abstract, philosophical ideas, was not just criminal but folly.

In the year following Burke's *Reflections*, Thomas Paine's *The Rights of Man* (1791) was published (subtitled 'An Answer to Mr Burke's Attack on the French Revolution'). 'Paine broke from the Whig tradition of the Glorious Revolution more sharply than any other radical ... there was nothing "glorious" in 1688 compared to the struggles of America and France' (Claeys, 1989, pp. 86-7). Just as Paine's *Common Sense* (1776), had called for an independent American Republic - in the year the American Revolution began - so *The Rights of Man* acclaimed the French Revolution and condemned the 'old governments' throughout Europe, and especially in England. Paine answered Burke's appeal to history, custom and tradition saying that history in fact recorded:

a wretched tale of aristocratic conquest and exploitation whereby a despotic form of government had arisen to serve the interests of a privileged minority. Reason demanded that the debris of history be swept away in favour of democratic government which would secure the rights, and represent the interests of everyone (Eccleshall et al, 1984, p. 42).

Paine therefore upheld the notion that individuals had 'natural rights' and an innate ability and entitlement to make rational decisions in all spheres of life; morality, religion, politics and economics. These beliefs necessitated the abolition of slavery, rights for women, free speech and religious tolerance. A related aspect equally a part of this Radical scheme of things was 'limited government'; governors subject to popular democratic control, and 'minimal government'; the restriction of the public sphere of politics and government so as not to intrude upon the individual's 'private sphere' (Eccleshall et al, p. 42. For a fuller discussion of Paine, see Claeys, 1989). Such was then the picture in eighteenth century Britain. However:

> by the end of the eighteenth century times were (again) unstable. New interests came into being which were outside of the established set-up. The middle classes, based on manufacture in the emerging industrial towns, and a working class made out of these self-same developments, gained a consciousness of the fact that they were unrepresented and politically disadvantaged within the eighteenth-century constitution... Long before the century closed, pressures were building up for constitutional change and for more profound changes in the social and economic system itself (Dearlove and Saunders, 1984, p. 17).

Thus, by the beginning of the nineteenth century, the differences between Old Tory and Old Whig thought had lost their relevance, since for each the defence of the unreformed parliament against demands for the extension of the franchise became paramount:

> The reform of parliament was a difficult matter for the tories; it implied an attack upon vested interests, and, particularly, upon the vested interests of tory members in tory seats (Woodward, 1988 p. 52).

Simlarly, in relation to Whig interests: 'The magnates of the party did not wish to lose their "pocket" boroughs' (Woodward, 1988, p. 57). It would be wrong however to see the dispute about the franchise as straightforwardly that between entrenched interests and the proponents of democracy; such would both imply clearer and more stark positions than were held on either side and would oversimplify the far more complex reality of the time. The franchise was in fact the focus for a general ideological clash between Old Tory/Whig and Liberal thought. But what is often underplayed if not totally ignored - and what I want to emphasize here - is the narrow conceptualization of 'democracy' which emerges from this dispute. Even Birch, who structures his work around the idea that British government could lay claim to being 'representative' (of 'interests') long before any serious claim to its being 'democratic' could be made, fails to make explicit the implications for British democracy which follow from the influential concepts of 'representative' and 'responsible' government. But since this is crucial for our purposes, let us divert briefly to consider how, Birch's work is nevertheless amenable to such a project.

Representative and responsible government

In a work first published in 1964, but which was to become a classic running to seven editions, Birch begins by considering the different aspects or meanings of 'representative' and 'responsible' government. He ascribes three different meanings to each term. Let us deal first with the least important meaning of 'representative' government: 'microcosmic' representation. In this sense representation or representativeness is measured by the extent to which the representative body could be said to be a microcosm of that said to be represented. Although parliament has often been criticized for failing to be representative in this manner (eg the legal profession is grossly overrepresented in this sense), there have never been any serious proposals put forward to make it so representative. Since this sense of representation has therefore failed to have any real impact upon the British political tradition, it need detain us no longer [2].

However, more importantly, the term representative is used, says Birch:

> to denote an agent or delegate, a person whose function is to protect and if possible advance the interests of the individual or group on whose behalf he (sic) is acting.

The point, in this sense of representation, is that 'irrespective of who they are, how they are chosen, or how much discretion they are allowed, their function is to look after the interests of the organisation, group or person they represent' (Birch, 1979, p. 14).

A second important usage is where the term is applied 'to describe persons and assemblies who have been freely elected' (Birch, 1979 p. 15). Birch refers to this as 'elective representation', because the definitive characteristic is that of election. But this is a characteristic of *selection*, rather than *function*, and not all elected people are to be regarded as representatives of those who elect them; the Pope is elected by the College of Cardinals but is not their representative. There are other such examples, and thus it would seem, says Birch, 'that elected persons can be described as representatives only if their election involves some obligation, however slight, to advance the interests and opinions of their electors' (Birch, 1979, p. 15).

Yet Birch also says that in Britain:

> the conventions of politics do not compel an elected representative
> to act as an agent or delegate of his (sic) constituents... only a small
> minority of politicians have argued that MPs should behave as
> delegates, and the accepted view has been exactly the opposite (Birch,
> 1979, p. 15).

So in fact the concept of representation stressed in relation to British democracy is 'elective' representation, which, as Birch himself says, concerns the selection of representatives rather than their function *as* representatives. Thus by implication a minimal and largely passive role is envisaged for the British electorate, with wide discretion and independence for representatives and government so chosen. Indeed, as if to confirm and even emphasize this, Birch says:

> There can be no doubt that in the prevailing view an MP is regarded
> as being the parliamentary representative of his (sic) constituency
> whether or not he takes any notice of the views of his constituents.
> So long as he has been elected, and is dependent on his constituents
> for re-election, he is looked upon as their representative (Birch,
> 1979, p.15).

In Birch's own terms this begs the question as to whether, without such an 'obligation' to advance the interests of their electors or indeed 'take any notice' of the views of constituents, British MPs are in fact properly described as 'representatives'! In turn this raises again the narrowness and elitism of British democracy. Yet such matters are there only by implication in Birch, who, in answer to such implied questions only asserts 'the prevailing view' in support of the argument that British MPs should properly be considered representatives.

Further questioning of Britain's democratic credentials can be found in Birch's consideration of three examples of 'responsible' government. In the first instance here, 'responsible' can be taken to mean 'responsive', that is; 'responsive to public demands and movements of public opinion'. It is useful I think to quote Birch at some length here, the significance of which will be brought out subsequently. He says:

> It is in this sense that the term is used to distinguish between liberal or democratic regimes, which recognise an obligation to be responsive to public opinion, and dictatorial or autocratic regimes, which may be responsive for reasons of prudence but generally regard leadership as a greater virtue than responsiveness. The difference of emphasis is clearly reflected in the attitudes taken to censorship: in liberal systems censorship is thought to be wrong because it distorts the public opinion on which government is presumed to be based, whereas in autocratic systems censorship is often regarded as a permissible weapon to use against those groups who try to undermine public confidence in the wisdom of those in power (Birch, 1979, p. 18).

It is therefore clear that good responsible government should be responsive to public opinion, should in fact 'recognise an obligation' to be so. This is complimentary to the sense in which to be a representative implies an obligation to further constituents' interests and opinions. But it is therefore in conflict with 'the conventions of (British) politics', which 'do not compel an elected representative to act as an agent or delegate'; 'whether or not he (sic) takes any notice of the views of his constituents ... he is looked upon as their representative' (Birch, 1979, p. 15). Birch mentions neither of these connections however, instead emphasizing (if not unreasonably) the difficulties involved in translating responsiveness into coherent government policy. More will be said of this later.

In Birch's second example, responsible government is focused on the way in which the nation's well being is entrusted to the guardianship of government. Government therefore has a moral duty to behave as 'responsible' guardians. In this sense, says Birch, 'the ministers in office are responsible for seeing that the government pursues a wise policy, **whether or not what they do meets with the immediate approval of the public**' (Birch, 1979, p. 18, my emphasis). This therefore seems to be at odds with the previous sense of (responsive) responsibility, and it is in this second sense of responsibility that the emphasis in the British political tradition on strong, initiatory and decisive government is most apparent. The idea (at its most favourable) is that it is sometimes government's lot to take tough decisions, which, particularly in the short term, will be unpopular. But it would be 'irresponsible' to shrink from taking those necessary decisions, and, having taken them, government must not be swayed by considerations about its unpopularity as a result; it must get on with the job. Thus once more a clearly elitist 'government knows best' attitude is to be seen; it is government's (independent) task to ponder the alternatives and then initiate policy. Only those with long parliamentary - and preferably governmental - experience, are qualified for such responsible decision making. Further, any questioning of those decisons (and here the next sense of responsibility is heralded), is to be undertaken by parliament, not the ordinary people. Parliament is then the outer limit of responsibility, with government being best qualified in this respect and the people not at all.

In the third sense of the term, 'responsible' can be taken to mean 'accountable'. In the British tradition, responsibility in this third sense is signified by 'the accountability of ministers, or of the government as a whole, to an elected assembly' (Birch, 1979, p. 20). Thus via 'ministerial responsibility' ministers are deemed individually responsible for the activities of their department, and via 'cabinet responsibility', they (even non-cabinet, junior ministers) are deemed jointly responsible for government policy. The point is that government policy, and its implementation through the civil service administrative machine, is said to be subject to parliamentary scrutiny and accountability. There are some serious flaws in such assumptions, which were indicated earlier (see p. 25), and will be taken up again in Chapter Five. Let me say here only that the reality is that just as the Executive dominates the legislative process in Britain, so too does it dominate the legislature's supposed means of holding it to account. But quite apart from the shortcomings of written and oral questions and even the oft-reformed Parliamentary Select Committees - shortcomings greatly understated by Birch and Beer et al - is the point that this is again a very narrow and elitist concept of accountability. That is, at best it is accountability to the 'representatives' of the people - if indeed given British conventions MPs may even be called representatives - rather than popular accountability of the governors to the governed.

This narrow elitism is related to the manner in which British democracy came about; first via the elevation of the Commons above the Monarch and the Lords, and subsequently via the extensions of the franchise, until the Commons was transformed into a chamber derived from popular election and from which government was drawn. We are hereby brought back to the importance of the historical consideration of the British political tradition, and the manner of the evolution of the British constitution. But before returning to that consideration we should first note that if government is not (directly) accountable to the people, then there is little reason for the people to be well informed as to the details of public policy. Nor, since it is parliament's role to scrutinize government decision making, is there any need for the unsophisticated public to be well informed about the details and internal dynamics of the policy making process. Indeed it could be considered 'irresponsible' to give too much information to the lay person incapable of responsible judgement. Thus, just as parliamentarians are not obliged to take any notice of the views of their constituents, so the operation of official secrecy is entirely complimentary to the underlying assumptions of British government. Let us be perfectly clear, 'practical difficulties' are sometimes cited as reasons why government does not behave more 'responsively'. We have seen that Birch points to the problems involved in clearly assessing public opinion and formulating coherent and consistent policy for example. But even where such difficulties do not apply (where for example a specific policy mandate can be said to have been given via a General Election victory), a party in government is still in no way bound to enact legislation based upon such a mandate, and in no way prevented from doing the exact opposite.

In fact, although 'dictatorial' or 'autocratic' may be going a little too far, by the criteria set up by Birch in the substantial section quoted earlier, Britain would seem to be more in the authoritarian than the liberal camp, since leadership is so prominent a feature of the British tradition. It would certainly seem to be regarded as 'a greater virtue than responsiveness'. Indeed later in the book Birch states quite categorically that in terms of priorities:

> the British political tradition would clearly determine the order as,
> first consistency, prudence and leadership, second, accountability to
> parliament and the electorate, and third, responsiveness to public
> opinions and demands (Birch, 1979, p. 245).

The fact that 'prudence' is also valued above 'responsiveness' also brings to mind Birch's statement that *autocratic* regimes may be responsive for reasons of *prudence* rather than principle or obligation. Indeed, after pointing out that the conventions do not recognise any obligation 'to act as an agent or (far less) delegate', Birch says that perhaps the best justification of the electoral process is that it 'tends to make MPs act in the interests (and further the opinions) of their constituents' (Birch, 1979, p. 15). In other words, it is prudent to do so!

It can therefore be deduced via even so brief a consideration of the work of an academic clearly favourable to the British system of government, that the most striking feature of the British political tradition and govermental practice is its elitist nature. We will now turn to see how this elitism is carried into the democratic era via certain principles of representation being maintained from Whig to Liberal constitutional norms, even though the individual rather than societal interests came to form the basis of political representation.

The emergence of liberal individualism

As was indicated earlier in the consideration of Thomas Paine, the democratic revolution was underway in America and France whilst the industrial revolution was transforming the nature of British society. Radicals like Paine spearheaded the democratic movement in this country but were met with determined resistance from traditionalists like Burke. With the Revolutionary and Napoleonic Wars (1792-1815) and in their aftermath, democracy and all forms of Radicalism came to be associated with alien, even 'enemy' thought; as had been the case with the earlier American Revolution, Radicals in this country were weakened and divided by 'the stigma of disloyalty' (see eg Claeys, 1989, p. 15). There was much suppression (see eg Watson, 1991).Indeed Paine's *The Rights of Man* had been banned as 'seditious' (Paine himself was tried *in absentia* for seditious libel in 1792). This was the background against which what would come to be called Liberalism would emerge.

This is to say that British Liberalism emerged out of the conflict between what is sometimes called 'Establishment Liberalism', emphasizing the principles of toleration, civil liberties and constitutional government upheld by Whigs, and the popular democratic principles of Radical Liberals like Paine. The thought of John Locke, Jeremy Bentham, James and John Stuart Mill reflect variously the tensions between individual freedom and democracy which had first set 'liberals' apart from democrats. In general, 'Establishment Liberals' (Whigs) and Radical Liberals agreed that there were legitimate and illegitimate forms of government determined by the concept of 'government by consent'. However, in relation to this legitimacy the former stressed constitutionalism (the basis upon which a government behaved), and particularly a government's upholding of freedom (from arbitrary rule and state encroachment):

> liberty alone was the basis of virtue, order and stability in governments
> and ... the best form of government ... required ... a strong, patriotic
> people loving liberty and uncorrupted by luxury and private interest.
> Preserving liberty also required maintaining rights. While man (sic)
> was born naturally free, liberty being 'exemption from the domination
> of any other', all governments required surrendering some natural

liberty. But the right of dominion was based on consent, and kings who exceeded their authority could be resisted ... (Claeys, 1989, p. 8).

Radicals on the other hand stressed democratic election and accountability:

The proper image of political society was one in which authority flowed inwards towards the centre from the mass of people ... (and) that centre is formed by representation (Eccleshall et al, 1984, pp. 43-4).

Further, a representative democracy 'could not be founded by an existing government, ... but only by a constitution through which a whole people installed a new government' (Claeys, 1989, p. 77).

Thus on the one hand we have the 'function' (or 'behaviour') sense of representation and on the other that of 'selection'. These, in part, formed the basis of the dispute between the two forms of Liberalism, and it was out of this conflict that British Liberalism emerged as a synthesis of the two. Indeed the 'liberal' aspect of the legitimacy of the British state and government emphasized the notions of minimal government and the defence of individual freedom (function), whilst the democratic aspect emphasized free elections as the means of *selecting* a government. But we have run ahead of ourselves somewhat, we need now to turn to examine how these tensions were resolved constitutionally.

By the time of the nineteenth century debate over the franchise the active role of parliament in policy making was generally accepted, if the justification for that role varied. As between Old Tory and Old Whig thought, Liberalism saw some elements of old thinking rejected and some retained, if in modified form. As indicated earlier, the idea that society was reducible only to corporate, community or other common interests - the notion which justified 'virtual' parliamentary representation - was rejected. Liberal theory instead based parliamentary representation on individuals and common opinion. Thus a wide extension of the franchise was implied, along with the equalization of electoral districts. This would seemingly suggest that a movement towards a more participatory rather than elitist, a more 'responsive' rather than 'responsible' nature of government, would begin to emerge. However, both the impetus to extend the franchise and its 'responsive' implications were countered by other Liberal principles. In fact, at this juncture, in the exactly opposite way to that occurring with the transition from Old Tory to Whig, the assumption of 'who' (or what) was to be represented changed, whilst the 'how' of representation was maintained; Liberals upheld Whig parliamentarism.

The embracing of parliamentarism is in my view something of a paradox deserving of closer consideration, even if others have not found it necessary [3]. Whilst debate and deliberation over the best policy to reconcile certain corporate interests with the common good seems appropriate, and therefore parliamentarism and Whigism are perfectly consistent, debate and deliberation by the few over what are the *opinions* of the many, seems somewhat less plausible. Both Birch and Beer point out for example, that once popular opinion rather than fixed interests became the rationale for representation, 'virtual' representation became untenable. Yet 'parliamentarism' - seemingly equally inappropriate as a representational theory of the new era - was maintained. To put this another way, if 'the logical implication of the new emphasis on opinions was that everyone capable of holding an opinion should have the vote' (Birch, 1979, p. 53), then popular voting is surely evidence of popular opinion. Rather than the role of MPs being to deliberate over the merits of alternative policies in relation to fixed societal interests, given that they owe their position to expressed popular opinion, they need only 're-present' the opinions of their constituents about policy matters in order to determine public policy. That is, a parliamentary majority, derived from the weight of electoral opinion, would decide public policy.

However, we have seen that the literal meaning of representation, 're-presentation' (to present again), what Birch referred to as the expectation that the representative would behave as the delegate or agent of those electing him or her, goes against the conventions of British politics. Indeed 'the accepted view has been exactly the opposite' (Birch, 1979, p. 15). Also, to say that MPs need only 're-present' the opinions of their constituents in parliament obviously puts the case at its simplest. For example, in order to avoid 'an aggregate of conflicting opinions and demands, which would not be a satisfactory basis for policy or legislation' (Birch, 1979, p. 34), we need to consider the role of opposing parties and their programmes in determining and presenting consistent policy alternatives. That Liberals attached low importance to the role of party, and lacked enthusiasm for presenting a programme to the electorate, lends important insights into the understanding of the 'paradox' of Liberal parliamentarism and its concomitants. We will examine these Liberal attitudes further, as well as looking at the 'middle class' view of the individual which completes the aspects of Liberal theory mediating against responsive, participatory government.

As mentioned earlier, the concern with the individual implied the extension of the franchise, but this was not carried to what might be thought its logical conclusion because a certain type of individual was envisaged as the basic unit of representation; the propertied middle class individual. Why? Well, often, says Beer for example:

> Liberals reasoned from the premise that the main end of government is
> the preservation of property. Not inconsistent is the view that property
> shows something about the individual that entitles him (sic) to political
> power: it is, so to speak, the best rough index of his (sic) intelligence
> and good will (Beer, 1982, p. 34).

Thus, as with hierarchy in Old Tory/Whig thought, so with property for Liberals. Liberal individualism signifies a break with, indeed freedom from, the old hereditary hierarchy. Yet it also establishes a new, if more fluid basis for social order, where the index of 'worth' and 'responsibility' is property.

But it was not just evidence of enterprize and practical ability which made the middle class individual the model citizen, and property the appropriate 'qualification'. There was no public provision for education at this time, so a good income was also a reasonable measure of learning and, by extension, of 'intelligence'. Hence early Liberals tended to emphasize the rights of those with property and hence a stake in society:

> with the related gloss that education was a prerequisite for the
> 'responsible' exercise of the franchise. Intellectuals of the age
> believed in parliamentary government, not a democratic system; in
> liberty, not popular government; and the spectre of social and
> economic equality itself was seen as the dark side of the claim for
> adult suffrage (Dearlove and Saunders, 1984, p. 25).

Beer therefore places the emphasis upon the concern with an educated and enlightened electorate, Dearlove and Saunders highlight a hostility to democracy; there is something of the Whig view here in that where the majority are uneducated and propertyless, 'democracy' means 'mob-rule'. Each emphasis is equally valid in my view, but it would seem worthy of note that there is also a similarity between this liberal view of the middle class and the Whig view of the aristocracy; each was thought to be fitted for a pre-eminent position in politics and government via their social position and environmental circumstances.

It is nevertheless the rational, independent individual, with a stake in modern society and respect for the law, which forms the ideal Liberal citizen and elector. The move from corporate, community and other fixed societal interests, to a certain kind of individual as the basis for representation, therefore led to uniformity, rather than variety, being the ideal of representation:

> On these premises, it was logical not only to extend the franchise to
> the rational and independent, but also to withdraw it from such poor
> and ignorant as had previously enjoyed it on the grounds of variety
> (Beer,1982, p. 35).

This suggests something of a political monopoly (in ideal) for the middle class. Indeed the Liberal reformers of this period are usually portrayed: 'as concerned mainly with the welfare of the middle class and with a reordering of the economy and policy that would favour the interests of the owners of industrial and commercial capital' (Beer, 1982, p. 36). As Beer says, there is 'much truth' in such a characterization, but much less well appreciated is the importance of the vision of the middle class as the model for the future. The liberal reformers, indicates Beer, 'felt peculiarly representative of the whole society... Suffering from neither the compulsions of poverty nor the temptations of great riches', they felt it encumbent upon themselves to 'strike down privilege and open the doors to economic, social and political advancement to all persons' (Beer, 1982, p. 37). Birch too notes this liberal view of the middle class as 'the most virtuous section of the community, as their publicists were not slow to suggest' (Birch, 1979, p. 84). Here there is a similarity between this liberal view of the middle class and the Marxist view of the proletariat, as Beer acknowledges the historian Asa (now Lord) Briggs to have noted earlier [4].

However, by the beginning of the nineteenth century the strongly individualistic Liberal view is challenging the established order, that challenge being focused upon the question of parliamentary representation and the franchise. The most significant aspect of this period, as I have argued, is that Liberal theory embraced parliamentarism, which was instrumental in maintaining narrow, elitist views of representation and the role of government into the coming democratic era. That this is generally unacknowledged in works on the British political tradition in my view demonstrates the norm of the top-down perspective outlined in the introduction to the present work. I also indicated there that this work would take the opposite, 'bottom-up' emphasis already evident, which suggests that the key to understanding the Liberal representative paradox, and thereby the further development of the characteristic British 'strong government' tradition, lies in the ideal of the rational independent individual. Strongly related to this is the Liberal attitude to the role of party, which could not be described as better than cool, and the fact that Liberals were in general hostile to the idea of a commitment to a specific electoral programme. It is to these aspects of the Liberal puzzle that we will now turn.

Responsible government, responsible electorate

The Liberal individualist ideal was consistent; whether thinking of the ideal citizen/elector or Member of Parliament, the qualities of rationality and independence were foremost. We have considered how this tended towards limiting the extension of the franchise to the pace at which a responsible citizenry might develop, with property being the appropriate measure of this. When we apply these ideas to the political representative they are equally instructive.

. If the ideal MP is 'independent' in 'rational' decision making, we see the strong implication of the 'deliberating' MP. This counters the suggestion of the Member 're-presenting' the opinions and policy choices derived from his or her constituents which I have suggested seemed to be implied by the Liberal commitment to parliamentary representation based upon individuals and common opinion. Prioritizing independence also ascribes a low role to party, most immediately appreciable in the sense of party discipline. This again counters the more participatory and 'delegatory' view of representation, since such requires an 'instrumental' view of party and programme. That is, so as to avoid the pitfalls of inconsistent and conflictual 'public opinion', it would be the role of party to formulate consistent policy and present it to the electorate in the form of a clear programme. Party discipline would then be needed in order consistently to reproduce in the Commons a parliamentary majority won in a General Election.

Such instrumentalist notions of party held little sway with classical Liberals. As for party as policy maker and programme presenter, even following the Second Reform Act: 'the party election manifesto was still a personal appeal from the party leader, not a statement of future policy prepared and endorsed by the leading men (sic) in the party'. Indeed, in office, party leaders were 'relatively uncommitted to any particular scheme of reform' (Beer, 1982, p. 55). Radicals in the Liberal Party believed in both popular intra-party participation in policy making and electoral commitments, but even at the height of Radical influence in the early 1890s, the leadership of Gladstone and Rosebery gave no clear endorsement to any programme as official policy, far less any commitment to such a programme. Thus:

> There is no doubt that in regard to policy-making the parliamentary leadership was firmly in control. The radical Newcastle Programme of 1891, adopted by the National Liberal Federation conference, was completely ignored by the Liberal government of 1892-5 (Ball, 1987, p. 31).

Beer in fact emphasizes that this went beyond defensively avoiding being hindered in the initiation of policy by being associated with a particular programme:

> After the fall of Rosebery's government, a reaction set in against policy-making by party conference and programmatic pledges by party leaders. In the campaign of 1895, Rosebery had warned against 'a many-headed programme', and later ... he attributed the government's fall in part to its overcommitment to pledges deriving from the party conference. As strenuously as Rosebery,Campbell-Bannerman refused to commit himself to 'any fixed programme for action'. What a liberal government would do, he told the Council for 1899, would depend on its majority (Beer, 1982, p. 58).

Neither was there much enthusiasm among Liberals for the role of party as reproducer of parliamentary majorities, or even for the General Election 'vote organizer' role: 'even after mid-century, leading men in the Liberal Party organization denounced the very registration societies that they directed' (Beer, 1982, p. 38). Thus the continuities with the past and the established views of government is clear; the Liberal view of the independence of the governors, and the traditional view of the independence and initiatory role of government, are so close as to have been synthesized.

To the Liberal mind then, government, as with the individual MP, must be independent, and therefore unfettered by electoral pledges. This is especially true of any such pledges and programmes originating outside of the leading circles of government and party leadership; conceived by those without the proper experience and 'responsibility'. Good government is strong, decisive government, so government must hold the initiative regarding policy (any tendencies to the converse being therefore regarded as 'weak' and 'indecisive' government). Their acceptance of such principles set Liberals apart from Radicals, which led to much conflict between the two strands of thought within the Liberal Party. But as we have seen, this conflict was resolved in favour of mainstream Liberalism and compatibility with traditional notions of British governmental practice.

For Beer, 'Both individualism and parliamentarism agreed poorly with the idea of party government' (Beer, 1982, p. 38). But I think it is more accurate to say that the two concepts are antithetical to the instrumental idea of party, and indeed this seems to be what Beer is really getting at above (ie, for 'party government' read 'party discipline'). This seems evident since Beer goes on to point out that the 'loose' idea of party as an 'association' of independent MPs had one great advantage in Liberal thought. 'Parties so conceived', says Beer, 'not only did not violate independence', but also positively enhanced it by attaching individuals to 'steady and lasting principles', thus 'protecting them against the seductions of money and patronage' (Beer, 1982, p. 39).

I'm not sure that this does enhance 'independence', if I can agree that the above effects would be advantageous. Nevertheless it seems clear that the loose idea of party was acceptable and the instrumental view not. In addition, party government so conceived 'made possible the passage of laws which had not yet caught popular favour' (Beer, 1982, p. 39). This of course does emphasize the independence of both individual MP and government from the people in the making of policy, and therefore 'responsible' government; government as arbiter of the national interest. Government policy is therefore deemed to embody the national interest, and as such is above the particular interests embodied in public opinion. It is therefore quite right and proper for government to 'lead' or be ahead of popular opinion, and to put consistent 'responsible' policy before 'responsiveness'. Once again, it is the loose concept of party which sees public opinion as upholding 'particular' and likely conflicting interests, in contrast to the instrumentalist view within which the party programme and electoral mandate determine the national interest. But the instrumentalist view was never accepted into mainstream Liberal theory and practice, and thus 'responsible government' is maintained via the Liberal era.

Having now considered fully the relationship between Liberal individualism and representational theory, we can better appreciate the conflict over the franchise between Whigs and Liberals, and the explanation of the paradox of Liberal parliamentarism. In any case, as Birch puts it:

> It is fair to say that Victorian discussions about representative government were dominated by Liberal ideas and that these ideas, at first held by only a minority of politicians and writers, gradually won widespread acceptance until by the end of the century they had come to constitute the prevailing constitutional doctrine (Birch, 1979, p. 52).

This gradual metamorphosis of ideas was matched by one in practice. As we have seen, it was The Great Reform Act of 1832 which 'broke the essentials of the eighteenth century constitution'. It was accompanied, if not pushed forward by 'massive political unrest, and a campaign of civil disobedience' (Dearlove and Saunders, 1984, p. 18). The 1832 Act began a process which, if not fully realized at the time, was unstoppable. The emerging ascendancy of the Commons and the greater importance of political and governmental organization both within parliament and in the country, meant that 'the parties gradually became more rigid and monolithic', (Bromhead, 1974, p. 100). With the term 'His Majesty's Loyal Opposition' having first been used (derisively) in 1826 (Beer, 1982, p. 39), thus began the rise of party and party government. Also, just as the power of the Monarch had been limited beforehand:

> The acceptance of the Commons as the "representative" chamber undermined the authority of the peers to challenge or negate the wishes of the other House. After the 1830s, the Lords tended to be somewhat restrained in their attacks on government measures (Norton, 1984, p. 42).

In fact the aspiration to a democratic basis for the legitimate authority of the Commons **required** the powers of the House of Lords to be limited. Thus, when in 1860 the Lords rejected a bill (repealing an excise duty on paper) passed by the Commons, the government began the practice of putting its whole range of tax changes in a single bill [5].

The Second Reform Act followed in 1867, making 'working-class males a majority of the electorate in the country at large' (Dearlove and Saunders, 1984, p. 26). It is with this reform that we might begin to speak of the transformation of the Liberal into the Liberal-Democratic constitution, but in addition:

> Whereas the 1832 Act helped ensure the dominance of the House of Commons within the formal political process, the passage of the Reform Act of 1867 began a process of the transfer of power from Parliament to Ministers (Norton, 1984, p. 42).

However, the Secret Ballot Act of 1870, and other acts which sought to outlaw the various forms of corruption still existing as well as limiting the amount of money that could be spent by candidates, and the institution of single-member constituencies, were followed by the further extension of the franchise in 1884. For the first time working class males formed the majority electorate, with 'the ancient communities of shire and borough ... (having) ceased almost entirely to be the basis of representation' (Beer, 1982, p. 34). But if 'two in three adult males - almost 4.5 million people - had the vote in England and Wales, whereas some 50 years earlier the electorate stood at little more than 650 000' (Dearlove and Saunders, 1984, p. 26), universal male suffrage did not follow until 1918, and women did not recieve the same voting rights as men until 1928. More important still though, and what is often 'glossed over' as Dearlove and Saunders indicate, is that if Liberalism was democratized:

> in the process democracy came to be 'liberalised' in that ... in practice, democratic politics worked within the prevailing system of power in economy and society' (Dearlove and Saunders, 1984, p. 26).

Thus the continuities with pre-democratic theory and practice are more marked than the discontinuities, and the nature of British parliamentary democracy closely mirrors that of the traditional elitist system. Indeed the universal franchise and the General Election as a means of deciding who will govern constituted little more than a 'bolt-on extra' placed in front of the traditional governmental system; government was still decided on the basis of who could command the support of parliament, but the make-up of parliament was now decided by popular vote. The people had won the right to choose **who** should govern them, if the essentials of **how** they were to be governed - 'responsibly' - survived.

The Radical challenge

Within the above consideration of the transition from Whig to Liberal dominance over constitutional theory and practice, we have touched upon the Radical challenge to mainstream Liberalism. Nineteenth century Radicalism was hostile to traditionalism but never captured the Liberal Party; far less did it transform British government. Nevertheless, it was influential for a time, indeed Birch cites Radical pressure as the key element in leading to the campaign to extend the franchise, and Beer finds it necessary to examine Radical and Liberal politics together.

The tensions and conflicts between Liberals and Radicals are in many ways crucial to our concern here with the maintenance into the democratic era of narrow, elitist notions of representation. Unlike mainstream Liberalism the Radical position took the move from (Whig) fixed, corporate and community interests, to individuals and opinions, to its logical conclusion. Beer notes for example that in standing for freedom of the individual, 'loosening his (sic) ties to the established social groupings with their fixed interests, and enhancing his ability to create new associations in pursuit of new demands', Liberals and Radicals were 'at one' (Beer, 1982, p. 33). But (reminiscent of the earlier 'Levellers'), Radical demands included shorter parliaments, electoral pledges from candidates and governmental commitment to carry out the programme submitted to the people. Thus the Radical, unlike the Liberal ideal, was truly one of popular government via popular participation and accountability; the delegatory sense of representation. Radical theory was therefore opposed to the Whig/Liberal 'parliamentarism'.

Radical rejection of parliamentarism is rooted in an alternative conception of the individual as the basis for representation. Indeed, the Radical view of 'the people' has little in common with the Liberal 'middle class' ideal of citizen elector. In the Radical tradition, as Beer tells us, rather than 'the people' meaning a miscellany of rational, autonomous, free willed individuals:

> it means rather a body of individuals bound together and guided forward by a unified and authoritative will. In spite of apparent diversity, this unity of will and direction is there, forming the ultimate and only sovereign in the polity - supreme, morally infallible, even sacred (Beer, 1982, p. 40).

Just how these individuals, 'the people', are 'bound together' by their collective will is something of a grey area in Radical theory to which we will return. For the moment, I want to emphasize that for the Radical 'popular government' and 'popular sovereignty' were not just slogans signifying opposition to old hierarchies. Rather, it was the will of the people that was sovereign; the Radical concept of democracy was inherently participatory. Thus whereas Liberalism showed itself to be amenable to traditionalist and pre-democratic ideas of 'representative government', Radicalism was premised upon direct democracy as the ideal; 'representative democracy' was a necessary compromise. Any idea of the House of Commons as a 'deliberative' chamber was therefore unacceptable. Instead, Radicals sought to transform the Commons into a truly representative assembly. These distinctions serve well to highlight the different attitudes of Radicals and Liberals to the nature of political representation and government.

Radical and mainstream Liberal principles thus emphasize the exactly opposite poles of the relationship between government and the people: Liberalism being about 'top-down' parliamentarism and a passive, legitimizing role for the electorate; Radicalism emphasizing 'bottom-up' active popular participation and the delegatory sense of representation. For Radicals 'responsible' government was little more than a front for maintaining the power and privileges of the elite. In order to combat the old hierarchies and entrenched interests a highly 'responsive' government was envisaged, with an active role for the mass electorate. The emphasis here is clearly upon the people, rather than the government, having the means to ensure that their views form the basis of public policy.

More specifically, Radical democracy demands that the views of the majority must prevail. Again we touch upon the 'grey area' of how the will of the majority is to be elicited and translated into government policy, but the time has not yet come to take this up. Instead, let us consider further this Radical attachment to the will of the majority. Beer gets straight to the heart of this question by asking, 'Did the Radicals believe that the majority has the right to do whatever it liked?' In reply to his own, rhetorical question, Beer seems quite sure that they did not; Radicals were not 'crude majoritarians':

> The majority should rule, not because it is arbitrarily sovereign but because it, and it alone, can be trusted to speak with the voice of the whole people. It is the one will in the community that can be trusted to speak the general will. The majority ... is the only body which has no interest opposed to that of the whole. It is therefore through the will of the majority that the people carry on their war against the special interests and for the national interest (Beer, 1982, p. 41).

The above passage provides both a succinct exposition of the basis of Radical championship of the will of the majority, and a good illustration of why Beer feels that Radicals should not be considered 'crude majoritarians'. Yet Birch seems to take the opposite view. In his consideration of utilitarianism as the most influential strand of Radical thought, Birch clearly feels that in being unable to take account of minority feeling, or the variations in the intensity of feeling, it was crudely majoritarian:

> the interests of the majority would always be put first, even if the majority were only mildly in favour of a proposal while the minority felt that it threatened their wellbeing and even their lives (Birch, 1979, p. 47).

But we should note that Birch (and sometimes Beer too) is speaking in terms of 'the majority' and 'the interests of the majority' rather than 'the majority view' or 'the will of the majority'. The importance of these subtle distinctions becomes appreciable once we remember that it is views rather than any 'fixed' characteristics which form the basis of Radical representational theory's support for 'the majority'. The spectre of 'the tyranny of the majority' diminishes somewhat if this is held uppermost. That is, the image of a minority persecuted by the majority is the more convincing if the majority is conceptualized in a more substantial and enduring manner than is suggested by 'opinion'. It is of course possible for a minority to be so persecuted (on perhaps religious or political bases for example), but again, this ignores the context of Radicals' support for 'the majority' and indeed the political nature of Radicalism. By this I mean that rather than the majority of 'the people', it is more accurate to think in terms of 'the electorate'; the majority view needs to be drawn out through the electoral process. Any potential or actually existing permanent majority is therefore irrelevant unless illicited through the electoral process. In turn, the Radicals' belief in the unity of the people as a collective body with a common purpose would rule out any encouragement of divisive prejudice or vested interest via that process or any other. As Liberals believed Liberal*ism* would create a Liber*al* society, so Radicals believed popular *enlightenment* would result from the following of Radical political principles.

It therefore seems to me that Radicalism (whether of the seventeenth, eighteenth or nineteenth centuries) is rarely given a fair hearing. In turn this seems symptomatic of the 'top-down' orientation common to most British government text books, and the preoccupation with actual outcomes rather than the analysis of such events in British political history. That is, because Radicalism failed to dominate British politics and constitutional practice, there is generally less interest shown. Hence the increased interest here in the reasons for the failure of a 'bottom-up' participatory challenge to the British political tradition, to which we will now return.

The above consideration of 'the people' and 'the majority' again touched upon what I have called the grey area in Radical thought. I have indicated that for Radical theory and practice to be fully consistent the role of the electoral programme is essential and prominent. We have seen that electoral pledges and the idea of the policy mandate feature in Radical theory, but I have also indicated that in these instances Radicals failed to transform the political practice of the Liberal Party, within which Radicalism was a minority current. Thus there is a severe weakness in the disparity between Radical theory and actual political practice. To this we must add a weakness within Radical theory itself, in that, despite the belief in popular sovereignty and its participatory and 'delegatory' implications, Radicals failed to present a consistent and unambiguous account of the practical application of such principles. They failed, in other words, to promulgate an agreed 'instrumentalist' idea of the party, and thereby failed to overcome a central problem: 'that of showing how a government can follow the dictates of the popular will without pursuing a set of contradictory policies' (Birch, 1979, p. 33). If Liberals favoured the 'loose' idea of party because of their cherished 'independence', Radicals had other reasons for failing to embrace fully any stronger conception.

Beer argues that although the attitude in this country was less hostile than in the USA, the Radical was far from a natural supporter of the party system. Given their belief 'in the unity, or potential unity, of the people, rival partisanship can only seem wicked' (Beer, 1982, p. 42). Yet Radical initiative also 'led to the founding of the National Liberal Federation in 1877' (Beer, 1982, p. 39), and to the attempt to assert the power of the extra-parliamentary party over the parliamentary leadership. In order to resolve the apparent contradiction of Radicals initiating the formation and championing the role of the party, whilst at the same time being opposed to the very principle of the party system, we must again refer to the context of 'the people'.

Radical hostility to the party ideal is attracted by and directed towards parties as representatives of 'special interests' (or, as Bentham would have it, the 'sinister interests'); the Conservative Party of the 'landed nobility', and even the Liberal Party seen as the vehicle of the new rising manufacturing class. The attitude is the same as that taken towards the interest group seeking advancement of the narrow interests of its own members, and thereby fostering the social divisiveness anathema to Radicals: 'For the unity of "the people" is not co-operative solidarity, but rather homogeneity, likeness, similarity of condition and wants' (Beer, 1982, p. 42). Thus the Radical attitude will be hostile to any claim to preference from 'leading' or 'outstanding' individuals, and especially where such claims seek to assert the right of the few to decide for the many. The Radical hostility to party as representative of a certain kind of special individual is on a par with that of the Liberal to fixed, 'corporate' interests; each are corrupting and divisive influences:

> Towards them the Radical is not, like the Liberal simply suspicious; he (sic) is positively hostile ... For they are ... selfish promptings seeking continually to breach the unified will of the people (Beer, 1982, p. 40).

Hence there is a clear antipathy to all claims of special interests and to politicians asserting their 'independence' from the people, and audaciously professing to 'deliberate' about the national interest on their behalf:

> The Radical ideal, with its appeal to direct democracy, confirms this right of the people to associate in order to *press their views on government* (my emphasis). There could be no question of such ... being 'unconstitutional' (Beer, 1982, p. 42).

Equally clear is that this puts Radicals in conflict with the central planks of British constitutional norms, and, given mainstream Liberalism's acceptance of these norms, the Liberal Party became the site of a protracted struggle over these issues. The Radical commitment to active, participatory democracy also led the drive to transform the organizational form of the Liberal Party so as to encourage and reflect popular involvement and activity. This too is contrary to the strong leadership tradition of prevailing political culture.

Given the above, although the extent of Radical influence was varied, in general classical Liberal influence was strongest, and Radicalism weakest, where Liberalism and existing political practice were compatible (whilst such political practice was incompatible with Radicalism). This is well illustrated in regard to the relationship between government and the people, within which Liberal principles can be summarized as 'independence', 'parliamentarism' and the 'deliberative' role of the MP at the governmental level, and 'passivity' and 'legitimation' at the level of the electorate. That the Liberal view of the constitution was clear and precise, and 'was so closely tied to existing institutions in Britain' (Birch, 1979, p. 66) is most important. Liberalism offered limited and gradual electoral and social reform - the great issues of the day - without the need to give credence to such 'dangerous' notions as popular sovereignty, with its egalitarian democratic implications. By contrast Radicalism, by its very definition, demanded fundamental change. At the same time it evidenced this grey theoretical area, and contradictions between its theory and practice which provided a perception of conflict both within the Liberal Party and between Radicals and the whole existing nature of society.

Political culture

I have suggested that many British government textbooks tend towards a preoccupation with actual political outcomes, at the expense of close analysis of the reasons for those outcomes. To some extent I think this is symptomatic of a common conception of 'political culture'. Kavanagh defines political culture for example as 'denoting the emotional and attitudinal environment within which a political system operates' (Kavanagh, 1972, pp. 10-11). Similarly, Birch and Beer hold that 'the way in which people behave in political situations depends very much on the values and political traditions of their society' (Birch, 1979, p. 241), and therefore political culture is 'one of the main variables in a political system, and a major factor in explaining the political behaviour of individuals, groups and parties' (Beer, 1982, p. xii). Thus:

> Political culture is the pattern of the individual's attitudes and
> orientations towards politics among members of a political system. It
> is the subjective realm which underlies and gives meaning to
> political actions (Almond and Powell, 1966, p. 50).

Further, this shaping of political attitudes and thereby of political behaviour, 'provides the stimulus for change and is the underpinning of stability' (Marsh, 1971, p. 453). There is general agreement as to the importance of political culture, and that it is derived from and constituted out of past trends and historical continuities. These trends and continuities are therefore often referred to in relation to the explanation of subsequent events. This is all perfectly reasonable, but it does lend itself well to simple acceptance of those continuities and trends rather than seeking to *explain* them, and to a lack of interest in that which does not 'fit' with prevailing political culture. Hence what we might call a negative or inhibitive role for political culture - how it might figure in relation to the failure of a given trend to materialize or to endure - is largely ignored.

We saw for example Birch's attitude to the demise of the Levellers prior to the Restoration, and similarly, that the stable Old Whig era was preceded by an unstable period during which relatively short lived new forms of political organization sprang up, but failed to endure. Others are little concerned with this period however, since it does not fit the framework of 'stability' and 'continuity' emphasized by the predominant approach to political culture. Instead the unspoken assumption is that since they were 'short lived' the 'new forms' of politics were simply inferior; stability returns given a suitable quality of theory and practice in a new constitutional settlement.

Even in relation to the settled, stable period of the 'balanced constitution', the concentration of emphasis tends to be upon the emergence of a new kind of governmental power. Beer for example stresses the loss of monarchical prerogative and the transfer of most political power from crown to ministry, and the implications for the maintenance of 'strong government' through the Whig era. First and foremost then, it is such concrete developments, 'outcomes', which form the predominant focus. But this leads to a lack of concern with possibilities of alternative paths of development indicated by contrary trends, simply because such did not endure. Any inhibitive role for institutionalized political culture, in combating 'hostile' counter-trends, therefore goes unexplored.

In regard to his consideration of the conflict between Liberal and Radical ideas, Beer notes the weakness of Radicalism in this country by comparison to the USA. But he neither seeks to explain why this should be, nor does he acknowledge its relevance to the maintenance of parliamentarism by Liberals. Indeed he never really goes beyond a straight forward historical account of the conflict caused in the Liberal Party by the active, participatory organizational principles of Radicalism. The fact that Beer does not seek to emphasize that these principles were in conflict not just with the established Liberal Party organization but with the whole institutionalized tradition of 'leadership' in British politics and government, indicates that he is 'reading' these events back through the known outcomes; such therefore become seen as virtually 'inevitable' and 'natural'.

I think this kind of orientation severely limits the adequacy of analysis. Norton hints at a more adaquate conception of the role of political culture in saying that it:

> cannot be divorced from the contraints of history and of physical and
> spatial resources. Each has a significant impact on the other. The
> impact has not been in one direction only: the political culture has
> served to shape political perceptions and actions, and hence to
> influence the nation's political history. Conversely, those actions have
> been constrained by the experiences of history ... (and) by Britain's
> geographic location and limited resources (Norton, 1984, p. 25).

Although Norton himself does not develop this viewpoint analytically in the manner that I think is required, this does seem to me to be a far more adequate starting point. What I want to suggest here, and will seek to further illustrate in subsequent chapters, is that rather than the success of political ideas and practice being determined by their intrinsic merit, rather than the competition between ideas being carried on in a kind of meritocratic vacuum, the context within which that competition occurs is both limited ('narrow') and biased ('elitist'); some ideas and conventions are favoured and some inhibited by the existence of prevailing political culture. Considering such an 'active inhibitive' role for political culture at specific conjunctures of development should therefore be recognized as an important explanatory aspect of both historical and contemporary developments. Having outlined this alternative approach, and its application in analysis, it remains only to summarize our conclusions from this chapter.

Conclusions

This chapter has indicated that from Absolute Monarchy to the advent of parliamentary democracy the debate about government has focused very largely upon **who** should govern, and on what basis of authority, rather than upon **how** government should be carried on. Initially the main concern was with whether authority should rest with the Monarch alone or be shared between the Monarch and the unreformed parliament. Subsequently the focus shifted and it was accepted that authority lay with an Executive drawn from the reformed parliament. However, the concept of govermental office and the role of government itself, has remained very largely consistent. Throughout, the office of government has been deemed to involve the reconciliation of the various 'particular' interests in society, with what today tends to be referred to as the 'national interest'; government policy, once made, thereby becomes sacrosanct.

The dominant view of the nature of governmental authority has of course conditioned, and been conditioned by, the idea of who should hold and undertake the responsibilities of government office. Under Absolute Monarchy for example, the idea of the Divine Right of Kings is inseparable from that as to who should perform the functions of government. When this basis of authority was rejected, a new consensus emphasizing the shared responsibility for government emerged, but the idea of what those functions of government were and should be was undisturbed by the change in the basis of either responsibility or authority. Subsequently the broadening of the basis of authority continued, with society as a whole increasingly being seen as the repository of that authority. To put all this another way: what has not been effectively questioned is **whether** government, in whatever guise, has the right to make decisions independently and on behalf of the people. We have seen that Radicalism represented such a questioning, and we have seen the manner of its defeat. In the next chapter we will see that the Labour Party represented another such challenge, and we will consider the manner of its 'constitutionalization'.

In general, writers dealing with the British political tradition take what might be characterized as a 'positive/continuous' view of political culture; concrete political outcomes seen as emerging out of powerful trends and continuities in ideas, values and attitudes. Such an approach little questions the narrowness of the historical debate nor its elitist nature. Indeed, it tends towards seeing the outcomes in each succeeding evolution of the constitution as straightforwardly favourable and perfectly natural. However, I have suggested a three way relationship within political culture: ideas do indeed prompt action, and therefore 'explain' political behaviour, but when a system of ideas becomes dominant, those ideas instigate institutions and conventions which then reflect their values in practice. Political traditions do not exist in a vacuum, but in an institutional context which expresses the acceptance that **these things must be done.** In turn this tends to confine questioning of the system in terms of whether these things need to be done **in this way** rather than another way; **how** a function should be fulfilled rather than **whether** it is still relevant or should be superseded.

Only by seeing political culture as this mutually supporting triangle of theory underpinning practice within institutions, can we appreciate an active-inhibitive role; limiting the range of possibilities by institutionalized bias. The greater the divergency from current practice represented by a proposed reform the less likely it is to be adopted or to be successful. Fundamental change must therefore be attempted through the overthrow of the system itself or within this, at best, incremental context. The former method would only be appropriate under the most extreme circumstances and over the most crucial of issues, two such examples suggested by our consideration thus far are the civil war(s) and the 'Glorious Revolution'. The latter method involves the in-built bias which we have seen to have been effective in marginalizing Radicalism, and will see to have been effective in constitutionalizing the socialist challenge.

Notes

1. There are now 159 members of the UN.
2. This is not to say that the idea has never had any currency. The notion of microcosmic representation is implicit in some Whig, Fabian and corporatist thought for example. My point is that these have never had a significant impact upon the political institutions and governmental conventions of this country.
3. Beer merely mentions the Liberal maintenance of parliamentarism (p. 19; p. 33). Birch has a more substantial section dealing with it (pp. 28-9) but does not question Liberal maintenance of parliamentarism at all. Perhaps, in crediting the movement for parliamentary reform to Radicals, Birch does at least imply - since Radicalism rejects parliamentarism - that parliamentarism is an idea not well suited to a movement for the extension of the franchise. Also, since Radicalism never gained dominance, the survival of parliamentarism is more understandable. But none of this is at all explicit. Greenleaf is particularly orientated towards state interventionism, and the realm of ideas he considers is largely limited to its relationship to this prime interest. Therefore, although he considers at some length 'The extension of the Franchise and its Effect', in Vol. 1, Chapter 4, he never questions the nature of representation at all.
4. Asa Briggs, 'Middle Class Consciousness in English Politics', in *Past and Present,* Vol. 1 (1956), pp. 65-74.
5. As a result of the Lords' rejection of the whole Finance Bill of 1909, the Parliament Act of 1911 was passed to provide that money bills should go for the royal assent one month

after being passed by the Commons, regardless of what the Lords might do. The position since the 1949 Parliament Act has been that any bill rejected by the Lords, or to which their proposed amendments are unacceptable to the Commons, can go for the royal assent in the next session of parliament, provided that it is again passed without substantial change by the Commons. A 'money bill' can be delayed by the Lords for only one month.

3 From unified Libertarianism to Libertarian form, Collectivist content

Introduction

As we saw in the last chapter, Liberal individualism is associated with the industrial revolution; the rise of industrial capitalism and the wane of the economic interests and political dominance of the landed aristocracy. There was nevertheless an alliance between the old and new dominant classes in regard to the attempt to restrain working class interests, aspirations and influence. Hence initially the extension of the franchise was limited to the propertied middle class. But a loose counter-alliance of Radicals and working class activism ensured that the democratic movement was unable to be stopped (if it was somewhat compromized). As this process grew and the franchise was further extended, so we are able to begin speaking of the movement from the Liberal to the Liberal-Democratic constitution, although universal suffrage was not attained until 1928.

In this chapter we will examine the manner by which the underlying orthodoxy of governmental policy orientation was transformed within this Liberal-Democratic framework. Importantly, this occurred *without* an appropriate institutional transformation; 'Collectivism' operated within the Liberal individualistic constitutional set up (hence Libertarian form, Collectivist content). The rise of Collectivism was related to the growth of democratic demands, and each was related to political, social, economic and ideological factors. The political demands of early Radicals like the Diggers and the Levellers can be said to have been sustained and renewed via Paine for example, and again, later still, through the Chartists. We have already considered Paine's powerful advocacy of popular, participatory democracy, less well appreciated however is that:

> Between 1791 and 1792 in particular, he decided that trade alone could not assure a subsistence to all and that government would have to promote a more extensive notion of rights than was implied by what we now term a 'negative liberty' conception of commerce and society, where individuals are considered 'free' primarily if the state does not interfere with them (Claeys, 1989, p. 95).

As we will see, the growing questioning of the adequacy of the 'negative' conception of freedom indicated above, is very influential in the transition from Libertarian laissez-faire assumptions, to the interventionist implications of Collectivism. Paine may therefore be a more important influence here than is often thought; his early advocacy of a broader conception of individual liberty is little appreciated. As Claeys (1989) has argued, most commentators have seen Paine's commitment to 'minimal government' as straight-forwardly requiring a laissez-faire approach.

In relation to the demands of The Chartist Movement of 1838-48, interestingly Birch considers Chartism to have been 'entirely compatible with Liberal principles':

> The six points of the Charter - manhood suffrage, annual parliaments, voting by ballot, equal electoral districts, the abolition of property qualifications for candidates, and payment for members - imply an acceptance of Liberal ideals rather than their rejection (Birch, 1979, p. 85).

Yet this seems again to be reading historical events through their subsequently known outcomes, rather than problematizing them in their proper historical context. That is, although what we now know as 'Liberalism' seems in the main to be compatible with these points of the Charter, at this time it was still in the process of being constructed out of the opposed tendencies of anti-democratic Whigism and popular democratic Radicalism. Not until 1868 did Gladstone first take office as Prime Minister at the head of a party formed 'by a fusion of whigs, Peelites and radicals, to which the term "liberal" was first regularly applied in England' (Ensor, 1988, p. 2).

Also annual parliaments had been a long standing **Radical** demand, just as the delegatory sense of representation and the active role envisaged for the mass of the people by Chartism were also associated with Radicalism. Neither should 'the stigma of disloyalty' (see Claeys, 1989, p. 15) which had been attached to Radical ideas during and in the aftermath of the Revolutionary and Napoleonic Wars be forgotten. Indeed only four years after Waterloo and less than twenty years before Chartism began, the 'Peterloo massacre' (1819) had seen a mass assembly around similar Radical demands brutally ended with eleven dead and hundreds wounded. Indeed Chartist riots and strikes coming to adopt the Charter at times led to establishment fears of revolution. It therefore seems somewhat naive to suggest that Chartism was completely compatible with 'Liberalism', particularly since no explanation is given for its failure. But again, we have seen that the dominant view of 'political culture' is unconcerned with explaining such 'failures', only with concrete 'outcomes'.

If Radicalism's most apparent contribution to the growth of Collectivism was through the championship of democracy, an economic and a social impetus were also to be seen. These arose out of the (often) widespread unemployment, poverty, ill-health, overcrowded and insanitary housing and poor working conditions, which the unrestrained capitalist economy had produced. All of these aspects combined in the undermining of the ideological orthodoxy of 'libertarianism'; the assumption of a natural self-regulating balance existing in society, and especially in economic affairs. Hence this old orthodoxy begins to give way to the view that such a balance required artificial construction. The role of the state was therefore transformed: whereas both Whigs and classical Liberals saw the state as the foremost threat to individual freedom, 'New' (or 'social') Liberalism begins to see it instead as the handmaiden and guardian of freedom.

The extent to which New Liberalism instigated or was itself a response to the rise of Collectivism is unclear, but certainly the significance and influence of the early Labour Party is crucial in intensifying the Collectivist challenge. How the Labour Party influenced the Collectivist outcome will be touched upon here, and further elaborated in the following chapter. The main purpose of Chapter Four will however be to demonstrate the manner by which the Labour Party was itself influenced profoundly by the institutional context within which it operated; that is, the chapter deals with the party's 'constitutionalization'.

Along with the movement towards a new Collectivist orthodoxy, both the breadth and depth of government intervention grew enormously. Yet even though what governments **did,** changed very significantly from the kind of policies favoured in the earlier period, this is less significant than may be thought because the **nature** of goverment changed little. That is, in regard to the institutions and processes of government, there were remarkably few innovations to facilitiate the Collectivist orientation of post 1945. Indeed all that really changed was that what governments considered **to be** in 'the national interest' changed radically, whilst the government's **role** as **arbiter** of the national interest (as a concept) changed hardly at all.

From Libertarianism to Collectivism

The work of W H Greenleaf (1983), whose first volume is entitled 'The Rise of Collectivism', provides a good starting point for our consideration of the transition from the dominance in ideology and governmental practice of Libertarianism to that of Collectivism. However, it should be said at the outset that as much as the transition *from* Libertarianism *to* Collectivism, Greenleaf's overall theme is that the 'character' of modern British politics is reflected in the continuing tensions *between* Libertarian and Collectivist tendencies. There is therefore some similarity between Greenleaf's and my own position stated above, if our conclusions are somewhat at odds. I will elaborate upon this subsequently, as it becomes appropriate.

Greenleaf points out that, as indeed I have indicated, the two phases of Liberalism reflect nicely the wane of the idea of a natural societal harmony - interference with which was not only harmful but futile - and the rise of the idea that government intervention was necessary to artificially create such a desirable societal harmony. The antithesis between Libertarianism and Collectivism was therefore that between 'two contrasting views of freedom, personal fulfillment, and the proper place of government in society' (Greenleaf, 1983, Vol. 2, Part 2, p. 19-20).

In upholding freedom for rational individuals to pursue their own self interest - taken to mean as little restraint as possible from government and state - Classical Liberals had thought that the optimum production of goods and wealth would be achieved. Despite wide disparities of wealth and income such a system would therefore represent the most advantageous position for all. But such beliefs were greatly undermined by the depth of poverty and deprivation apparent in the second half of the nineteenth century. Indeed Henry George's *Progress and Poverty* (1884), provided a thorough critique of the previously dominant view that the benefits of economic growth would 'trickle down' to all. George was deeply pessimistic about the 'wedge' of poverty being forced through and starkly dividing society. By the 1880s a movement away from Gladstonian laissez-faire was apparent, and hence 'New Liberalism' no longer saw the state as a necesary evil to be kept firmly in check, but as a tool of reform. This signifies the shift in the perception of the meaning of liberty, and how it might best be furthered and maintained by government, which Paine had perceived as early as 1792. That is, rather than the 'negative' conception of freedom as 'absence of restraint', freedom begins instead to be defined as 'absence of impediment'. The state is then able to be seen as the means to **remove**:

> those conditions which inhibited the full life for the mass of the citizens, the poverty and distress brought about by unregulated economic growth and technological change (Greenleaf, 1983, Vol. 2. Part 2, p. 27).

This new conception of freedom thus demanded not just a new role for the state, but one far broader in scope and increasingly more detailed and systematic in depth. This is clearly indicated by for example: the rising level of public expenditure and taxation required to pay for it; the increase in employment in public authorities and the machinery of government and administration; and the inevitable vast increase in the volume of legislation. Similarly, in Robertson's consideration of the emergence of official secrecy, we saw that the relationship between government and administration evolved after the introduction of entry to the civil service via competitive examination, and as Ensor puts it:

> From then onwards may be traced a steady and rapid expansion in the size, number, and efficiency of the government departments, which - followed at short distance by similar expansions on the municipal side - revolutionized the scope and role of government itself (Ensor, 1988, p. xxii).

In turn, and again as already indicated, Greenleaf considers this effect of the increasing influence of democratic demands to have been crucial in furthering the growth of Collectivism.

It would therefore seem that 1870 is an early marker of a new era during which the old laissez-faire orthodoxy would give way to a new interventionist and Collectivist one. Marking the onset of the process of change is far easier than assessing its completion however. For example:

> It is possible, by listing a long series of nineteenth century Acts of Parliament dealing with child or female labour in factories, or public health in congested or ill-planned cities, or elementary education for children whose parents could not afford to pay for it, to suggest either that the Victorian period (had in any case) not (been) an age of laissez-

faire, or that it had ceased to be so long before the end of the century
(Peden, 1988, p. 5).

Yet it is more generally agreed that the Collectivist era proper does not begin until after the
Second World War. We will therefore first consider in some detail the rise of
interventionism, before looking more closely at its culmination in the post-1945 Collectivist
era.

It is clear that 'During the nineteenth century the density of population more than trebled',
and the impact of demographic and industrial expansion 'altered the face of the land and
closely affected the condition of the people working in the new factories and living in the
mushrooming towns' (Greenleaf, 1983, Vol. 1, pp. 79-80):

> this rapid concentration of people in growing towns - there were parts
> of Liverpool in 1884 with a density of 1200 persons to the acre -
> entailed many problems of housing, disease, water supply, drainage,
> sewage disposal, lighting, poverty, and so on... what was done by
> private or local initiative proved woefully inadequate and overcrowding
> and general squalor resulted (Greenleaf, 1983, Vol. 1, pp. 93-4).

Thus, in common with others, Greenleaf cites a multitude of social problems associated
with the development of industry and urban growth as against the relative decline in
importance of agriculture, and also the necessary greater 'responsiveness' of government
due to the widening of the franchise, as important factors giving impetus to this increased
state activity. But he also cites **war** as foremost among them, something which will be
more appreciable in the following chapter.

In relation to these factors giving impetus to New Liberalism, increased state intervention
and the rise of Collectivism, the Conservative leader Benjamin Disraeli has a significant
place. If 'Born of Disraeli's (1867) extension of the franchise', Gladstone's first 'Liberal'
government of 1868 set in motion 'the greatest reforming parliament since that born of the
original extension in 1832' (Ensor, 1988, p. 2), it was nevertheless in decline after about
1870. This period also sees the beginnings of the rise of the Irish Home Rule Party, which
would undermine the two-party system in the House of Commons for some time.
Following the dissolution Disraeli won the General Election of 1874; the Conservatives
winning 350 seats to the Liberals' 245 and 57 for the Irish Home Rule Party (Ball, 1987,
pp. 14-15). This put Disraeli for the first time at the head of a government with an assured

parliamentary majority, though he had led the Conservative Party in the Commons for twenty five years.

The Conservative Party leadership continued to be drawn overwhelmingly from the aristocracy and the upper middle class. But since the First Reform Act of 1832, financial, industrial and commercial interests and forms of wealth had greatly increased their representation in the party, at the expense of the landowning interests; a reflection of rapid industrialization. Following the 1867 extension, and particularly that of 1884, that section of landed interest previously giving its support to the Liberals also turned to the Conservatives (see eg Beer, 1982, pp. 252-3, Ball, 1987, pp. 32-41). So despite the largely aristocratic parliamentary leadership, the base of Conservative support was widening. But Disraeli, and after him Lord Randolph Churchill, represented a strand of Toryism - mindful of the increasing role of 'the people' - that sought to extend the base of the party's support still further, urging 'that the cause of the common people should be espoused by the traditional landed classes or by the enlightened among their mercantile successors' (Greenleaf, 1983, Vol. 1, p. 298). Indeed, in emphasizing concern for 'the condition of the people', a working class appeal was constructed; an appeal reformulated by Randolph Churchill as 'Tory Democracy'. This progressive appeal was spearheaded by a series of social reforms.

Disraeli thus argued that the fulfillment of the duties of the 'natural leaders' was a matter 'not only for individual and voluntary charity, but also for action by the state' (Beer, 1982, p. 268). The Liberal idea of 'personal responsibility', in absolving the better off (middle class) from any responsibility for the poor, had created 'Two Nations'. The governing class must recognize and discharge its proper responsibilities in order that One Nation might ('again') be created out of the two. Ever present in Disraeli's writings and speeches was this ideal of charismatic leadership dedicated to recreating One Nation. However, his election address of 1874 made only a brief reference to his concern with 'all measures calculated to improve the condition of the people' (Beer, 1982, p. 265), and having won the election:

> He could not skate so boldly in office as he had in opposition over the
> thin ice between his own reforming ideas and the property interests of
> those who had made him their champion (Ensor, 1988, p. 30).

Indeed, few of his followers in parliament supported him for his commitment to social reform, particularly as when in opposition Disraeli had rallied support against Gladstone's reforms on the basis that they menaced 'every institution and every interest, every class and every calling in the country' (Ensor, 1988, p. 31).

Nevertheless, Disraeli's 1874 government did embark upon social reform, and many significant and trend-setting pieces of legislation derive from this period, including: a Public Health Act, which established sanitary authorities throughout the country; an Education Act, which, building upon the Act of 1870 which had made elementary education national, now made it, in effect, compulsory, and obliged local authorities to appoint attendance committees; an Artisans' Dwellings Act, giving local authorities powers to tackle the housing problem; a Sale of Food and Drugs Act, which was the first comprehensive measure on the subject; an Agricultural Holdings Act, giving compensation to displaced tenants in a programme of agricultural improvements; a Land transfer Act, establishing the general lines upon which land registration was henceforth treated in England; a Merchant Shipping Act, which provided for the safety and protection of seamen, with the Board of Trade empowered to detain unsafe ships; a Conspiracy and Protection of Property Act, which (despite its title) extended legal protection to the right to strike; and The Employers and Workmans' Act, which improved the position of employees in regard to the law governing breach of contract (see eg Ensor, 1988, pp. 33-40; Beer, 1982, pp. 262-6).

This programme of reform and intervention seems clearly to have driven 'a remarkable number of nails into *laisser-faire'* s coffin' (Ensor, 1988, p. 36). As one enemy of the Conservative Party, the Lib-Lab MP Alexander MacDonald, said at the time, the Conservative Party had done more for the working class in five years than the Liberals had in fifty (Beer, 1982, p. 264). However, Disraeli was in fact always more concerned with foreign affairs and the empire than with social problems (see eg Ensor, 1988, pp. 35-65), if in his famous Crystal Palace speech of 1872 for example, he linked the two, emphasizing the need for good health, housing and factory reforms to sustain (One) Nation and Empire (see eg Ball, 1987, p. 40). He was in any case adamant that no matter how desirable social reform might be, it should not lead to new taxes. Indeed, a sense of perspective on the scope of this programme is gained by the recognition that the civil service at this time numbered only some 50, 000 and income tax was only 3d (barely more than 1p) in the pound (Beer, 1982, p. 270).

It is therefore the case both that increasing state intervention (and thereby the Collectivist cause) was 'legitimized' and encouraged (however ambiguously) by Disraeli, and that following this high point of Conservative interventionism, after their defeat in the General Election of 1880, the party retreated from it. Further, despite the presence of 'Radical Joe' Chamberlain (and the 1884 extension of the franchise) the Liberal government which followed was hardly marked by its progressivism, and what little it did attempt was opposed by the Conservatives in the Lords.

There followed an unsettled period, with elections in consecutive years, 1885 and 1886, and the dominance of the Irish Home Rule issue:

> the Irish Home Rule Party increased its representation, and for a short time it held the balance of power in the House of Commons with crucial political consequences for government stability... the Liberal Party's espousal of Home Rule led to the 1886 split in the party with opponents ... leaving to constitute the Liberal Unionists, who soon became indistinguishable from the Conservatives (Ball, 1987, p. 15).

The split Liberal Party contributed to a long period of Conservative domination (with the exception of a weak Liberal Government between 1892-5) lasting until 1905. In relation to our main interests here it seems that Lord Randolph Churchill's youth prevented him from acceding to the Conservative leadership. Rather than the Disraelian tradition being renewed therefore, 'at a period when swiftly changing conditions called for legislative action' the new leader, the 'anti-progressive' Lord Salisbury 'stood nearly always on the side of doing nothing' (Ensor, 1988, p. 90). Other important contributions to the undermining of libertarianism and laissez-faire nonetheless require mention.

The period between the ending of the Revolutionary and Napoleonic Wars (1815) and the Great Reform Act (1832) was one of depression and increased unemployment. The Poor Law response was in line with the general orientation of the time, which saw unemployment as caused very largely by the moral defects of 'work-shy individuals, work was available for those who truly wanted it and looked for it, and poverty could be avoided by regular employment:

> Despite the experience of booms and slumps throughout the nineteenth century, economists, following Ricardo, argued that the economy would always tend towards full employment. The community's income from production (wages and profits) would always be spent on consumption or invested. There might be an over-supply of a particular product, because of miscalculation or because of a change in taste, but there would be no general glut of goods, so that, by implication, there could be no general unemployment (Peden, 1988, p. 4).

This individualist, laissez-faire orientation did not begin to be effectively challenged as the basis for government policy until the detailed empirical work of Charles Booth in London between 1886-1903, and Seebohm Rowntree in York in 1899-1901 (following Henry George's intellectual critique in *Progress and Poverty* mentioned earlier). Booth's *Life and Labour of the People of London* (1902) indicated that one third of the London working class were on or below the poverty line. He offered systematic evidence that (at least not all of) the poor could be blamed for their own poverty. Rowntree undertook a similar, if indeed more rigorous, survey of the poor in York (see eg Peden, 1988, pp. 11-12). He concluded that almost as high a proportion of York's working class also lived in poverty, and not primarily because they were 'work-shy' or because they misspent their wages. These findings were important in challenging the libertarian assumptions that individuals and not the workings of the capitalist economy itself were responsible for unemployment. In turn, they contributed towards the perception of the inadequacy of the 'negative freedom' approach which sustained non-intervention.

The same period, following the 1885 General Election and temporary rupture of the two-party system mentioned earlier, was also one during which Socialist and labourist influence began to become significant. Again, this will be dealt with in detail subsequently, but for now we will remain with the two old parties.

As indicated, the Conservative Party lowered the banner of social reform following Disraeli's defeat in 1880. Ten years of Conservative government from 1895-1905 did nevertheless produce some notable reforms, including for example: The Workmens' Compensation Act of 1897, which established the principle that employers were liable to pay compensation to workers in cases of industrial accidents; The Factories and Workshops Act of 1901, which implemented legal minimum conditions; The Education Act of 1902, which made permanent the national system of 'provided' and 'voluntary' schools under local Education Authorities, and empowered these to provide for secondary and technical schools; The Shops Act 1904, which authorized local authorities to shorten the shopworkers' working day; and the Unemployed Workmen Act 1905, which broke from the old 'poor law' tradition, establishing an administrative structure of local committees authorized to set up labour exchanges, assist in emigration, and other employment related functions (see eg Beer, 1982, pp. 271-72; Ensor, 1988, pp. 237, 355-58, 379).

There is certainly some important legislation passed during this period then, but in its social reform content this **decade** does not compare favourably with the single parliamentary session of 1875. The Conservatives were in fact soundly defeated in the General Election of 1906, and following this defeat the winding down of the emphasis on social reform and 'Tory Democracy' continued. Indeed with the accession of Bonar Law to the leadership of the party in 1911 it was effectively ended, if to be revived in the inter-war period when the party would again swing against laissez-faire. The Great Reforming Liberal Government of 1906, which included Lloyd George, Winston Churchill and William Beveridge (the latter as an advisor not an elected politician), was therefore often frustrated by the Opposition's utilization of their majority in the Lords to defeat their legislative programme:

> During the ten years of Unionist (Conservative) rule since 1895, the second chamber had, as such, lain dormant, and allowed its power of revising bills to rust in almost complete disuse. Now it was to become wide awake again, and was to re-employ that power in order, as in 1893-5, to prevent a liberal government from carrying its bills (Ensor, 1988, p. 386).

Nevertheless Campbell-Bannerman's government passed a wealth of progressive legislation: The Trades Disputes Act 1906 gave trades unions immunities from legal action for damages arising out of the pursuance of their interests in a trade dispute, and in the same year free school meals were brought in with the Education (Provision of Meals) Act; the following year saw provision for the medical inspection of schoolchildren, with the Education (Administrative Provisions) Act 1907, and in 1908 came a Children's Act, establishing children's rights and community responsibilities, and dealing with parental neglect and juvenile offenders; a formal age of retirement was specified (at 70) and old age pensions first introduced with the Act of 1908, and the same year the Coal Mines (8 hours) Act was passed; in 1909 labour exchanges were introduced by statute and trade boards set up to regulate wages in low paid industries via the Wages Board Act. The flagship of reform was however the first scheme to compensate for loss of wages through sickness or unemployment, which began with the Health Insurance Act of 1911 (see eg Peden, 1988, pp. 16-35). Lloyd George intended this to be the beginning of a campaign against poverty, and, unlike Disraeli before him, he sought to secure new taxation revenues in order to extend social reform still further.

This period, between 1906 and the onset of the First World War, thus saw a profound change in the basis of welfare provision and state intervention; a significant move away from the norms of laissez-faire and towards Collectivism. The work of Booth and Rowntree in revealing the extent of poverty, and undermining the dominant perception of its causes as lying in defects in the character of individuals, has been mentioned as being influential in this respect. Not just Socialists but some Liberals and Conservatives too became so persuaded. But there was also a profound concern about the risk of economic and military decline. The poor physical condition of the British working class revealed by the low standard of recruits to fight the Boer War, had begun to jolt the national leadership out of its complacency; laissez-faire was not 'optimizing' in the way that had been envisaged. Thus there arose the 'national efficiency movement':

> National efficiency could be concerned with Britain's ability to compete in international trade as well as on the battlefield. Already in the 1880s there was concern in the Board of Trade about Germany's superiority in technical industries, and it was not necessary to believe in social justice to believe that the British working man (sic) should be provided with an education equal to that of his German counterpart (Peden, 1988, p. 12).

As Disraeli had linked social reform and empire, subsequently the Conservatives had been enthusiastic flag wavers in their imperial policy from the 1870s; there was therefore a natural tendency towards support for national efficiency. Their exploitation of patriotic fervour during the Boer War led to electoral success in the 'khaki' election of 1900, and such has remained a strong element within the Conservative Party. So too was there support for national efficiency in 'Liberal Imperialism', upholding the 'consolidation of Empire based on strong foreign and defence policies' (Ball, 1987, p. 34). Thus the working class needed to be better fed and better educated if for no other reason than because otherwise Britain would be unable to compete with her imperial and industrial rivals!

Libertarian form, Collectivist content

The rise of Collectivism is therefore clearly related to that of democracy and to the decline of the 'negative' conception of freedom; 'New Liberalism' and 'One Nation' Conservatism each sanctioned greater interventionism. Initially this was confined to piecemeal intervention in social policy areas, but the demands of 'national efficiency' would combine with other emphases to stimulate more broadly Collectivist approaches, ultimately including intervention into the economy. I said in the introduction to this chapter though, that the underlying orthodoxy of governmental policy orientation was transformed **within** the Liberal-Democratic framework, that is, without a corresponding institutional transformation. We should therefore be very much aware that even despite the growth of intervention and the influence of Collectivism, the underlying libertarian assumptions of laissez-faire survived, and certainly so at the time period thus covered.

Thus the general free market, laissez-faire position espoused by Adam Smith in *The Wealth of Nations* (1776) was still dominant, if Smith himself had made exceptions to this general principle. He supported protection for British shipping for example, due to its importance in time of war, and the public funding of education and the arts, to offset widespread and debilitating tedium, and enhance individual personality. Intervention was therefore quite possible whilst maintaining laissez-faire as the general principle. As Peden argues, the legislation regulating conditions in factories for example, 'was designed to prevent the exploitation of women and children', who, it was assumed, were not fully capable of 'self-help'; it was not intended 'to interfere with agreements freely arrived at by employers and adult male workers' (Peden, 1988, p. 6).

Even Radicals like Jeremy Bentham and John Stuart Mill were enthusiastically individualistic opponents of interventionism and Collectivism. Bentham's ideas were still very influential, and he had assumed that:

> state intervention was to be regarded as a necessary evil which would
> be acceptable only when there was no other way to secure the greatest
> happiness of the greatest number ... Such a philosophy could lead to
> acceptance of more state intervention, as social problems, such as
> disposal of sewage or prevention of disease, were exacerbated by
> urbanisation. However ... central government action was a last resort
> ... self-help by individuals or local communities was to be preferred
> (Peden, 1988, p. 3).

Similarly, Mill, in his *Principles of Political Economy* (1848) held that, 'letting alone should be the general practice, every departure from it unless required by some great good is a certain evil'. Libertarianism was therefore the **form**, within which intervention would increasingly provide the **content** of British government and politics [1]. Again though, this seems to be unappreciated within the general writings on British government and the British political tradition.

Greenleaf for example is thorough in charting the increased scope and role of government from the beginning of the nineteenth century to modern times, and in his consideration of the factors prompting the massive increase in state activity and intervention. In this manner he explores the interrelationship between ideas about government, how and why they changed, and how government changed as a result. Significantly, the norm of gradual and limited change that we have seen to characterize the earlier period of development is seen to hold for the latter. Similarly, as only the civil war(s) and the 'Glorious Revolution' as extreme situations had prompted more extensive change, so it took two further major wars to usher in the post-1945 'Collectivist consensus'. Greenleaf covers this ground well, if, in my view, sharing the deficiencies of others (eg Birch and Beer) having gone before.

Greenleaf's consideration of the development of the uniquely British 'parliamentary sovereignty' is, for example, introduced in terms of the British system of government involving a high degree of concentration of legal power coupled with little formal restraint upon its use; perfectly true in my opinion. But rather than considering the implications of this for the nature of British democracy, Greenleaf is initially content to point out that the idea of natural or fundamental law implies/requires some effective restraint on the exercise of parliamentary power. Again, this is a good and valid (if rather abstract) point. However, parliamentary sovereignty and the absence of a written constitution are set up by Greenleaf in terms of their being favourable to a government's Collectivist aims, and are thereby used to 'explain' the 'ease' with which Collectivism was able to be adopted in this country. This seems a similar example of the utilization of hindsight, 'reading back' historical developments via known subsequent outcomes, to those I have identified in regard to Birch and Beer.

However, given his orientation towards the significance of any development being in its relationship to state intervention, it is in this manner that Greenleaf considers the changing nature of government and governmental relations, and the narrowing of the decision making base. That is, in regard to Greenleaf's major theme, the transition *from* Libertarianism *to* Collectivism: the increasing centralization of government; the ascendancy of the Executive over the Legislature; the narrowing of the decision making base; the limitation on the public and the legislature's ability to scrutinize and hold government to acount for its decisions; for Greenleaf these are all **part of the development of Collectivism.**

Greenleaf thus treats developments in the field of state intervention and those relating to governmental power distribution as being directly related, yet comparison with Sweden for example, suggests that such is a dubious proposition. That is, Sweden, with a written constitution rather than parliamentary sovereignty, saw decision making become concentrated among an elite of corporate presidents, government ministers and trade union leaders in a classical corporatist manner never achieved in Britain. Indeed this system successfully transformed Sweden from a poor agricultural nation to an affluent modern industrialized society (whilst Britain on the other hand was unable to properly operationalize Corporatism/Collectivism or stem relative economic decline). That Collectivism became far more deeply rooted in Sweden than in Britain would therefore seem to fault Greenleaf's argument, and suggest that the level of state intervention and the distribution of governmental power are independently subject to pressures which are as likely to lead to the **diffusion** of power and **greater** accountability being associated with a high level of state intervention; let us not forget Sweden's position at the opposite pole to Britain on the 'Robertson scale'.

Thus, although he is critical of the concentration by others on institutions, and I have said that his idea that the 'character' of modern British government being derived via the *continuing* tensions *between* Libertarianism and Collectivism is a good one, Greenleaf's focus upon ideas is limited. Greenleaf does not take up a discussion about different concepts of democracy or representation, and analytical specifics in the relationship between Libertarianism and Collectivism are absent. I will first provide another example of the drawbacks of the former, and will then take up further the distinction I have suggested in regard to the latter; that between form and content.

In Part Two of his second volume, 'The Transition to Collectivism', Greenleaf is considering J S Mill's attempts at 'weaving anew' the fabric of old Liberal thought. A particular concern of Mill taken up here is the danger of excessive concentration of power with government, and Greenleaf paraphrases Mill's views saying:

> The task of the state is thus, not to tolerate no experiments or institutions other than its own, but to act as the emollient of any difficulties that arise through allowing people to tackle their own problems (Greenleaf, 1983, Vol. 2, p. 108).

This is treated as showing the antithesis between Libertarianism and Collectivism and the tension between classical and 'New' Liberalism. Indeed, there is a lengthy discussion as to whether the new was a 'betrayal' of the old values, and as to the correct place for Mill in such a continuum.

However, it is significant that rather than arguing for the greater participation of the people in the business of government (or conversely justifying the role of 'leadership' and/or 'responsibility') - as would befit a discussion about the nature of government focused on representation rather than intervention - Mill argues for as little participation as possible by government in the business of the people. Mill therefore substitutes delineating the scope of legitimate activity by government for a discussion about the nature of British democracy; he is concerned with the 'liberal' rather than the 'democratic'. This is unsurprizing, given the fear and suspicion of powerful government as a threat to individual freedom, coupled with a less than wholehearted embracing of popular sovereignty and accountability that we have seen to be a feature of early Liberals. It is no less significant for its predictability however, since it is another clear example of an analysis from the 'top-down' rather than the 'bottom-up'. Further, Greenleaf's failure to recognize this suggests again that, as Mill himself (and Birch and Beer), he is writing within the traditional mould that I am seeking to expose and criticize as inadequate.

In recalling here the point that the development of Collectivism took place *within* the established governmental framework, rather than transforming it, both Birch and Beer acknowledge this, if largely implicitly [2]. Also, this parallels Greenleaf's theme that the 'character' of modern British government derives from continuing tensions between Libertarianism and Collectivism. I think Greenleaf's is a good theme, which might be expanded and made more explicit, and I think more analytically useful, via the idea that Collectivism developed as *policy* - **content** - within a *system* - **form** - that was constructed out of Libertarianism. This would of course ensure that tensions and conflicts between the two would continue, and hence Greenleaf's characterization is accurate if incomplete.

As has been said, the rise of Collectivism was both aided by, and itself further aided increasing government intervention, each being related to the increasing importance of the Labour Party (if not directly or straightforwardly so). But if the onset of rising intervention is located in the 1870s-80s, it is nevertheless not until after 1945 that Collectivism attains dominance. Indeed, in distinguishing between form and content, I have stated my reservations as to the completeness of this 'dominance' even then. In order to further illustrate and analyze the above, and the implications (both in regard to 'Thatcherism' and the modern Campaign for Freedom of Information), having considered the origins of Collectivism's rise it is instructive to divert to the position of its assumed dominance.

A Collectivist consensus?

If not as directly as Greenleaf, Birch and Beer nevertheless also take the historical transition from Libertarianism to Collectivism as an organizing theme of their work; each refers to the modern (post-war) era as Collectivist. We do need to remember that these are (originally) works of the (in my view uncharacteristic) consensus period in British politics and government. But having said that, Beer sees the ideological clash betwen Conservatism and Socialism (or 'Tory Democracy' and 'Socialist Democracy'), as best understood in terms of dialectical opposition within the context of Collectivism. To illustrate this broad Collectivist consensus, Beer cites the common acceptance of the existing political, administrative and legal structures, and points to the extent to which Tory and Socialist views 'agree on how political power is to be organized within this legal and constitutional framework'. 'This agreement', says Beer, 'sets both Tory and Socialist Democracy apart from nineteenth century political individualism and constitutes a common theory of politics in the Collectivist era' (Beer, 1982, pp. 70-71).

Birch echos these views, both in regard to the consensus over political, legal and constitutional matters, and in that 'the individualistic assumptions about society on which the traditional doctrines were based' have been rejected (Birch, 1979, p. 81). He also points out that, as with the Conservatives, the most influential Labour Party views - 'including (those of) all those who have held the office of Leader of the Parliamentary Party' - have regarded 'the maintenance of the parliamentary system ... as an essential aim of Labour policy', and that 'Labour is as determined as the Conservative Party to uphold the established institutions of representative government' (Birch, 1979, p. 89). Thus, 'there is little practical difference between the two parties ... in the importance that they attach to party management or in the day-to-day means by which they carry it out' (Birch, 1979, p. 114).

If 'Collectivism' is taken to refer to political and governmental practice rather than as a philosophical orientation uniting the parties, Birch and Beer agree that a Collectivist consensus over means at least came to exist in the modern era (in fact the actual proposition goes further, showing the now dated suggestion of the consensus extending to economic means and ends also). However, one thing which is in my view crucial once such a consensus is posited, is to explain - given the sharp antagonism between Conservative and Socialist views in general - how such a consensus could arise. Yet this question, as such, is largely ignored by both Birch and Beer. Perhaps, given the foregoing analysis of their orientation in the previous chapter, this is not too surprising; they are interested in what was most notable in regard to contemporary British politics, the outcome of historical conflict being one of a Collectivist consensus. We however again need to keep to the forefront the context (the form) within which the proposed Collectivist consensus (the content) emerged. As I have said, this is to some extent acknowledged by Birch and Beer (see note [3] eg) and more so by Greenleaf, but none draw out to the full the implications.

In regard to 'Socialist Democracy' for example, being a participatory and popular accountable conception of political representation, the elitist, individualistic form of British politics and goverment ('political culture'), would be antagonistic. 'Tory Democracy' on the other hand, would be compatible and complimentary to 'the established institutions of representative government' (Birch, 1979, p. 89). Thus, 'Socialist Democracy' would have to transform the established institutions and their underlying philosophical ideas, or be itself transformed by them. The constitutionalization of the Labour Party can be seen as representing the latter outcome, seen as 'natural' in one way or another elsewhere, but considered here to require systematic explanation.

Party government and functional representation

Birch and Beer are again agreed in regard to the themes of the modern era: party government and functional representation. These, for Beer, mean that both Tory and Socialist Democracy 'reject parliamentarism'. Both theories, he says:

> reject the notion that Members of Parliament should freely follow their own judgement when deciding how to vote and the House of Commons is, or should be, in Bagehot's phrase, in a 'state of perpetual choice'. On the contrary, both demand that the MP be not a 'representative' but a 'delegate' (although to be sure, a party delegate, not a local delegate), and that the Government's majority should stand stoutly with it, as should the Opposition's minority (Beer, 1982, p. 70).

Thus party government, with its implication of party discipline, is seen as the rejection of 'parliamentarism'. Yet, by the words in parentheses, Beer indicates that (unlike the Radicals') this 'rejection' of parliamentarism leaves intact the idea of the MP's independence from constituents' views and opinions. Again then, the view from the top-down rather than from the bottom-up is what is emphasized. The change is at the 'top' end of representation; concerning the role of the MP in a parliament dominated by party demands, deriving from the firm roles of Government and Opposition.

From the bottom-up, there is consistency. Conservatives have retained the traditional view of the MP's role vis-à-vis constituents, that is, the assumptions of independence, deliberation and decision making 'on behalf' of the people. The Labour Party on the other hand explicitly rejected this traditional view with its adoption of the 1918 constitution, which instead saw the role of the electoral manifesto and mandate, and the 'instrumental' view of the party and its parliamentary leadership emphasized. In fact even the pre-1918 party represented the instrumental view strongly, upholding a popular participatory and accountable concept of representation. Again, since the eventual outcome was one of 'convergence' between the parties in regard to their constitutional behaviour, the manner by which traditional views and practices gained ground (or that by which the old Labour Party was abandoned), is, if not ignored, certainly played down by the Birch/Beer school.

However, having established that in upholding party government both Tory and Socialist theories of democracy reject political individualism, Beer argues that each instead legitimizes a concept of functional representation. This merits closer investigation, so let us first be clear about what is meant by 'functional representation'. Beer defines it as:

> any theory that finds the community divided into various strata, regards each of these strata as having a certain corporate unity, and holds that they ought to be represented in government ... (since) they are regarded as performing an important function in the community as a whole ... Moreover, the unity of such a stratum is not that of mere voluntary association ... On the contrary, its integration is seen as arising especially from objective conditions that give its members a function and are the ground for deeply rooted, continuing - even 'fixed' - interests. Recognizing this function and these interests, the members act as a unit and find in the group a sphere of moral fulfillment and an instrument of political action (Beer, 1982, p. 71).

Beer argues that the (theoretical if not institutional) abandonment of political individualism makes functional and interest representation quite compatible with the territorial representation upon which the House of Commons is based (see Beer, 1982, pp. 71-73). Whereas Liberal individualism upheld a state - individual dichotomy, Tory and Socialist Democracy uphold a more complex analysis of society within which functional and corporate interests intervene between the individual and the state. This shared, if varying perspective, gives rise to what Beer calls 'the new pluralism', within which the principal difference between the two views ('Tory Democracy' and 'Socialist Democracy'), is the advocacy by the Left of the representation of 'the workers', and the Right's 'familiar plea that "all classes, all interests" be given a share of power' (Beer, 1982. p. 74). Beer's lengthy historical foray identifying twentieth century developments accompanying the (partial) overturning of nineteenth century individualism and legitimizing the new pluralism from Left and Right does not really go beyond this initial distinction. But in my view something more explicit does need to be said about each of these two views.

Tory Democracy

The maintenance of 'parliamentarism' by Conservatives - the traditionalist 'independence' of the governors from the governed - owes much to the influence of Edmund Burke. Indeed, although a Whig, Burke is widely considered to be the father of traditional Conservatism [3]. His fear of the threat of 'mob rule' typified Conservatives' historical hostility to democracy, or more particularly to 'crude majoritarianism' or the 'arithmatical' view of democracy. Birch points out in this respect that it was largely as a result of the popularity of Liberalism that Disraeli introduced the Second Reform Bill, 'and later Conservative leaders accepted, somewhat reluctantly, that sooner or later everyone must have the vote' (Birch, 1979, p. 66). Beer in fact begins his consideration of Tory Democracy by noting the extent to which traditional Conservative ideas of authority have been adapted to the requirements of mass suffrage; traditional constitutional ideas of representative and responsible government shaping the modern 'democratic' era rather than being superseded by the concept of democracy. This gives a more specific character to the anti-individualist bias of Conservatism, and although Beer notes, as we saw earlier, that 'Tory Democracy' refers to 'the concern that Conservatives have sometimes shown' for 'the condition of the people' (Beer, 1982, p. 91), neither he nor Birch explicitly distinguish this 'concern' 'sometimes shown' from adherence to democratic principles [4].

The first principle of Toryism old and new is that order requires hierarchy, 'whether it be a nation of a family, a factory or a farm, there must be those who exercise authority and those who obey' (Clarke, from Beer, 1982, p. 92). Here is indicated the Tory view of the natural 'political class', the 'governing class'. To the Tory, authoritative leadership, which can only derive from such a class of natural leaders, is as relevant and necessary within modern democracy as in the age of monarchy and aristocracy. Although neither Birch nor Beer acknowledges it, there is surely a similarity between this view of a unique political class best fitted for the role of government and the Liberal view of the middle class as the universal class particularly suited to that role; there is at least in each case a view of a 'natural' hierarchy. Despite the former view being initially associated with the landed gentry and the latter drawing strength from oppositon to such an association, the basic idea that there exists a special category of persons best suited to the practice of government, upholding a 'fitness to govern' is shared.

This is in fact related to a further Liberal agreement with the Tory idea that government is something of an 'art', which requires certain skills and rare character. Successful government can thus only be achieved 'if its practitioners are given a large discretion' (Beer, 1982, p. 93); the initiative and independence of these specially talented individuals, the natural governors, must therefore be given free rein. These attitudes have gone hand in hand with the traditional Conservative idea of the need for 'balance' between the various interests in society, as relevant to Disraeli's 'One Nation' concerns as to Burke's earlier corporate ideal. No one interest - even that of 'the majority' - should therefore be given preference or allowed to dominate. How successfully this has been upheld in practice is a moot point, but the concept of balance is a consistent feature of Conservative theory, the implications of which are I feel also underemphasized, particularly by Beer. For example, in considering the 'new pluralism', Beer quotes L S Amery as follows:

> Manual labour, important as it is, is after all only one element, one function in the life of the nation, and it would be entirely contrary to any true interpretation of democracy if that one element should by its numerical majority occupy a preponderating place in the House of Commons (From Beer, 1982, p. 76).

As well as showing the functionalist flavour of Conservatism - Beer's purpose - the above quote shows as well the implications for the view of (Tory) Democracy which Beer fails to follow up. Yet it is clear that rather than being *more than* just about the majority, Tory Democracy, as a 'true' interpretation of democracy, is *not even about the majority* but more about balance. Can we conclude otherwise if a 'numerical majority' should not expect to find itself reproduced via representation in the House of Commons? Indeed, although not in this context, Beer again quotes Amery as having 'sharply distinguished' Tory views from those giving the initiative to the people and which make political power 'wholly a delegation from the voter to the legislature and the executive':

> A British government ... is an independent body which on taking office assumes the responsibility of leading and directing Parliament and the nation in accordance with its own judgement and convictions (Amery, from Beer, 1982, p. 96).

British democracy therefore is, again quoting Amery 'democracy by consent and not by delegation'. It is a system of 'government of the people, for the people, with, but not by, the people' (from Beer, 1982, p. 95). Government 'with, but not by' the people, clearly indicates a passive rather than participatory role for the people, indeed this conception is opposed to popular participation.

However, though independent and unfettered, government should not be undertaken in isolation. Indeed 'balance' requires that government maintains consultations with party, with parliament and with the nation, in making policy. So too with the role of leadership. Policy and decision making is the prerogative of the leader, but the good and wise leader exercises this prerogative after consultation with groups and leading individuals, and with the benefit of their views and advice. In the Tory mind then, rule by the best suited is the only guarantee of good government; it will produce effective and efficient decision making. Any concept of popular participatory 'self government' will therefore be rejected as utopian folly, at best threatening inefficient and ineffective government.

The Tory view thus sees the national interest as arising out of the deliberations of a govermental team and the initiative of a leader drawn from a political class of natural leaders. Authority derives from governmental office itself, and its exercise is dependent upon the electorate's wise choice of governmental team rather than its programme. Another continuity between the views of Conservatives and Liberals is in that:

> Neither ... have ever embraced the view that a party should go to the
> electorate with a set of concrete proposals which, if successful, it is
> therefore mandated to put into practice (Birch, 1979, p. 116).

Although, as Birch says, the principle of 'honouring' an electoral programme **has** been invoked by both Liberals and Conservatives, 'when political conditions made it tactically appropriate ... (they) have felt free to ignore it in other circumstances' (Birch, 1979, p. 117).

To sum up the Conservative attitude to democracy we might do no better than to consider the words of a traditional Conservative of today, Ian Gilmour. Gilmour points out that:

> Conservatives do not worship democracy. For them majority rule is a
> device ... Majorities do not always see where their best interests lie and
> then act upon that understanding. For Conservatives therefore,
> democracy is a means to an end not an end in itself ... And if it is
> leading to an end that is undesirable or is inconsistent with itself, then
> there is a theoretical case for ending it (Gilmour, 1978, p. 211).

Thus Tory Democracy, if seemingly a synthesis of Conservative and Liberal governmental principles, is certainly and markedly elitist. Further, this synthesis of Conservative and Liberal assumptions seems quite clearly to underpin the operation of the modern British constitution, if neither Birch nor Beer is prepared to say as much. This point will be the better appreciable after having considered 'Socialist Democracy'.

Socialist Democracy

By contrast to the above, a large part of the Labour Party's championship of the working class has been on the basis of that class's status as the majority class and interest in society. British 'Labourism' always emphasized this view rather than that deriving from Marxism, of the working class as the 'revolutionary class' [5]. The party has a long 'crude' democratic tradition in its foundation, structure and ideology. Labourism and Socialist Democracy have inherited from earlier Radicals the notion of popular sovereignty and participatory democracy which Tory Democracy explicitly rejects. The anti-individualist bias of Socialist Democracy is therefore of a different order to that of Tory Democracy; where Tory Democracy is more about balance than the majority, Socialist Democracy is more about the (working class) nature of that societal majority.

Beer's failure to focus upon this difference leads him to treat as inconsistent Labour politicians' staunch advocacy of the working class on some occasions, and on others their having 'lapsed' into 'typically Radical' appeals to 'the people' (Beer, 1982, pp. 82-6). He explains this ambiguity first by reference to the party's 'mixture of traditions'. He also points out though that since electoral considerations tend to lead any parliamentary party to avoid offence to any section of the electorate, this might account for a softening and broadening of the party's appeal. This brings to mind the attitudes alluded to earlier; such a development is seen as a 'natural' result either of entirely sensible maturity, or a betrayal of the working class equally naturally (inevitably) arising from the party's operation within bourgeois structures. In either case, this has become all the more relevant with the decline of the view of the working class as 'the majority', and the widespread acceptance that the class structure is now far more sophisticated. Yet, as a relatively recent development, this does not justify the failure to acknowledge the early importance of the idea of the working class majority.

As Beer acknowledges, a continuity between Radical and Socialist thinking is evidenced in the outright rejection of the deliberative role of parliament. In the Socialist view the Commons is the means of ventilating grievances, and providing responsible criticism of government through the organized Opposition. But is is quite definitely seen as a representative assembly:

> its function is not to deliberate and decide on major questions of policy
> or - except in the rarest circumstances - the fate of Governments. For
> that would be usurping the role of the electorate, which by giving a
> majority to a party has endowed it with authority to govern (Beer,
> 1982, p. 79).

A Socialist government and its policies therefore derive legitimacy and authority largely
through the electorate's mandate; the participatory view is clear in that this is a policy
mandate, not, as in the Tory view, a broad 'mandate to govern'.

Thus Socialist thought 'profoundly alters and strengthens the foundations of party
government' and, despite the common origins between Socialist and Radical
representational theory, party becomes 'a political formation quite different from that
conceived by Radicals' (Beer, 1982, p. 79). The strengthening of the role of party is at
both top and bottom. Since sovereignty resides with the people and government's authority
derives from the electoral mandate:

> the old problem of whether the MP should represent his (sic)
> constituency or the nation is given a new solution. The function of
> representing the national interest, once attributed to the Sovereign and
> later to Parliament, is now performed by party (Beer, 1982, p. 88).

So the deliberative role is carried out within the institutional context of the party, and within
the ideological context of what constitutes the interests of the workers (the majority).

The party programme, or more specifically, the election manifesto, thus represents the
party's view of the national interest, and its endorsement by the electorate confirms its
legitimacy as such and endows the Parliamentary Labour Party (PLP) with the authority to
carry it out. Birch puts it well and succinctly, in saying that in this view:

> electors now decide how they will vote according to the policies of the
> parties rather than according to the personalities or individual opinions
> of the candidates... a general election gives the victorious party a
> mandate to put its policies into effect, and ... MP's ... elected on that
> party's platform have an obligation to support the party in Parliament
> even though its policies may occasionally conflict with their personal
> views. Only by acting as a disciplined block ... can these MP's ensure

that the popular will expressed at the polls is translated into legislative
and executive action (Birch, 1979, p. 115).

In terms of the earlier consideration of Radicalism, this conception of political
representation and governmental procedure might well be seen as Radical democracy plus
the instrumental view of the party. Thus what was a 'grey area' in Radical theory, at odds
with the political practice of the Liberal Party, is brought into sharp focus, providing a clear
alternative political practice for the Labour Party. Such 'system thinking' (Beer, 1982, p.
81) involved in this conception of the transformation of society would require
comprehensive and continuous planning and administration. Beer is indeed concerned to
establish that these 'were not the views only of early ideologues or left-wing extremists'
but constituted the orthodoxy (see Beer, 1982, p. 81). The point is that in order to achieve
such a mammoth task, tremendous discipline would be required within the PLP in order to
avoid policy intentions being subverted by parliamentary defeats and/or amendments. The
Socialist end was therefore clearly integrated with the Socialist means; Socialist
Democracy.

If less explicit, Birch is in broad agreement. He certainly stresses the central role of the
mandate in Labour Party governmental theory, and that for the Socialist 'politics is not a
matter of compromising between interests and opinions, but a matter of advancing towards
known objectives' (Birch, 1979, p. 118). This itself indicates how Socialist Democracy is
at variance with the traditional constitutional view, and Birch more directly points to this by
referring to the Labour Party Constitution. This, in giving 'the formal power to make party
policy' to 'the Party's Annual Conference and, between conferences, ... its National
Executive Committee', can, he says, be 'said to conflict with the principles of the British
Parliamentary system' (Birch, 1979, p. 90), since it represents the subjugation of
parliamentary leaders to external authorities. More directly still, Birch then cites the
expressed views of certain Labour theoreticians, including the Webbs, Harold Laski, John
Strachey and Stafford Cripps, which posit the incompatibility of Labour's Socialist project
with Liberal parliamentary institutions. Laski, in 1932 for example, considered that to
prioritize the maintenance of such institutions 'gravely exaggerates the power of reason
over interest in society', and in fact:

> In any society ...the state belongs to the holders of economic power;
> and its institutions naturally operate, at least in the main, to their
> advantage. But by establishing political democracy they offer to the
> masses the potentiality of capturing the political machinery and using it

to redress the inequalities to which the economic regime gives rise. Where that position arises, they are asked to co-operate in the abolition of the advantages they enjoy. Such co-operation has rarely been offered deliberately or with good-will; and it has been necessary, as a rule, to establish by force a new legal order the institutions of which permit the necessary adjustments to be made. It appears likely that we are approaching such a position at the present time (from Birch, 1979, p. 91).

For his part Beer substantiates thoroughly, as indicated earlier, that the Labour Party was wedded to Socialism as its orthodoxy. Today's perception of the party is of course very different, and we need to remember that the above and similar statements were emanating not from a left wing clique but from among the party's parliamentary leadership [6].

Birch and Beer therefore provide much evidence to support the view that Socialist Democracy was in conflict with the institutions and practices of the modern era, whereas Tory Democracy was perfectly compatible and/or complementary. The more such is stressed however, the more important is the need to explain the Labour Party's constitutionalization. I have indicated that in my view Birch and Beer are not very adequate here. It is therefore unsurprizing that they play down the conflict between Socialist Democracy and the operation of the British govermental system, and similarly, that the change in the party's orthodoxy is treated as a result of a natural maturity of the party.

As if to minimize the impact of his earlier points for example, Birch points out that these seemingly extreme views were expressed against the background of economic crisis, and that Laski later repudiated such views, as did Cripps - who would become the 'austerity' Chancellor of the post-war government. Thus Birch subsequently comes to say that it is 'stretching things rather too far to suggest that the Labour Party's mode of organization is in conflict with the British constitution' (Birch, 1979, p. 124). This is to sidestep the point however. Of course the Labour Party has proved in practice that it can operate in a manner compatible with the British constitution. That is not at question. The important point is how did this compatibility arise?

The first aspect of Birch's above point is in that the extreme views were expressed against the context of economic crisis, and that this somehow means they were not typical or not to be taken too seriously. This puts Birch in conflict with Beer's plainly stated and well supported argument that there was a broad and deep orthodox Socialist commitment. But more importantly, rather than being a reason to doubt the orthodoxy, the existence of crisis would in fact attest to the orthodoxy rather than extremism of such views. Socialism was always envisaged as emerging out of capitalist economic crisis, so for Birch to cite the existence of such in the attempt to explain away 'extreme' views which were later repudiated, is something of a non-starter [7]. This being so, the repudiation of such views, the second aspect of Birch's point, must signify the repudiation of the aims as well as the means. To ask what explains the movement back to labourism from Parliamentary Socialism is to return to the fundamental question of interest here.

Beer acknowledges that Socialist commitment and 'system thinking' is a good deal less common in the Labour Party of more recent years (Beer, 1982, p. 81). Indeed, since the time of Beer's writing this is all the more true - what was the orthodoxy *is* now the mark of the 'left wing extremist'. But rather than seeing any need to focus upon the explanation for this, as with Birch, the change is noted but not properly analyzed. On the one hand for example, Beer notes the unique nature of the Attlee government as unified, programmatic and purposeful (as does Pelling), but on the other, since the Socialist end was not achieved, the party's old orthodoxy was either tried and failed or failed to be tried. The former case would in turn prompt either the formation of a new Socialist strategy, or the retreat from Parliamentary Socialism back to the rationale of the parliamentary representation of 'the interests of labour'. It could of course - and I will argue that it did in fact - produce both conclusions simultaneously; the former among the left and the latter the right of the party. Equally, the extent to which the old orthodoxy went untried, or was not tried sufficiently determinedly, is also a measure of the strength of the right wing view in the Parliamentary Party.

In relation to the above, Beer takes the view (see Beer, 1982, pp. 153-216), that the Socialist orthodoxy was abandoned because it was found to be impractical. It was thus (in good pluralist-liberal form), modified in the light of experience; of practical problems in regard to the role of the trade unions, nationalization and other matters, coupled with the existence of the Keynesian economic alternative. In my view this gravely underestimates ambiguities within the Labour Party's conception of Socialism and the extent to which the belief in the means and ends of the old orthodoxy had been undermined *before* 1945. Worse, the manner by which these problems arose is either not focused upon at all, or is misfocused.

The following chapter will elaborate upon these points in tracing the historical development of the Labour Party from its origins. However, it is relevant to mention here that neither Birch nor Beer consider properly the relationship between Socialist and Tory views in the context of the operation of the British constitution. Beer declares 'the authorities are divided' (Beer, 1982, p. 960), and then considers the compatibility of each view with the British constitution only quite briefly and sometimes tenously. Birch, although including much that is relevant and useful, does not even do that explicitly. Yet if, instead of seeing *compatibility* as the issue, we pose the question 'does the operation of the constitution provide for the prerequisites of a Tory or a Socialist view' ? I think the answer is much more straightforward. For example, the Radical/Socialist view of the electoral mandate is not upheld in British constitutional practice. Members and prospective Members of Parliament, a Prime Minister and a prospective Prime Minister, can 'promise' anything they like. Despite such endorsement of an election manifesto however, upon election a government or individual MP can act in a manner completely inconsistent with any such pledges with impunity. A British government *is* therefore 'free' to initiate policy, and *is* 'independent' of the views and opinions of the electorate. In each case these constitutional realities depart fundamentally from the participatory, popular accountable Radical/Socialist conception of democracy, whilst reflecting clearly the top-down, elitist Liberal/Conservative principles.

This does not mean that a government is simply compelled - by the nature of the institutional framework - to abandon bottom-up views and practices. A government can act differently if it feels itself bound by other principles. So other principles may indeed be 'compatible' with British constitutional practice. The fact remains however, that the Radical/Socialist view is not the one underpinning the British system of government, and this has far reaching consequences for those attempting to operate participatory principles within elitist structures.

This can be illustrated by hypothesizing a situation whereby a Conservative government is suffering a prolonged unpopularity. A Labour Opposition may certainly use the language of participatory, popular accountability in condemning the government and calling for its resignation. But upholding 'responsible' rather than 'responsive' notions of good government, the encumbent Conservative administration would simply ignore such calls. The Opposition would be more likely to embarrass the government by accepting the constitutional reality and concentrating their criticism upon the government's 'irresponsible' record in office.

If we switch the hypothesis to one whereby a Labour government finds itself widely unpopular, we find an even clearer incentive to support traditional notions of government. Such a loss of popularity might well be attributed to hostility from the centres of industrial and financial opposition to Socialist policy being instigated and manipulated by a biased media, so that ordinary people come to lose faith in 'their' government. To the Socialist mind this would therefore be evidence of private vested interest - which they are duty bound to oppose - being illegitimately mobilized against government policy. In this manner, a 'temporary' suspension of the higher participatory principles would be justified, in order that the government is enabled to 'weather the storm'. After all, if the Tories recognized no compulsion to resign due to unpopularity, for Labour to do so would be to give them an unfair advantage. *There is of course no constitutional obligation to do so.* So Labour ministers and backbenchers justify the government's continuation in office via the same arguments as the Conservatives.

So the tendency will be towards accepting, and thereby giving greater credence to and legitimizing the constitutional realities, which is to undermine the participatory views. It can be easily appreciated that the next step in the process of convergence - and a very short one - is for participatory, popular accountable *reforms* proposed by the Labour Party in Opposition, to be abandoned in government. Labour ministers will not wish to strengthen the hand of those seeking to undermine confidence in Labour's programme and 'team'.

This is in fact a simplified version of the argument I will be proposing in relation to the explanation for the constitutionalization of the Labour Party in the following chapter. The main point is that the institutional and constitutional context accounts, in large part, for the dilution of the Socialist project and the marginalizaton of participatory practices. Bottom-up views are constantly undermined within the parliamentary arena. This being so, we would expect to find them less in evidence among long standing Labour parliamentarians than in the extra parliamentary party. Likewise, we would expect oppostion to the party's participatory practices to be widely shared within - if not actually instigated by - the PLP. These propositions do indeed seem well founded. The Freedom of Information issue for example, was a feature of Labour Party policy whilst the party was in Opposition in the early 1970s (and is again now). But the last Labour government failed to implement a Freedom of Information Act. Similarly, as Chapter One indicated, a distinct cleavage is identifiable between ministers and ex-ministers (and to a lesser extent, shadow cabinet members) on the one hand, who are resistant to such a reform, and the newer intake of (particularly Labour) MPs who are strongly in support.

In looking at the Labour Party's constitutionalization, the next chapter will therefore take account of the differing 'environmental contexts' within which the Labour Party's parliamentary and extra parliamentary wings operate, and at the manner by which their influence and prestige has varied. Looking at what they have in common will be instructive in accounting for the conception of Socialism and the strategy by which it was to be achieved; looking at what sets them apart will provide the basis for the explanation of the manner by which both means and end in the old orthodoxy were overturned.

Notes

1. Lenin for example used this distinction in relation to 'bourgeois democracy', which he considered to be a sham; a 'democratic form' distorted and made worthless by its 'class content'. A rather different example of the general idea, though certainly close to my own, comes from Sir Ivor Jennings, who held the view that the British constitution was elastic; it might be stretched by New Liberalism and Socialism but would return to its former traditionalist character.

2. This is easier to read into Birch, particularly through his short Chapter Five, 'The Liberal View of the Constitution', than Beer. Even so, Beer certainly shows that the institutions of British government developed their basic 'modern' character during Liberal pre-eminence in the nineteenth century, and that political practice evolved in a Collectivist manner during the twentieth century. Even if only by implication then, we may deduce that Collectivist political practice developed within the Liberal individualist institutional context.

3. Beer in fact warns (see eg p. 9) that some confusion is unavoidable given that membership of Whig or Tory party did not necessarily denote adherence to what has come to be known as 'Old Whig' or 'Old Tory' theory. Indeed most of those who articulated the Old Whig theory were Tories, but 'this theory was derived from the Whigs of the previous century' so it is right to call it Old Whig, given the warning about confusion.

4. To reiterate the distinctions made regarding representation via Birch (in Chapter Three), the former stresses 'function' and the latter 'selection'.

5. That is, the class who, in achieving their class interests, also transform society; in abolishing the distinction between capital and labour, class itself is abolished.

6. Beer quotes eg from MacDonald in 1928:

> The Labour Party, unlike other parties, is not concerned with patching the rents in a bad system, but with transforming Capitalism into Socialism ... Industry must be converted from a sordid struggle for gain into a cooperative undertaking, carried on for the service of the community and amenable to its control (Beer, 1982, p. 136);

From Morrison in 1933:

> Socialism for me is a policy for today and not for some indefinite day after tomorrow... The function of Labour Governments in the future will be to secure the socialisation of industry after industry under a

management which can be broadly relied upon to go on with its work
(Beer, 1982, p. 134);

From 'For Socialism and Peace' 1934:

the choice before the nation is either a vain attempt to patch up ... a
capitalist society in decay at its very foundations, or a rapid advance to
a socialist reconstruction of the national life. There is no halfway house
(Beer, 1982, p. 136);

From Attlee in 1937:

The evils that capitalism brings differ ... but ... the remedy is seen to
be the same ... The cause is private property; the remedy is public
ownership (Beer, 1982, p. 134);

From 'The Old World and the New Society' 1942:

Common ownership will alone secure that priority of national over
private need which assures the community the power over its economic
future (Beer, 1982, p. 136);

And from 'Let Us Face The Future' 1945, which denounces 'the chaos of do-as-they-
please' anarchy, and continues to proclaim:

The Labour Party is a Socialist Party, and proud of it. Its ultimate
purpose at home is the establishment of the Socalist Commonwealth of
Great Britain (Beer, 1982, p. 137).

7. The movement from old to new orthodoxy is that from 'Parliamentary Socialism', ie the
achievement of Socialism by parliamentary means - parliament as a means to an end - back
to 'labourism', the representation in parliament of 'the interests of labour' - as an end in
itself. In fact Birch seems to lose this distinction.

4 The constitutionalization of the Labour Party

Introduction: the founding of a new party

The Labour Party has something of a paradoxical place in relation to the development and operation of Britain's Liberal-Democratic constitution; it both aided it's emergence yet also represented a serious threat. But just as we have already seen how during the Liberal era the demands of democracy were made compatible with traditional British governmental practice, so, operating within that context, the Labour Party became 'constitutionalized'. In order to begin to appreciate this and its explanation, we must consider the party's foundations towards the end of the nineteenth century.

As was said in the last chapter, the period after 1885 saw Socialist influence begin to become significant. The Labour Party began life in 1900 as the Labour Representation Committee (LRC), but this organization was itself assembled out of earlier bodies, each of which had been in existence for some time. There were in fact four distinct sources from which the LRC emerged: the trades union and labour movement; the Fabian Society; the Independent Labour Party (ILP); and a small Marxist grouping, the Social Democratic Federation (SDF) [1]. We will briefly consider each of these.

The Labour Party's origins as the infant born of the trades union movement - or as having 'grown out of the bowels of the TUC' (Bevan, in Beer, 1982, p. 113) - are well known and well documented. Almost as well known is the extreme sectionalism of British trades unionism, the leading Fabians Sidney and Beatrice Webb writing in 1894:

> the basis of the association of these ... wage earners is primarily sectional in its nature. They come together, and contribute their pence, for the defence of their interests as Boilermakers, Miners, Cotton-spinners, and not directly for the advancement of the whole working class (from Beer, 1982, p. 111).

The process by which the Labour Party was gradually assembled was one governed by trades unions affiliating as and when they considered that the LRC/Labour Party offered them something not previously available or thought necessary. Pragmatism was therefore more influential than ideology. Thus the wider interests of the trades union movement as a whole - despite the rhetoric of solidarity employed in regard to economic interests - was very much a secondary consideration. Beer for example substantiates thoroughly both this sectionalism and the instrumentalist norm. That is, having affiliated, unions would submit resolutions to Conference which were directly related to their own sectional interests, thus regarding the Labour Party as the means of furthering these usually quite narrow interests (see Beer, 1982, pp. 113-114). Beer also establishes that the assumption that these specific 'instructions' should be *followed* largely governed the operations of the early Parliamentary Labour Party (PLP):

> the concerns of the parliamentary party corresponded closely to those of conference, a very heavy emphasis falling upon direct trade union interests (Beer, 1982, p. 119).

'Official' party policy therefore originated in individual unions' concerns with 'nuts and bolts' issues of workers' conditions under contemporary circumstances. The significance of the extent to which the Labour Party emerged as a product of the position of workers within the existing capitalist framework, rather than representing an ideological revolt against the system itself, will be considered subsequently. For now the point is that not only was the trades union movement not Socialist, but its sectionalism detracted even from a general condition of 'trade union consciousness' [2]. The specifics of pragmatism being more influential than ideology, even for 'vague general Collectivism' to be translated into 'practical proposals', required their expression 'in projects for the advantage of a particular trade'. As a result, argued the Webbs, 'the most momentous question of contemporary politics' was whether it was possible to 'counteract the fundamental sectionalism of Trade Union organisation' in order 'to render the Trade Union world ... an effective political force in the state' (from Beer, 1982, pp. 111-112).

However, just as the trades union movement bequeathed its organizational traditions to the Labour Party, so it had itself inherited those traditions largely from Methodism and the Free Churches. Thus:

> The early unions were, in the Webbs's phrase, 'primitive democracies', and the 'essential feature of primitive democracy was that everybody took part in the making of decisions' (from Birch, 1978, p. 122).

This clearly evidences the entirely separate and contrary nature of Labour and trades union organization to those of the old parties originating in parliament (as well as the elitism of the British political tradition itself). Nevertheless, since the 1870s working class and trades unionist representatives had been elected to parliament as Liberal Members, particularly in concentrated working class and mining constituencies; 'Lib-Lab' (or 'Laberal') MPs elected by virtue of working class votes would be expected to actively further the interests of the labour movement as it saw them.

The success of a party dedicated to the representation in parliament of the specific interests of labour therefore required this association with the Liberal Party to be superseded. But, given that the unions did not want to overthrow the capitalist system and transform society so as to create Socialism, there seemed little urgency for such a break. Similarly, their long standing organizational forms - based upon the 'delegatory' and 'instrumental' sense of representation - made them allies of Radicals in the Liberal Party. But then these Radical organizational principles were never adopted in that party, and we have seen these principles and practices to be opposed to the mainstream British political tradition. Worse, and related to this latter point, the middle class dominated local party associations (despite exhortations from the Liberal leadership), tended to reject working class candidates. Thus towards the end of the nineteenth century the viability of a 'labour party' seemed to be strengthening.

The second source from which the nascent Labour Party was constructed was the Fabian Society. Founded in 1884, the Fabians were (and are) a gradualist, constitutionalist Socialist organization. If the trades union movement provided the working class base for the Labour Party the Fabians were distinctly middle class, and largely intellectual. Whereas the basis for working class support was the hope to improve (or even transcend) their harsh conditions of life, middle class Fabians believed in the superiority of Socialism on moral grounds as well as those of efficiency; Socialism was not just about social justice and equality, but it would be a more rational and efficient distribution of national talent and resources. Their strategy for achieving Socialism therefore depended upon rational people coming to appreciate, as had the Fabians, the superiority of Socialism as a means of organizing society; Socialism would gradually *permeate* through society initially via the commitment of the social elite (not least as represented in the Liberal Party).

The Fabians' strategy was therefore not based upon the working class (although many of their members worked voluntarily with the poor). The working class were generally seen at best as the passive recipients of reform handed down from above, and at worst, their inability to properly comprehend their own position and the complexities of the social whole, were impediments to Socialist progress. Thus before 1900, the Fabians had stayed aloof from any attempt to secure independent working class representation. Indeed, this disdain, added to frustration born of impatience, was sometimes translated into actual hostility towards the working class; the almost obsessive constitutionalism was tinged with an element of 'enlightened authoritarianism'. George Bernard Shaw for example, a prominant Fabian, held the view in 1895 that the middle class Socialist would be the saviour of the 'mob of desperate sufferers abandoned to the leadership of exasperated sentimentalists and fanatical theorists'. Only a little later he became convinced that the principal obstacle to Socialism was in fact 'the stupidity of the working class' (Lichtheim, 1978, pp. 206 -207). This Fabian elitism and middle class conception of Socialism and the nature of the working class will also be shown subsequently to be significant in creating ambiguities in the Labour orthodoxy.

However, the third source of the Labour Party's origins was the Independent Labour Party, founded by Keir Hardie in 1893. The ILP, like the Fabians, was a Socialist organization, and no less wedded to constitutionalism. But by contrast to the Fabians, they were certainly orientated towards the working class. Indeed, as their very name signifies, the ILP was very much in favour of the independent representation in parliament of the interests of labour.

The Parliamentary Socialists of the ILP upheld a vision perhaps best described as 'Ethical Socialism'. Their commitment to the collective ownership of the means of production, distribution and exchange was 'interpreted in the light of Christian nonconformity rather than Marxism or Fabian elitism' (Foote, 1986, p. 32). They thus represented a principled if moralistic condemnation of the injustice, corruption, and degrading effects of the capitalist system on ordinary decent people.

The ILP has sometimes been accused of 'naivety'; most seriously, in their lack of an adequate theoretical or analytical basis for their critique of capitalism and strategy for its transcendence. The ILP's 'utopian' position; 'incapable of delivering what it promised' (Foote, 1986, p. 37), nevertheless provided the most influential theoretical basis for the Labour Party's conception of Socialism. Certainly the ILP represented 'the mainstream of British socialism' and made 'the most significant contribution of all the socialist societies to the setting up of the Labour Party' (Ball, 1987, pp. 46-47). Again, we will subsequently examine how the above points are important in terms of the Labour Party's ambiguous conception of Socialism and, thereby, the understanding of the evolution and 'constitutionalization' of the party.

If the ILP could claim Keir Hardie as a leading political figure of the day, many who were to become leading figures in the Labour Party began their political lives within the Social Democratic Federation; George Lansbury, Ramsay Macdonald and Herbert Morrison among them. The SDF was founded in 1881 as an independent party of the working class based on Marxism. Its advocacy of an independent party of labour was therefore qualified by its equally strongly held view that such a party must be based upon the class analysis of Marx. Yet, for a working class party its membership was decidedly middle class. Further, the SDF was not in any sense a good exponent of Marxism. Its leader, H M Hyndman upheld a narrow, crude version of Marxist dogma, and imposed - via authoritarian means if necessary - a stifling conformity within the party. Thus the SDF was as sectionalist (and sectarian) as it was dogmatic, and in this sense it was as elitist as the Fabian Society:

> Hyndman's Marxist terminology concealed a crude national chauvinism
> and a belief that socialism could be achieved by the existing state. Marx
> found him personally and politically abhorrent, while Engels eventually
> derided the SDF as 'purely a sect... incapable of ever becoming
> anything else ... ' (From Foote, 1986, pp. 21-22).

The SDF thus tended to force its best and most able members out, often because of their disagreements with Hyndman; examples being William Morris, Eleanor Marx, John Burns and Tom Mann. It always remained a small organization with limited influence, being particularly weak outside of London. 'Its failure to merge with the ILP in 1893 and 1897 and its early secession from the newly born LRC in 1901' - both of which are unsurprizing given the foregoing - 'ensured its relative weakness in terms of working class representation' (Ball, 1987, p. 46, see also Foote, 1986, pp. 19-24).

The Labour Party was therefore something of a disparate coalition right from its origins in the Labour Representation Committee; a mixture of elitist constitutionalist Socialism and participatory Labourism. Yet right from its origins too, it represented not just an intensification of the Collectivist challenge, but a challenge to the traditional workings of the British constitution. As a consequence of its bottom-up structures and assumptions it 'gave its extra-parliamentary wing much more policy-making power', yet 'in the long term this power was no match for the growth in prestige of the parliamentary party' (Ball, 1987, pp. 26-27). Again, these contradictions will be taken up and analyzed subsequently.

The British government textbook 'norm' is to see the Labour Party as something of a success story; the party's rise to prominence during the twentieth century being emphasized. What we might call 'liberal/pluralist' accounts (Birch/Beer eg) therefore concentrate upon the extent to which, *as an institution*, the Labour Party can be said to have been successful in challenging for governmental office. But what is far more important in my view is how, in the process, *what it stood for* changed radically. The changed orthodoxy is of course recognized by all, but rather than being problematized - seen as requiring detailed   explanation - the liberal/pluralist works treat it as a perfectly natural occurrence: a party simply having 'changed with the times'; a case of 'modernism'. Marxist works on the other hand (eg Miliband, 1973), do emphasize the 'move to the right' and the need to explain it. But there is nevertheless often little more than another version of its being 'natural'; this time the inevitable consequence of a bourgeois reformist perspective and political practice [3]. I regard neither of these approaches as adequate, and as indicated,   will seek to problematize the whole process of the Labour Party's 'constitutionalization'.

'Socialist Democracy', 'Labourism' and 'Socialism'

From the Labour Party's foundation as the LRC in 1900 until the adoption of the 1918 constitution, the matter of to what extent Labour MPs should be tied to Labour Party Conference decisions was continually to the fore. This is indicative of the party being founded upon an 'instrumentalist' orthodoxy. It was entirely consistent, given the 'delegatory' sense of representation allied to such an instrumentalist conception of the party, for the electoral manifesto to come to be perceived as a contract between the party and its supporters. Beer associates this with what he calls 'Socialist Democracy', but such a general acceptance and practice of delegatory representation and party instrumentalism **pre-dates** the party's adoption of Socialism.

Beer highlights the problem of pluralist interests existing within a party needing to operate as a unitary entity. He suggests that the adoption of Socialism provided a means of bridging this gap (Beer, 1982, pp. 105-107), but considers that this merely masked the 'contradiction'; Socialist Democracy conceives the party as something it was not, a unitary entity such as would be necessary for the attainment of the end via the means. His emphasis is thus upon the labourist party which became a Socialist party. But this approach is faulted given that the *means* of 'Socialist Democracy' were established long before Socialism was adopted as an end. In fact, not only did the pre-Socialist Labour Party operate under these principles but, as indicated, so too did individual trade unions.

The adoption of Socialism was in this sense then only the addition of a final goal - where one previously did not really exist - to the existing nature of Labour Party activities. The key problem of the Labour Party's ideology, practice and structure is in my view located in the 'labourist' conception of Socialism itself; the problem is one of labourist conceptions being carried over into the Socialist period. More specifically, the conception of Socialism which the Labour Party came to uphold was one which confused and conflated combating the rigours of capitalism with the strategy to bring about Socialism; such a conception deriving from the character of the pre-Socialist party and the environments within which it operated. Thus rather than being a rupture with the past, as implied by Beer ('This change in purpose made the Labour Party a different kind of political formation', Beer, 1982, p. 127), the 'manifestoism' associated with the adoption of Socialism is merely the extension of the participatory policy making and delegatory representation from the labour movement into the political and electoral arena.

Some form of instrumentalism was certainly accepted from the earliest then, if, in relation to such means, there were equally two views as to the party's actual ends. On the one hand the party existed for parliamentary representation of 'the interests of labour': labourism. On the other hand, the Socialists in the party believed that the only way that conditions for the working class could be improved significantly and permanently was via the abolition (albeit gradual, cumulative) of the distinction between capital and labour itself. Having introduced the key relationships between Socialist Democracy, labourism and Socialism, let us consider in some detail how these are related to the party's development between 1900 and 1918.

Given the participatory and popular accountable means of both pre- and post-Socialist Labour Party, correspondingly, the role of 'leadership' in the party - even in the PLP - was minimal in this early period. Indeed, the existence of a 'Leader' of the party was not recognized, there being only a 'Chairman' of the Parliamentary Party. Based on Snowden's explanation, Beer puts it thus:

> The Labour Party ... had always set its face against a permanent
> Chairman, and had insisted that the Sessional Chairman should not be
> regarded as the 'Leader'. It was considered undemocratic. The Party
> must not permit one man (sic) to dictate the policy of the Party. The
> Chairman was simply the mouthpiece of the Party, stating its decisions
> in the House of Commons (from Beer, 1982, p. 122).

This remained very largely the case for the party's first two decades, after which time the role of leadership became increasingly more prominent (as did conflict between parliamentary leaders and extra-parliamentary opinions and practices).

Against the background of the conflict between these bottom-up participatory and popular accountable principles and the top-down elitist perspective of parliamentary and governmental convention, within the party a struggle over strategy was ongoing. This turned initially on the question as to whether or not the party should make its independence from the Liberals permanent and irreconcilable, by pressing for Socialist restructuring and rejecting the kind of piecemeal reform compatible with Liberal progressivism. There were powerful advocates on both sides of this argument, but on the whole the party itself managed, in this period, to keep a foot in each camp.

The general situation is well illustrated by considering a resolution put to the 1900 Conference by the SDF. This called for the Parliamentary Party to 'have for its ultimate object the socialisation of the means of production, distribution and exchange'. It is difficult to think of anything less compatible with Liberalism than this, and in addition, the resolution's mover argued that the party's MPs should not be left free to abandon their cause at any particular moment of history (Labour Party Annual Conference Report [LPACR], 1900, p. 11). The 'foot in each camp' strategic reality of the day is demonstrated in that this resolution was amended out of all recognition. But equally, the idea that its MPs should be accountable (in some way) to the wider party was clearly present at the very foundation of the Labour Party. Interestingly, the terms of the resolution also indicate that there was thought to be a quite straightforward relationship between instrumental mandatory policy implementation and ideological commitment. Indeed, the most left-wing members of the party saw ideological commitment (rather than delegatory and popular accountable intra-party democracy) as the crucial thing, assuming all else would follow quite naturally. This may have been somewhat naive, but certainly at this time there was a confused and complex relationship between Socialist and non-Socialist views as to policy and operational principles.

At the following year's Conference (1901), the SDF again demonstrated the 'primacy of commitment' idea, by attempting to stop the LRC supporting candidates who were not 'pledged ... to the recognition of the class war as the basis of working-class action' (LPACR 1901, p. 20-21). The debate again turned upon support for a broad Collectivist policy and the principle of the Conference mandate. This time the Conference avoided the issues via a procedural motion: it decided not to take a decision rather than to amend or defeat the resolution. Before the next Conference the SDF had withdrawn from the LRC, regarding it as an insufficiently Socialist organization to merit further interest.

There was nevertheless deep hostility to capitalist injustices, which sometimes apparently took the party beyond mere Collectivism. The 1902 Conference for example saw a resolution calling for the overthrow of capitalism defeated by only 295, 000 to 291, 000 votes (LPACR 1902, p. 36). At this Conference too, although at the time there were only two LRC MPs, a resolution was submitted calling for the National Executive Committee (NEC) to draw up a programme to be submitted to all affiliated bodies for their consideration; the original draft plus amendments to be put to the next Conference. Although this motion was in fact defeated, it established a momentum over these issues which would see similar resolutions appear at the 1903, 1905 and 1906 Conferences; the debates over programme and mandating were prominent in all three.

Despite the complicating dispute over policy itself, the relationship between popular participation in policy making, the manifesto and mandatory policy implementation was clear; a consistent feature of the party's instrumentalist perspective. However, the cautious 'foot in each camp' position of the party at this time is also indicated by the fact that the General Election Manifestos between 1900 and 1906 had been issued in the name of the NEC, but had not actually committed anyone to anything. But when the issue arose again at the 1907 Conference - the LRC now having become the Labour Party and increased its parliamentary representation to 29 - a compromize position was accepted. The position established since 1900 whereby the Labour Group in the House of Commons maintained its own whips and followed its own policy was transcended. A resolution was passed which suggested:

> That resolutions instructing the Parliamentary Party as to their action in the House of Commons be taken as the opinions of the Conference, on the understanding that the time and method of giving effect to these instructions be left to the Party in the House, in conjunction with the National Executive (LPACR 1907, p. 49, also in Minkin, 1980, p. 5).

This recognizes that the 'opinions' of the Conference **should** be given effect in the House of Commons, and therefore that Conference **can** 'instruct' the PLP. But it also gives to the PLP discretion regarding priorities, timing and strategy. A 'conscience clause', giving 'freedom to members of the party who felt a difficulty in accepting a majority decision either to abstain from voting, or even to go to the length of voting against the majority of the party' (Snowden, in Beer, 1982, p. 121), was also introduced at this time. According to Snowden's account, this was introduced in 1906, following differences of opinion in the Parliamentary Party. Pelling (1982) says however, that the clause resulted from Hardie's threat, in 1907, to resign from the PLP rather than vote in opposition to women's suffrage based on a property franchise, which was Conference policy. What is clear is that, beyond the formal position outlined, such a conscience clause gives considerable scope to members of the PLP who wish to 'go their own way'.

Thus instrumentalism was accepted whether in regard to labourist or Socialist ends; if there was a continuing tension between the attempts by the party outside parliament to determine the actions of the party's MPs, and the attempts by the parliamentarians to maintain - albeit within certain minimum parameters - their autonomy. It is the movement in the balance of these forces and the consequent strength or weakness of the positions associated with each 'environment' which characterizes the subsequent development of the party.

This tension is evident in 1909, when, in speaking against another resolution, J Ramsay MacDonald put the case that, rather than Conference, it was the PLP which 'ought to lay down in the shape of a programme the sentiments and the principles expressed from year to year at the Conferences'. Conference was therefore the way in which the extra-parliamentary party could 'indicate their point of view - indicate to the Party in the House of Commons the large questions in which they were interested' (LPACR 1909, p. 85). The increasing acceptance that the party should have a programme is indicative of greater confidence in its independence from the Liberals. Similarly, the argument that the PLP should formulate such a programme would seem to indicate *its* greater confidence in its ultimate decision making autonomy. But again the PLP can be seen as simply wishing to formalize its autonomy regarding priorities, timing and strategy in the Commons. Alternatively, it can be seen as reducing still further the weight of Conference policy; from 'instructions' at its strongest and 'opinions' at its weakest, to mere 'sentiments', 'principles' and 'questions of interest'. This interpretation would see Conference as little more than mere agenda setter and advisor for the PLP.

The resolution which MacDonald was arguing against was indeed defeated, but the tide of feeling in the party's first decade was on the whole against a formal programme -

whoever was to draw it up. The argument had thus moved from whether the party should have a programme, to whether the party's MPs and candidates should be bound by it, to who should draw it up, to back again to whether the party should have a such a programme at all.

The general theme of the Labour Party's activities at this time was then for the representation in parliament of 'the interests of labour'. The effort to reverse a judicial decision of 1901, following from the 'Taff Vale' case, had therefore been given top priority. Prior to this case it had been believed that the Trade Union Act of 1871 not only protected union funds from employers' claims for compensation for damages, but also that a union was thereby protected from court injunction. However, when the Taff Vale Railway Company sued the Amalgamated Society of Railway Servants, Mr Justice Farwell found in the employers' favour, thereby reversing both assumptions. The ASRS eventually had to pay £32, 000 in costs and damages:

> The effect on the trade unions was frankly disabling; the more so since
> an almost simultaneous case ... appeared considerably to extend the
> liability of a strike organizer to find his acts adjudged tortious. The
> whole trade union world rose up to demand remedial legislation ...
> (Ensor, 1988, p. 378).

Bills seeking to reverse the situation were introduced, unsuccessfully, in 1903, 1904 and 1905. A success was achieved however, when the Liberal government elected in 1906, 'yleldiiig icadily to pressure from its own supporters as well as the Labour Party', adopted Labour's bill in place of 'its own rather milder version'. Hence 'Parliament enacted the Trades Disputes Act of 1906' (Beer, 1982, p. 123).

The next major priority for the Labour Party was to reverse another judicial decision: the Osborne decision of 1909. This arose out of the unwillingness of the secretary of a branch of the ASRS to pay, as part of his union subscription, the levy in support of the Labour Party. W V Osborne was a member of the Liberal Party, whose 'views were not altered by the fact that a very large majority of his fellow members had voted in favour of the society using funds for exactly that purpose'. Further, he had 'strong financial backing from interests opposed to the Labour Party' (Williams, 1950, p.175). Thus it was that he attempted to get an injunction against the practice of such compulsory contributions. The same judge as in the Taff Vale case, Mr Justice Farwell, granted the injunction:

The decision was upheld (28 November 1908) by all three judges in the court of appeal, and (21 December 1909) by all five judges in the House of Lords. After the latter date injunctions were obtained restraining a number of unions from continuing a compulsory levy. Some sixteen MPs found their salaries cut off. Attempts were made to replace compulsory levies with voluntary, but with poor results (Ensor, 1988, pp. 437-38).

This was therefore the major issue for the labour movement at the time of the December 1910 General Election. Along with the demand that the House of Lords be abolished and that MPs be paid, it was prominent in the Labour Party Manifesto. The Manifesto itself was issued in the name of the Labour Party Executive 'on behalf of a million-and-a-half organized workers', but neither in the name or on behalf of the fifty-six Labour candidates.

Between 1910 and 1914 the party's fortunes were mixed. As was outlined in the last chapter, much legislation was passed in which the Labour Party had a close interest. The Trades Disputes Act of 1906 has already been mentioned. Local authorities were given power to provide school meals in 1906, and medical inspection of school children followed in 1907. Conditions for coal miners were improved, as were those in the 'sweated' industries. Acts established Labour Exchanges, Trade Boards, Old Age Pensions and a national scheme of sickness payment. In addition, the Parliament Act 1911, although falling far short of the Labour Party's aim of *abolishing* the House of Lords, did at least severely curtail their Lordships' political power. At almost the same time one of the longest standing Labour demands was also achieved: the payment of MPs. An annual salary of £400 was instituted, and parliament thereby ceased to be the preserve of the rich. The Osborne decision was also effectively overturned with the Trade Union Act of 1913. Yet, seemingly paradoxically in the face of the above, there was also much disillusion with the party's progress, and it suffered reversals in by-elections which suggested that the aim of a Labour *government* would be far more diffficult to achieve than such individual pieces of legislation.

Conference during these years concentrated on policy discussion, but the debate regarding the balance between Conference and the PLP seemed to move more in favour of Conference:

In 1911 and 1912 the parliamentarians came under pressure from the Conference to submit a formal report on their activities for question and debate at the Conference. It was introduced in 1913. And in 1914 a

special Conference was held to examine the policy and performance of
the group. It was at this Conference that J R Clynes produced a
statement of Conference sovereignty with which few in the Party dared
quarrel. He assured the delegates that 'The Conference - and no one
else - had the right to judge and decide what the Parliamentary and
electoral policy should be' (Minkin, 1980, p. 7).

Of course it could still be argued that the PLP had the right to determine the timing and
interpretation of Conference policy, but equally, this authoritative statement gave far more
status to Conference than MacDonald's attitude regarding 'sentiments', 'principles' and
'questions of interest'.

On the other hand, the Labour Party's involvement in the wartime coalition government
seemingly produced a contrary movement, since Labour ministers did not always follow
Conference policy. Indeed, the NEC showed itself to be sympathetic and tolerant in this
regard, as is evident from an NEC minute from August 1 1918 :

> On behalf of the NEC it was pointed out that there was every desire to
> recognise the difficulties of Labour Ministers in having to support
> measures and policy at variance with decisions of Annual Conference
> and the National Executive (Labour Party Archives, also quoted by
> Ron Hayward, see LPACR 1979, p. 190).

Since the party had adopted a new, Socialist constitution in *February* 1918, this might
seem to suggest a swing back to the Hardie/MacDonald position on the heels of that
constitutional change. However, the minute recognizes that Labour Members *ought* to
follow Conference policy, but that the very special circumstances of the wartime coalition
justified a deviation from *the norm*. A more reasonable interpretation would therefore be
that it actually amounts to 'special dispensation' in trade union terms. Labour's
involvement in the coalition had after all been debated and (though not without controversy)
approved by the Conference.

The 1917 revolution in Russia had given impetus to the adoption of the party's Socialist
constitution [4], and Labour's involvement in the wartime coalition had also led the
parliamentary leadership to now think seriously in terms of government rather than the
mere representation of labour interests. The two things were of course directly related:
'the adoption of the new ideology was not so much a cause as an effect of the hardly
avoidable break with the Liberals' (Beer, 1982, p. 145). Similarly, the Lloyd

George/Arthur Henderson 'doormat incident' signified the party's belief in the primacy of Conference. This incident is so termed as it refers to the manner in which Henderson was kept waiting outside the door of the cabinet office whilst the cabinet discussed his advocacy of British delegates being sent to the International Socialist Congress in Stockholm. Given the full support of the Conference for the proposal, when the cabinet turned it down Henderson indignantly resigned from the government. As a consequence of all of the above, from 1917 to 1918 the party went through major changes.

The mature 'Socialist' Labour Party

The inter-war period saw the party formalize its Socialist perspective and the participatory mode of organization allied to it. Paradoxically though, the period also saw the emergence and development of factors which were to undermine and overturn both. We will consider each of these aspects in turn.

At the end of 1917 a 'Memorandum on War Aims' was published which stated Labour's faith in a new international order. This was to be ushered in via the League of Nations' machinery for the mediation of international disputes as the basis for preventing war and securing joint action to deal with economic crises:

> These far sighted recommendations ... won such an overwhelming endorsement from the unions as a whole that they had much influence in the world, both upon Lloyd George and upon President Wilson... Lloyd George soon afterwards made a statement on war aims to a conference of trade unionists, and although it was in studiously vague terms it seemed to show some Labour Party influence: and President Wilson's Fourteen Points, which were enunciated a few days later, followed the same lines (Pelling, 1982, p. 43).

Such a highly influential document could not but help improve Labour's credibility as an alternative government.

Following closely in the wake of the 'Memorandum' came the adoption by the party of it's new Constitution. This was prepared by Henderson and Sidney Webb, and embraced Socialism as an ideal and as the goal of Labour governments. More will be said of this subsequently. However, via the new constitution the party was for the first time opened up to individual membership through the constituency parties, and the relationships between these, the trade unions, the Socialist societies and the PLP was formalized. In stating clearly that 'The work of the Party shall be under the direction and control of the Party Conference' (Appendix LPACR 1918), the Constitution showed how it was to be decided which reforms were to be supported and promoted by the NEC and the PLP. It also laid down clearly that it was the duty of every Labour MP to be guided by meetings of the PLP, which should give effect to Conference decisions. Under Clause V (part 2), the PLP and the NEC together were to produce the General Election Manifesto. This was to be based on the Party Programme, itself derived from Conference policy. The 'Clause V meeting' would also 'define the attitude of the party to the principal issues raised by the Election which are not covered in the Manifesto' (Appendix LPACR 1918).

Thus the role of the Annual Conference in defining election issues for the party. which had been accepted in 1914 was formalized quite specifically with the new constitution. Though there was some tension at a joint meeting of the NEC and PLP in August 1918, the 'Clause V meeting' on Wednesday November 27 seems to have gone smoothly (NEC minutes in Labour Party Archives). The 1918 Election Manifesto, 'Labour's Call To The People', was clearly based on Conference policy and included such items as freedom for Ireland, withdrawal of Allied forces from Russia, an end to conscription, land and housing reforms, equal rights for both sexes and industrial democracy.

Four months after the adoption of the new Constitution, at another Conference, the party endorsed a policy statement which would form the basis of its policy for the next thirty years. 'Labour and the New Social Order' contained four major proposals. The concept of 'The National Minimum' included the demand for full employment, with a 48 hour maximum working week, a minimum wage. and minimum standards of conditions in employment. 'Democratic Control of Industry' was basically a call for cumulative nationalization. 'The Revolution in National Finance' was based on the principle of progressive taxation to subsidize the extension of social services. Finally, 'The Surplus to the Common Good' called for the balance of the nation's wealth to be devoted to expanding the people's educational and cultural opportunities.

These three major developments between 1917 and 1918 - the 'Memorandum', the new Constitution and 'Labour and the New Social Order' - aided the party's challenge for government. That challenge would not be fully successful for nearly thirty years however, and the aims at this time envisaged were never truly achieved. The explanation for the latter lies in the long period between this formalization of the party's ends and means and its actually achieving a majority government. A number of factors combined during this period to overturn Labour's orthodoxy both in regard to ends and means. In continuing to chart the party's progress, these factors will be identified.

In the 1918 General Election the party fielded 361 candidates and won 57 seats. In an election perceived by and large as being a vote for or against Lloyd George as architect of British victory, although not a great advance (42 Labour members were returned at the last election), it was a respectable result. More significant was the number of seats where Labour came second; henceforth it was the Labour Party which would be regarded as the main Opposition party. The party's progress was continued in the 1922 General Election, where 414 Labour candidates stood, and the party won 142 seats. Thus:

> Although there was a clear Conservative majority in Parliament, in many ways the rise of the Labour Party to a total exceeding that of the broken segments of the Liberal Party was the most important single feature of the election (Pelling, 1982, p. 50).

There was now no doubt that Labour had replaced the Liberals in the two party system; the Labour Party was now the official Opposition in the House of Commons.

This development marks the onset of a process by which a concept of leadership, comparable to that existing in the Conservative and Liberal parties, would be imported into the Labour Party. This in turn would aid significantly in undermining and overturning the old Labour orthodoxy; a paradox whereby the party's very success undermined its project and mode of organization. The PLP's new status as the official Opposition of course raised the prestige of the PLP and its shadow cabinet members, in relation to the extra-parliamentary party. But beyond this, parliamentary convention demanded a Leader of the Opposition to confront the Prime Minister in the Commons. Following the 1922 election, Ramsay MacDonald was elected in place of Clynes as Chairman of the PLP. From 1922 then, MacDonald was described as 'Chairman and Leader' of the Parliamentary Labour Party, rather than simply 'Chairman', as had been the case previously.

This subtle change of title need not, in itself, have had any effect upon the 'Chairman's' role of course. He could still have been, to reiterate Snowden's term, the 'mouthpiece' of the party. But tradition and convention can be powerful moulding agents, particularly for an individual whose personal and party ambition is seen through a strong sense of history. MacDonald was such a man. He saw himself as stepping into the shoes of historical predecessors, and, believing that it enhanced both his own and the Labour Party's credibility, he was perfectly willing to accept the traditional role of Leader of the Opposition. Pelling indicates as much in quoting from a letter by MacDonald to an American friend:

My real difficulty is that with a very small income I have stepped into a job that has never been filled before by anyone who had not a command of much money; and also that whereas my predecessors inherited secretaries and a going machine, I inherited nothing and am having to make everything (Pelling, 1982, p. 50).

The instinctive reaction on reading the above is sympathy for the man struggling with the job he has been called upon to do. Yet *it did not have to be done in that way*. MacDonald shows here that he had accepted the personalizing of what, to be consistent with the Labour Party's alternative conceptualization of representation, should have been seen as something of a symbolic position and role. But rather than making the role conform to the Labour Party's demands and general orientation - which would leave him still a 'mouthpiece' - MacDonald accepted the personalized 'leadership principle', and thereby saw the problem in terms of how to make his personal and political position fit that of a traditional Leader of the Opposition. Hence a greater role for leadership enters the Labour Party's norms via those of the British political tradition and system.

Such a development was in fact aided by the particular choice of MacDonald as 'Chairman and Leader'. No-one was better placed to achieve acceptance for leadership from above, since he was seen in the party as epitomizing the trustworthiness which flowed from ideological commitment. His consistent and principled opposition to the War, and its political consequences for him, gave him the aura of a martyr. This 'moral authority' provided a unique justification for 'loyalty'. But also, with the party the official Opposition, party discipline became more important than ever; a united front against the government was essential. Submission to discipline, giving 'loyalty' - as with producing an outstanding parliamentary 'performance' - were routes to recognition and promotion to the Front Bench, and thereby, to the possibility of future cabinet membership. Hence patronage from above - very much against the labourist/Socialist grain - nevertheless came to play a significant part in the establishment of a leadership principle comparable to that existing in the other parties.

However, in the snap General Election at the end of 1923, the Labour Party won an extra 49 seats, bringing their total to 191. The Conservatives (with 258 seats) were still by far the largest party in the Commons, but were without an overall majority.

The election had been called by Baldwin (the Conservative leader) on the Tariff Reform issue, but the swing had been decidedly against the Conservatives - the Liberals also having gained 43 seats, giving them a new total of 158. Baldwin declared himself willing to accept a minority Labour government (with Liberal support), on the face of it because the Conservatives' election platform had been rejected. There is no doubt however that he would also have wanted to encourage Labour's moderate 'constitutionalists' and undermine the 'extremists'. After all, here was a way by which Labour could be given 'office' whilst denied *power* ; the Liberals could be relied upon not to support any Socialist programme. Dependent upon Liberal votes, Labour would therefore be tamed. Miliband emphasizes this picture, and indeed quotes Asquith assuring the Parliamentary Liberal Party on 18 December:

> whoever may be for the time being the incumbents of office, it is we, if we understand our business, who really control the situation ... if a Labour Government is ever to be tried in this country, as it will be sooner or later, it could hardly be tried under safer conditions (from Miliband, 1973, p. 100).

Be this as it may, the fact remained that just a few short years after the War, and its equipping itself for government via the changes outlined earlier, a Labour government, albeit a minority one, had been elected.

Socialism undermined by office

Just as the status of official Opposition had prompted the development of the leadership principle, so the election of a Labour government intensified that trend; the conventions of government itself being all the more based upon elitism. For example, it was traditionally a party leader's own choice as to whether to accept the Monarch's commission to form a government. At the other end of a parliamentary term, it is for the Prime Minister to decide when to call a new General Election, and to name the date for that election. Similarly, the selection of cabinet members was a matter for Prime Ministerial prerogative. In cabinet, far from being bound by the majority viewpoint (as a 'mouthpiece'), the Prime Minister is able to make policy decisions and, if necessary, impose them upon even a dissenting cabinet majority. Given that ministers hold their posts through Prime Ministerial patronage they are constantly aware that dissenters can be replaced. Practical limitations do exist in regard to most of these powers, but not firm constitutional ones.

The British constitution therefore leaves a Prime Minister free (if not obliged) to take such decisions alone. That is, in each of these matters a Prime Minister could consult with colleagues and perhaps take advice. Without impinging upon constitutional practice

MacDonald could therefore have consulted with colleagues and chosen to bow to majority views. In this sense then Labour Party principles were compatible with the traditional operation of the British constitution. But as we have seen, tradition and convention weighed heavily upon MacDonald, certainly a proud man and perhaps even 'aloof' in his *lack* of consultation (see eg Minkin, 1980, p. 14). What is clear is that the British tradition emphasizes strong, decisive 'responsible' government, and thereby regards the opposite tendencies as demonstrating weak, indecisive government. MacDonald would thus not have wished to be thought a weak Prime Minister, nor would he have wished the Labour Government to be thought weak. In any case he made these decisions alone, even going outside of the Labour Party for some of his appointments (see eg Beer, 1982, p. 157, inc, note 7, and Pelling, 1982, p. 56).

Thus: first through parliamentary convention requiring a 'Leader' of the Opposition to confront the Prime Minister; then in the choice of MacDonald - particularly well placed to demand loyalty and discipline - as that leader; and subsequently, through MacDonald's susceptibility to the underlying assumptions of the British governmental tradition; the participatory and popular accountable practices upon which the Labour Party was founded came to be undermined by its 'success'.

It is important to note however, that initially this was within the context of *carrying out* policy, and particularly a Manifesto, *derived from the Conference*. This principle, and the concomitant idea that members of the PLP - 'Leader' included - were the servants of the party rather than its masters, was unchallenged at this time. It was only a few years after all since the new constitution had spelled this out. The emerging elitism therefore did not yet justify a hierarchy from 'lowly' trade union branch or constituency party members up through the PLP to the parliamentary leadership. There was no attempt to implement policy making by the leadership, and therefore the role of leadership could be said still to be greatly restricted by comparison to the practice of the other parties. Again then, the leadership principle in the PLP could be seen as simply being within their own established prerogative in regard to setting priorities and strategy in the parliamentary domain. This could also be said of a highly significant debate within the party's parliamentary leadership prompted by the Labour government's minority status.

This discussion, primarily between MacDonald, Snowden, Thomas, Henderson and Webb, concerned the appropriate strategy for the party and government to follow under the prevailing circumstances. One choice would be to follow a 'maximalist' strategy, by attempting to implement some 'bold Socialist measures' (Snowden, quoted in Beer, 1982, p. 158). This would of course alienate Liberal support and thereby lead to parliamentary defeats. But such an outcome could then be made the focus for a new election and a new campaign for Socialism in the country, with the possibility for a new *majority* Labour government. On the other hand a 'minimalist' strategy would put forward only those ameliorative reforms which could attract Liberal support, and thereby a parliamentary majority. This would rule out any Socialist measures, but such a demonstration of 'responsibility', showing the party 'fit to govern', would be the means to improve the chances of re-election with a majority. Perhaps unsurprizingly from what we have seen of him: 'MacDonald's preference was clearly for the latter alternative, and throughout his period of leadership he had his way in spite of opposition from sections of the parliamentary and extra-parliamentary parties' (Beer, 1982, p. 158).

It is important to remember however, that, as with the wartime coalition's 'special dispensation' for Labour ministers regarding government policy, this development regarding strategy was necessitated by special circumstances: the party's dependency upon Liberal support. Had the first Labour government had the envisaged overall majority there is every reason to believe that it would at least have attempted to carry out the full programme decided by Conference. As it was, it should also be said that MacDonald's view was shared by the other parliamentary leaders and by large majorities in the PLP and the Party Conference.

The adoption of MacDonald's preferred, and very much 'traditionalist' position, would prove to be significant in relation to the Labour Party's constitutionalization. This is particularly so since an alternative bottom-up strategy to power, encapsulated in the term 'Poplarism', had been materializing at the same time. 'Poplarism' signified the determined resistance of the Labour councillors in the London Borough of Poplar to the policies of first the Lloyd George coaliton and then, after 1922, to those of Bonar Law's Conservative government (see eg Branson, 1980). Poplar flouted the Poor Law assumptions of the time by maintaining a much higher than average level of unemployment relief, failing to implement the 'labour test' - usually breaking stones for roughly half the prevailing wage - and thereby making it easier for unemployed people to avoid the 'workhouse'. The council also modified greatly the requirement to implement the 'household' or 'family' means test, by which levels of relief were to be assessed. In its unmodified form this had meant that if the eldest boy or girl in a family worked, the whole of their earnings could count as 'family income' in the assessment of the need for relief of parents and other children.

Herbert Morrison, leader of the Labour Group on London County Council criticized Poplar for being 'impractical' under the prevailing circumstances. He also made it clear that he thought such 'irresponsibility' would damage Labour's electoral prospects by scaring off 'moderate' opinion. With the election of MacDonald's minority Labour Government, and it's courting of respectability via showing itself as 'responsible', Poplar was an embarrassment. Only John Wheatley within the government gave any support, if cabinet responsibility made this somewhat muted. The bottom-up, local to central campaigning strategy to power represented by Poplarism was certainly at odds with the 'responsible' strategy of the parliamentary leadership. But it should be noted that, aside from the new government's minority status, the choice between the two strategies was, from the perspective of the day, one of *preference* rather than practicalities. That is, 'Poplarism' seemed a viable strategy. In the 1922 elections for Boards of Guardians for example, the highest turnout in London was in Poplar, and Labour losses throughout the rest of London were confounded by Poplar's increased Labour representation. Similarly, when the coalition government fell Labour won *all* the Poplar seats!

Nevertheless, at the close of 1923 Labour had achieved office and with the New Year the leadership had chosen it's strategy. In the event the government introduced legislation which reinstituted minimum wages in agriculture (abolished in 1921), gave significant encouragement to secondary education (reversing the 'Geddes Axe', which had cut popular educational provision), and established, via Wheatley's Housing Act, the foundations of council house provision. All of these were in line with the principles of 'Labour and the New Social Order', and all had been discussed and endorsed at Conference. The government had also attempted to amend the law on rent control and to prevent evictions where rent arrears had resulted from unemployment, but in these cases the lack of a parliamentary majority saw the proposed legislation fall.

In general, the government's handling of these matters was popular in the party, and the minimalist strategy seemed therefore to be having quite a respectable result even in putting forward domestic Labour policy. It was in foreign policy however where both its greatest success and its early downfall were located. The success was in regard to Franco-German diplomacy:

> the French were persuaded to evacuate the Rhur, the Dawes plan for
> scaling down reparations to a more practical level was accepted and the
> need for a modification of the Versailles Treaty generally agreed
> (Williams, 1950 p. 307).

The government's downfall, however, came via the issue of British-Soviet relations. Worse still was that the manner of the government's defeat totally destroyed the aim of the minimalist strategy.

Initially, the intervention of a group of Labour MPs in attempting to restart talks between the Foreign Office and Soviet emissaries led to Conservative charges of left-wing interference. Similar charges were levelled at the government in relation to judicial procedings over the 'Campbell case':

> J R Campbell ... had published an article urging soldiers not to 'turn your guns on your fellow workers' in industrial disputes. The Attorney-General ... decided that this was seditious and a prosecution was initiated. Later on, however, he changed his mind and withdrew the prosecution. The Conservatives, scenting left-wing interference with the judicial process, secured a debate on the issue ... Although Hastings effectively answered the charges, MacDonald's defence was unsatisfactory ... and a combination of Conservative and Liberal votes defeated the government on a demand for a Select Committee. MacDonald decided to dissolve parliament and a new General Election took place (Pelling, 1982, pp. 58-59, see also Taylor, 1965, p. 225).

Thus the 'responsible' government was charged with irresponsible and illegitimate activities!

Things were to get much worse yet however. Anti-Soviet propaganda was rife at this time, and the 'Daily Mail' for example had campaigned vigorously against the Labour Government, suggesting that the Communist Party was its secret paymaster. This campaign was intensified in relation to the 'Mail's' opposition to the Anglo-Soviet Treaty, which guaranteed loans of millions of pounds to Soviet Russia. Four days before the General Election of 1924, in banner headlines ('MOSCOW ORDERS TO OUR REDS', 'GREAT PLOT DISCLOSED YESTERDAY', 'PARALYSE THE ARMY AND NAVY', 'AND MR MACDONALD WOULD LEND RUSSIA OUR MONEY'!), the 'Zinoviev letter' was 'exposed' by the 'Daily Mail'.

This, so called because it appeared to have been signed by Grigori Zinoviev, head of the Comintern [5], seemed to confirm the 'Mail's' warnings about Communist influence and the Labour Government. In fact, it was a forgery. It was the culmination of an idea concocted by four White Russian émigrés horrified by Britain's willingness to, as they saw it, prop up the Bolshevik regime with economic aid. Exactly how the Letter got to London and to the Daily Mail is less clear than the effect that it had, which was to significantly undermine Labour's chances of re-election (Hurt and Worth, 1991, pp. 26-29). Indeed, the Conservatives won the election handsomely, with a majority of 221 over Labour (151) and the Liberals (40) combined, and an overall majority of 209. Despite the worries of Labour extremism however, the Liberals faired far worse than Labour, losing 118 seats and never to be a major force in British politics again.

Conservative offensive, MacDonald 'treachery'

During the ten month term of the Labour government effective liaison between ministers and the TUC had not been maintained. The 'National Joint Council', specifically set up for this purpose in 1921 and consisting of representatives of the TUC General Council, the PLP and the Labour Party NEC, had hardly been used. This had not endeared MacDonald and the PLP to the TUC General Council. Indeed:

> Ernest Bevin, leader of the recently formed Transport Workers' Union,
> led an attempt to put curbs on the leadership as regards its freedom to
> form minority governments in the future, but the attempt was easily
> defeated at the 1925 Conference (Ball, 1987, p. 110).

It was then something of an unsettled period for the party, which also saw the new Conservative government more determinedly attack Poplar. In the prevailing climate the Labour councillors now accepted (as indeed did the government) a compromize. The Labour leadership at this time also formalized its 'responsible' strategy; capturing 'the centre' was to be through the traditional and 'normal' route, rather than via the kind of local to central campaigning style of Poplarism.

Yet the end of the Labour government also saw union leaders more inclined to dig in their industrial heels. Increased trade union militancy ensued, and culminated with the General Strike of 1926. This was however soon abandoned by the TUC General Council, (if to widespread disbelief among the strikers, who thought they were winning!). In the wake of this defeat, and egged on by cries of 'back to Taff Vale' among his supporters, Baldwin, the Conservative leader, pressed home his advantage by implementing The Trades Disputes and Trade Union Act of 1927. This Act:

> made any large-scale sympathetic strike illegal and imposed heavy
> penalties for all who declared, instigated, assisted or took part in them.
> It curtailed trade union picketing and compelled Civil Service trade
> unions to withdraw from their affiliation to the Trade Union Congress
> (Williams, 1950, p. 328).

Also, under the 1913 Act which overturned the Osborne Judgement, political funds were able to be set up and maintained by a trade union. A member not wishing to so support the Labour Party could 'contract out'. The 1927 Act reversed this position:

> Instead of the minority who did not want their union to engage in political activities and affiliate to the Labour Party having to 'contract out', the majority who did had to 'contract in' (Williams, 1950, p. 329).

The movement thus looked once more to constitutional means of pursuing and defending its interests. The PLP fought a quite creditable rearguard action against such anti-trade union legislation, without which things might have turned out even worse.

A damaging split in the party nevertheless opened up between the always influential ILP and the MacDonald leadership. The ILP policy document, 'Socialism in Our Time', was debated at the 1927 Labour Party Conference, but was opposed by MacDonald and Snowden, as well as some of the trade union leaders. It was not adopted. The ILP then refused to nominate MacDonald as party treasurer, a post he had held since 1912. The rift between the old ILP stalwart MacDonald, and the contemporary ILP widened further when the 1928 Conference adopted 'Labour and the Nation'. This was not only mild by comparison to the ILP's 'Socialism in Our Time', but also to the earlier 'Labour and the New Social Order'. Worse still, MacDonald seemed to go beyond the pale in announcing (speaking on India):

> There is one thing I would like to say ... As long as I hold any position in the Parliamentary Party - and I know I can speak for my colleagues also - we are not going to take our instructions from any outside body unless we agree with them (LPACR 1928, p. 174, also quoted in Minkin, 1980, p. 14).

There was therefore tremendous conflict and animosity at this Conference, which was unresolved when the 1929 General Election was announced.

Labour's 1929 Manifesto warned electors against being misled this time by the 'scaremongering tactics' which 'gave the Tories a majority at the last Election', asserting that 'The Labour Party is neither Bolshevik nor Communist. It is opposed to   ... revolution ...'. There was also 'an unqualified pledge to deal immediately and practically with ... unemployment' ('Labour's Appeal To The Nation', in Craig, 1975, pp. 81-82). Under headings such as 'National Development and Trade Prosperity', 'Maintenance' and 'The Young and the Old', detailed plans were laid out to deal with the problem. The Manifesto committed a Labour government to intervention in the economy and to planning, and included specific proposals on housing, pensions and agriculture. One section was headed 'NO PLEDGES WE CANNOT FULFILL', which evidences the party's view of the status of the Manifesto. It was clearly seen as a series of proposals which, 'if it has a majority', the Labour government would act upon and turn into legislation.

The election saw the number of Labour MPs in the new parliament rise to 287. For the first time the Labour Party was the largest party in the Commons. But with the Conservatives with 260 and the Liberals 59 seats, Labour was still without an overall majority. The basic problem of the last Labour government therefore remained. Again MacDonald followed the traditional practice in choosing his cabinet, though at least not going outside of the party this time. The rift with the ILP was evident however, in that although most of those who had served in the first government were recalled, 'Wheatley and Jowett, who were identified with the policy of the ILP, were both dropped' (Pelling, 1982, p. 64).

The government was beset by insoluable problems almost from the start however. It was unable to get Liberal support in the Commons for its legislative programme, and in the Lords Conservative dominance ensured a similar fate. The government therefore seemed (as indeed it was), powerless, and all the time unemployment - the major issue for the Labour Party and its supporters - continued to rise. The cabinet could not even agree on a course of action which could be put to the House for approval, or, failing this, would justify the government's resignation.

The crisis intensified the splits in the party. Mosely put forward a radical programme including state control of foreign trade and expanded domestic purchasing power. The Cabinet's rejection of this plan led to its author's resignation. The 1929 Labour Party Conference showed itself unhappy with Prime Ministerial prerogatives by resolving that a Labour cabinet should be selected by the PLP (Beer, 1982, footnote p. 157). Things got no better. At the 1930 Conference a programme very similar to Mosely's was only narrowly defeated. Not only Mosely but many others therefore continued their opposition to the government's perceived timidity. The ILP attempted to tie its members to its own rather than Labour Party policy decisions where there was a divergence. Such was the state of affairs when the international financial crisis following the 'Wall Street Crash' led to the collapse of the government.

It may seem strange that taking Britain off of the Gold Standard, the alternative to accepting the pay and benefit cuts required by the New York bankers in return for the loan needed by the government, was so unthinkable to a Labour Prime Minister. Yet MacDonald's choice *was* to defend the Gold Standard and accept the necessity of implementing the cuts. He thus attempted to secure the agreement of the cabinet, the Labour Party NEC and the TUC General Council for that course of action. He failed in each case. What followed was that rather than resign and thereby force the Tories and Liberals (who between them had a majority) to take responsibility for such a policy, MacDonald abandoned the Labour Government in favour of heading a National Coalition Government. Pelling describes it thus:

> On the 23rd August MacDonald resigned office, and early next morning he accepted the King's commission to form a new government with the support of the Liberals and Conservatives. He announced his decision to his astonished Labour colleagues later the same morning. No discussion took place ... (Pelling, 1982, p. 67).

To some this episode represents simple class treachery [6], but what remains to be explained is how MacDonald came to think and act in a manner incompatible with his background as a defender of the working class and a Socialist. We need to understand how MacDonald came to be incorporated into the elitist mould of a traditional 'responsible' Prime Minister; *consulting* but then making his own decision, and, in traditionalist ideal, 'putting the nation before party and class'.

Only a very few Labour Members followed MacDonald. Indeed the vast and overwhelming majority of the Labour Party in all its sections, much to MacDonald's surprise, shared neither his view of what was best for the nation nor the elitist manner by which he came to that conclusion; they thus steadfastly refused to join him. Hence the bitter charge of 'traitor' levelled at MacDonald, which even today is the general view within the Labour Party of its first Prime Minister.

Very soon after its foundation the National Coalition Government took Britain off of the Gold Standard [7]. The very rationale of MacDonald's abandonment of the Labour Government was therefore completely broken. Pressure from the Conservatives for a new election then increased, much to MacDonald's unease. On September 28 MacDonald, along with Snowden, Thomas and Lord Sankey, who had followed him into the National government, were expelled from the Labour Party. A General Election was announced for October 1931. It was an uneven contest, with the former Labour members of the now

'National' government engaging, along with their new colleagues, in vilification of the Labour Party and the misrepresentation of its aims:

> MacDonald waved worthless mark notes in the air, declaring that the pound would have a similar fate if Labour were allowed to rule; Snowden described the mild ... Labour programme as Bolshevism run mad; Runciman, the Liberal leader, accused the Labour Party of taking Post Office deposits - 'the savings of the poor' - to finance extravagant payments to the unemployed (Williams, 1950, p. 342).

In addition to this, Labour Candidates in almost every constituency were opposed by a single 'National' Candidate, who could be expected to obtain the combined Liberal and Conservative vote as well as those of electors disposed towards 'National Labour' Candidates. Consequently, the 1931 General Election saw only 46 Labour Candidates elected. The ILP, having failed to win control over their MP's voting behaviour whilst part of the Labour Party, had fought the election as a separate group, thereby winning another five seats. This took the party's parliamentary strength back to somewhere between the positions of 1910 and 1918, although this by no means adequately conveys the full impact of the situation.

The post-MacDonald 'convalescence'

There were many repercussions for the Labour Party in the aftermath of the shock of 1931. The disagreements that have been mentioned, and a general dissatisfaction with the too-moderate response of the Labour government (and Party) to the crisis, led to the ILP's disaffiliation in July 1932. The 1932 Conference resolved that Labour ministers should be subject to decisions of the PLP. Strangely though, perhaps, there was no new attempt to curb the freedom of the parliamentary leadership to decide whether the party should form a minority government. But there were more attempts to limit the freedom given in the British governmental system to a Prime Minister:

> In 1933 a resolution was passed providing that a Labour Prime Minister, in forming his (sic) Cabinet, should consult with the Secretary of the Party and three MPs elected to advise with him; that a Labour Prime Minister should be subject to majority decisions in the

> Cabinet; and that he (sic) should recommend the dissolution of
> Parliament only on the decision of the Cabinet confirmed by a meeting
> of the PLP (footnote in Beer, 1982, p. 157, quoting from McKenzie,
> 1955, p. 321).

Perhaps MacDonald simply represented 'one bad apple', but nevertheless such precautions seemed wise. Indeed, in the light of the 1931 episode a Special Report, 'Labour And Government', was commissioned by the party. This attempted to bind a Labour government still more closely to the policies of the Party Conference and the principles of the labour movement. 'Provision 7' for example stated:

> The policy to be pursued by the Labour Government would be that laid
> down by Resolutions of the Annual Conference and embodied in the
> General Election Manifesto. The King's Speech would from year to
> year announce the installments of the Party's policy with which the
> Government proposed to deal. Where questions arose for decisions on
> which Party Policy had not been decided they would be dealt with by
> discussion with the appropriate bodies (LPACR 1933, pp. 8-10, also
> quoted in Minkin, 1980, p. 19).

This provision was accepted by the 1933 Conference, but was not written into the Party Constitution. It is clearer as to the origins of, and need to implement 'official' Labour Party policy, than the position laid down in 1907 (whereby the PLP and NEC jointly were given discretion regarding priorities and parliamentary strategy). In some senses then, it might be said to go beyond the position of 1907. But it still gives no guidance as to whether Labour should form minority governments.

Further evidence of the party's apprehension about the 'leadership principle' in the aftermath of MacDonald's betrayal, can be seen in an apparent return to the pre-MacDonald position as to the role of a Labour 'leader'. The immediate post-MacDonald party leader was Henderson, but he was soon succeeded by Lansbury. At the 1934 Conference, Lansbury said that he did not regard himself as the 'leader' of the party, but rather as no more than its 'spokesman'. Also, when Henderson resigned as Secretary of the party, it was decided that, in order to avoid any concentration of power in the hands of one person, henceforth no MP would be allowed to be the Party Secretary.

More generally, Pelling, as others, characterizes this period as one during which the TUC General Council 'abandoned its usual role of being the sheet-anchor of the party and instead moved in to take the helm' (Pelling 1982, p. 77). It was quite natural that this should be the case: the disillusionment with the labour movement's 'political wing'; the sheer scale of its defeat destroying the new-found prestige of the PLP; and in general, with Labour out of office, the industrial sphere would be bound to be prominent once again. A period of convalescence was required. The 1931 Conference had reaffirmed, as indeed the 1931 Labour General Election Manifesto echoed, that 'Socialism provides the only solution for the evils resulting from unregulated competition and the domination of vested interests' (Labour Manifesto 1931, Craig, 1975, p. 95). The party's attempt to regain credibility and the potential for government was launched in consistent fashion, with, to quote a 1933 policy statement, 'a nation-wide appeal' restating that Socialism was only possible by 'democratic methods and machinery' (LPACR 1933, p. 4).

In fact, between 1931 and 1933 the party embarked upon a remarkably broad review of policy; the NEC taking the lead. This resulted in a number of Reports being submitted to the 1932 Conference. The left of the party were quite critical of this process, preferring a more open derivation of policy to that by which Conference was simply presented with documents for acceptance or rejection. Certainly the constituency parties had had no real role in the drafting of these Reports, and although the TUC had been consulted before publication of the Report on 'Industrial Insurance', their actual involvement in producing it was minimal.

The party's participatory democracy does therefore seem to have been somewhat curtailed in this instance, but this should not detract from the extent to which participation and popular endorsement was necessary for policy to be 'official'. We need also to remember that the party's fight back to credibility was marked by the moves to greater accountability of the leadership. Further, whatever 'deviation' might have existed at this time is tempered by comparison to the fate of the Liberal Party following its splits and dissention; it is hard to believe 'that either of the older parties could have suffered such a defection among its leaders without being split from top to bottom' (Beer, 1982, p. 161). The *party* (as opposed to the parliamentary leadership), was therefore still not greatly attached to the leadership principle at this time. That is, MacDonald had been sucked into the elitist mould via his position of 'leadership'. This, to a large extent, separated him from the great body of the party and its doctrines, which, given their own close unity, were not susceptible in the same way. Thus, few were persuaded to follow MacDonald in his defection.

By burying itself in policy formation the Labour Party thus managed to re-establish political credibility quite quickly. One concrete example of this was to be seen in 1934, when, under the leadership of Herbert Morrison, Labour won a clear majority on the

London County Council. Moreover, the party was able to repeat this success in subsequent LCC elections, and:

> If victory in the LCC election was the most spectacular evidence of Labour advance, it was far from being the only one. In the London Metropolitan Borough Elections Labour had a net gain of 472 and won a clear majority on fifteen of the Metropolitan councils ... And in the country generally Labour gained control of twenty-one County Boroughs and eighteen non-County Boroughs and won 117 seats in the provincial county Council Elections (Williams, 1950, p. 350).

The 1935 Conference followed Mussolini's attack on Abyssinia (now Ethiopia) by just a few days. A resolution drafted by the NEC called upon the government, in co-operation with other members of the League of Nations, to use 'all necessary measures' to combat Italy's attack upon a fellow member. Lansbury, an avowed pacifist, and Stafford Cripps, (on 'anti-imperialist' grounds), opposed this confirmation of support for 'Collective Security'. When the resolution was overwhelmingly carried, Lansbury therefore felt honour-bound to resign the leadership. However, the long debate and Lansbury's resignation seemed to be more influential upon the public than the actual vote. Thus, when Baldwin called an election to seek, as he put it, a mandate for British support for Collective Security, this apparent ambiguity in the Labour Party's position was to its disadvantage. Nevertheless, with Attlee taking the leadership in the wake of Lansbury's resignation, the party's recovery continued. In the 1935 General Election 154 Labour Candidates (facing both 'National Government' and Liberal Candidates) were elected, but the National Government was returned with 420 members. After the election Attlee was confirmed as leader, and so began the era which was to provide the party with its first majority government, though not for another ten years.

The Attlee era

With the return to the PLP of some of its former glory, so the question of its autonomy (in interpreting policy priorities and the appropriate means of their implementation) also returned. In 1937 for example, Attlee could on the one hand proclaim:

I am not prepared to abrogate to myself a superiority to the rest of the movement. I am prepared to submit to their will even if I disagree ... the Labour Party Conference lays down the policy of the Party, and issues instructions which must be carried out by ... its representatives in Parliament ... the final authority of the Labour Party is the Party Conference (Minkin, 1980, pp. 20-21).

Yet he also asserted that:

Action in the House is a matter for the Parliamentary Party, the members of which decide on the application of Party policy. The Labour Party Executive is the body to interpret policy between Conferences, but in its own sphere the Parliamentary Party is supreme (Minkin, 1980, p. 21).

So the party continued seemingly to face both ways at once on this issue. Nevertheless, despite Provision 7 of 'Labour And Government' not having been incorporated into the Party Constitution, there was a tacit understanding in the mid 1930s between the PLP and the wider party that Conference policy was binding. In any case the matter was somewhat academic, since Labour was out of government.

The outbreak of war with Germany in 1939 intervened before another General Election had been called, and this soon led to another wartime coalition government. It is significant that the decision to join the coalition resulted from just the kind of 'discussion with the appropriate bodies' proposed in 'Provision 7'. When Attlee was asked by Chamberlain whether the Labour Party would join the government, he immediately referred the question to the party's NEC. Thus it was decided that Chamberlain's resignation was the price demanded, and agreed, for the Labour Party to join the coalition in 1940 (see eg Pelling, 1982, p. 86).

Labour was very well represented in this government, indeed, in terms of its parliamentary strength at the time, it was grossly over-represented. Involvement in the coalition enhanced further the status of the PLP, and as the war progressed Attlee's personal standing was similarly raised; a high public profile accruing from his dominance in domestic affairs. In addition to the raised prestige and governmental credibility, the party during the War also gained tacit approval for much of its policy principles; the Beveridge Report on social insurance and the Butler Education Act 1944 for example, upheld many principles important to party in these policy areas. Likewise, the principle of full employment being secured by government action was accepted and acknowledged in a 1944 White Paper.

But despite the considerable gains of this period, the old party orthodoxy had been greatly undermined, something no less true for its failure to be acknowledged explicitly. There were many reasons for the new reality. Minkin points to a process which 'so often happens with Social-Democratic and Labour politicians', namely:

> experience in governmental roles had had a profound effect on their
> attitudes. They gained in confidence, but also in the appreciation of
> 'difficulties'. They acquired more knowledge and administrative
> sophistication, but they also became more cautious and 'moderate'. As
> a result they also lost something of their vision and zeal for change,
> becoming even more wary of antagonising the electorate with 'extreme'
> policies (Minkin, 1980, p. 21).

I am sure this is valid, and something of the sort may well be virtually inevitable. I am equally sure however that we need to look beyond lack of political will, to ambiguities in the party's very conception of Socialism, and inadequacies in the envisaged means of its implementation. It was also the case that by now the old Treasury othodoxy of 'balancing the books' had been largely overturned by the 'official' acceptance of a Keynesian 'deficit financing' approach. The latter seemed to offer a means of achieving major goals of the Labour Party, such as full employment, decent housing, and a comprehensive welfare state, whilst being compatible with the basic nature and traditional practices of British government. This was of course not true of the party's old Socialist orthodoxy. These matters will be taken up and considered more fully subsequently. It is clear however, that even though the PLP had consistently acted upon Conference decisions, the shift in the perception of the party's ends and means among the leadership can be identified at this time.

In regard to ends, for example, the leadership in 1944 submitted to Conference an Economic Resolution which made no mention of the nationalization proposals included in 'Labour's Immediate Programme' 1937. Conference responded by pressing, against NEC advice and much PLP dissention, for a vote to be taken on another resolution calling for a range of industries to be nationalized. This resolution was then overwhelmingly carried:

> the reaction of Labour's leaders was typical of the style of that
> generation. Several (*but not all*) of the industries specified were

included in the Party Programme of 1945 *Let Us Face The Future*. This was then taken back to the Conference and duly authorised. It became Labour's election Manifesto (Minkin, 1980, p. 21, my emphasis in original parentheses).

The leadership were therefore able to achieve some compromize, but, this said, proposals which were unpopular with the leadership did find prominence in the 1945 General Election Manifesto.

However, an example of a shift in regard to means can be evidenced in that, on the eve of the election, the old tension between PLP 'autonomy' and its subordination to the wider party flared up once more. This was precipitated by a statement from the then NEC Chairman, Harold Laski, that the party would not be bound by any agreement reached at the Potsdam Conference of the 'Big Three'. This formed the immediate basis for Churchill's eve-of-election charge that a Labour victory would see Attlee, as the nation's Prime Minister, actually under the control of Laski in the first instance, and ultimately, that of the Labour Party Conference. As we saw in the last chapter, the Labour Party Constitution does in this matter seem to be clearly at odds with the British political tradition and accepted governmental norms. But Attlee strongly rebutted Churchill's charge, saying:

> At no time and under no circumstances has the National Executive Committee ever sought to give, or given, instructions to the Parliamentary Labour Party ... The Chairman has not the power to give me instructions (Pelling, 1982, p. 93).

This seems to be evidence of the shift in the Labour orthodoxy; the accepted extent of autonomy of the PLP and Party leader seems considerably overstressed. No doubt a large part of Attlee's motivation in responding thus relates to the wish to appear 'responsible', and, in the traditional sense, 'fit to govern'. But in another sense the statement hinges on the interpretation of the word 'instructions'. That is, since the NEC and the PLP are *jointly* to decide priorities and strategy, Attlee's insistence that he could not be given instructions by Laski - but would have to *agree* - may be justified. On the other hand, since that agreement is in regard to priorities and details relating to a programme already decided by Conference, and the Constitutional role of the NEC is as custodian of Conference decisions, then Churchill certainly had a point.

The real point though is that, whatever the Labour Party's Constitutional position may be, a Labour Prime Minister *can* simply ignore it, and, as MacDonald, act in the traditional manner of British Prime Ministers. This may or may not have been in Attlee's mind, but he would be hardly likely to say it publicly. Likewise, no-one in the Labour camp would at such a crucial juncture be likely to challenge Attlee's interpretation, and thereby give support to Churchill's critique. In any case, the assumed tacit understanding regarding 'Provision 7' made this unnecessary; enabling mandatory and non-mandatory politics in the party to coexist without the tensions leading to a party split.

Despite this - and indeed the more onerous charge by Churchill that, should Labour win, as a necessary part of their new order 'They would have to fall back on some form of Gestapo' (from Ball, 1987, p. 143) - the 1945 General Election was a spectacular success for Labour. The party's MPs in the new parliament numbered 393, giving a majority of 146 over all other parties. Attlee did not always comply with the procedures as laid down by the party for its leader between 1945-51 however. He paid no attention to 'Provision 7' when forming his government. Similarly, the PLP sometimes exercised an extent of autonomy beyond that which could really be justified by 'Provision 7'. Yet by comparison to later periods there was little dissention from the extra-parliamentary party. This is probably best explained in that, on the whole, they felt that the instrumentalist nature of the party was holding; the PLP was attempting to carry out the Party Programme. Indeed, Beer considers that the extent to which government legislation was dictated by a party programme at this time was 'unprecedented in British political history' (Beer, 1982, p. 179). We might bear in mind however, that given the anti-programmatic nature of the British governmental tradition, it was not too difficult to be 'unprecedented' in this respect.

Criticism of the PLP was largely good natured, if sometimes a little impatient, during this period. There were for example calls for 'greater workers participation' in the running of the nationalized industries. For example, Arthur Latham, later to become MP for Paddington, not only argued that policy in this respect was wrong but criticized the way in which government was attempting to gain workers' support. He also referred to further criticism in the constituencies (LPACR 1949, p. 129). More often there were 'coded' criticisms of government policy. For example, immediately after the 1946 Conference had passed a motion congratulating the government on its record, a resolution on 'Publicity' was taken, which called for 'radically improved presentation to the general public of the policies and achievements of the Government' (LPACR 1946, p. 128). Although the resolution itself did not criticize government policy, all four speakers from the floor clearly felt that the government had not done all that it might. The resolution was passed despite platform opposition.

This is really the outer limit of criticism of the government at this time however, as said, in general criticism was friendly and Conference gave its support to the government. There certainly was not the kind of bitter recrimination which would increasingly come to characterize subsequent periods, and 'Provision 7' was never in fact brought up. Beer's view is that:

> there was a corpus of principle and program whose acceptance by leaders could be taken for granted; they did not need continually to be instructed by the organization, but could be trusted with wide discretion in meeting the exigencies of prolonged and intense political combat (Beer, 1982, p. 156).

In my view this is to overstate the case a little, but if Beer is correct the acceptance of such 'wide discretion' for leaders is clear evidence of a major characteristic of the British political tradition and governmental system being imported into the Labour Party from without. However, I tend to favour the view that the *general* acceptance that the party orthodoxy was *holding* prevented serious dissention and damaging splits; there was no overt abandonment of the Socialist goal, and in spirit if not in the letter, the procedures governing the relationship between the parliamentary and extra-parliamentary parties were maintained.

The explanation for the subsequent increase in the intensity of internal division surely then lies in the perception that the 'trust' in leaders was being betrayed, or in the recognition that the orthodoxy was being broken - whichever of the above analyses is favoured it therefore leads to the same conclusion. The Party Constitution and its interpretation would become the battleground upon which opposing views of the party's purpose and mode of operation would clash; either in the attempt to reassert the old or to establish a new party orthodoxy. This is of course exactly what did happen, in the coming struggle between 'revisionists' and 'fundamentalists'. But before taking up that development we need to return to the reasons for the breakdown of the old party orthodoxy.

Beer's view here revolves around the fact that in large part the old orthodoxy grew out of the solidarity of political alienation, and would therefore inevitably be undermined with the ending of that alienation and the achievement of power. Trade union solidarity thus served as a sort of model for the 'new society', and, continues Beer, early party members' sense of 'alienation and class exclusion' prepared them to demand 'not merely amelioration', but the Socialist reconstruction of 'the system' (Beer, 1982, p. 150). The above does seem to indicate the ambiguities and theoretical poverty of the Labour Party's conception of

Socialism that I will subsequently be taking up (if Beer fails to do so). However, to complete Beer's point:

> if the thrust for power was the main driving force behind the adoption
> of Socialism, it might be expected that when and as power was won by
> organized labor (sic) the concern with Socialist ideology would decline
> (Beer, 1982, p. 152).

I am sure that Beer's is an important point, and he goes on to support it in relation to the 'practical problems' encountered by the Labour government in the attempt to implement the old orthodoxy. However, I do not believe that either of the above points, nor their aggregation, provides a sufficient or adequate basis for the explanation of the changed Labour Party orthodoxy. To say that it simply became less relevant and not worth the problems involved in its attempted implementation, is to fail to undertake the major part of the analysis. That is, rather like nineteenth century Radicalism, with its grey area and conflict between theory and current practice, as I have already intimated, the old Labour orthodoxy was itself internally faulted. Not least important here is that it was founded upon a 'quantitative' idea of Socialism.

Such an idea derives from the labour movement's early experience of Conservative and Liberal governments' favourable relationship with the employers and often positively hostile attitude to labour interests. The aim to achieve a government with favourable labour policies was therefore the motivation for labour representation in parliament. Socialists in the party had always argued that any gains so derived could only be properly defended and consolidated via the achievement of Socialism, but at the same time they embraced labourism in order not to alienate the largely non-Socialist movement and leadership. Thus by the time Socialism was officially adopted by the party it was associated with labourist governmental policies rather than with a different structure of government and society. Government office was conceptualized as basically meaning the same as for the Liberal and Conservative parties, except that what a 'Socialist' government would *do* would be different. This is Socialism as policy rather than system.

Socialist 'content' shaped by environmental 'form'

In looking more closely at how this quantitative conception of Socialism arose we in fact return to something alluded to earlier, namely the Labour Party as a product of the environments which spawned it: participatory labourism and elitist constitutionalist Socialism. In turn this leads us to the apparent paradox of a party built upon participatory and popular accountable democracy coming to operate nonetheless with a centralized, bureaucratic and elitist conception of it's Socialist goal.

In relation to the first point, we have seen that the participatory practices of the Labour Party derive from it's labour movement roots. I have also shown that the adoption of Socialism added a final goal for the party, and a clearer rationale to the programmatic extension of the party's instrumentalism into the parliamentary arena. This parliamentary arena is however intrinsically elitist and hostile to participatory, popular accountable assumptions and practices, whereas they were sustained by and within their own, labour movement environment. We have seen the importance of this in relation to the party's ability to hold itself together following the defection of MacDonald to the elitist camp. With the return to Opposition the extra-parliamentary environment became once again the primary one. It thus retook the helm and, since the 'alien' ideas of the parliamentary arena were marginalized, the party was able to regroup and recouperate without a serious split. Yet, as a result of the very success of that 'convalescence', the antagonism between the party's parliamentary and extra-parliamentary wings once again came to the fore.

Such an analysis also provides the basis for understanding the paradox of a party built upon popular participation and accountability adopting a centralized, bureaucratic and elitist conception of Socialism. In this respect too we need to recall the Labour Party's origins. The trades union movement provided the impetus to the idea of attaining parliamentary influence so as to further the interests of labour. The gradualist, constitutionalist Socialists added to this moderate aim that of attaining governmental office; the idea that the basis of the economy might be changed in favour of the majority working class. A Socialist Labour Government would do this 'on behalf' of labour and its Socialist allies [8]. Thus we see both a tendency to confuse and subsequently conflate labourism and Socialism, and that each source of this confusion accepts an implied form of elitism in relation to the rationale of the party. This is less surprizing than may be thought, given the various natures of elitism apparent among the Labour Party's founding organizations. The role of the workers themselves would thus be passive, and all activity subordinated to the overriding goal of the election of such a (Socialist or otherwise) Labour government.

Such a concept of Socialism derived largely from trade union *leaders,* and Socialists who recognized the necessity of an accommodation with them and the realities of a non-Socialist trades union movement. It was therefore a Labourist/Socialist strategy based upon *institutionalized* working class support; through the affiliation of workers' organizations, and the assimilation of union and TUC *hierarchies* into the Labour project. It was thus an elitist, bureaucratic and centralized conception of Socialism, dependent upon capturing the existing centres of political power in society for the *representatives* of the people.

Clearly this is a top-down view of the governmental rationale of the Labour Party, despite the party itself being organized along bottom-up principles. It is also a strategy for change firmly located in the existing political, economic and social institutional framework, and which accepts implicitly the Liberal/Conservative conception of the state. It implies for example the now very dated and simplistic view of the neutrality of the state, its organs and personnel, and their straightforward subordination to the policy objectives of an elected government. There is a wealth of evidence to demonstrate the inadequacy of such a conception of the state, and, as I indicated in the 'Introduction' to this work, Dearlove and Saunders' (1984) standard text on British government is actually organized around the need to dispel such myths.

The significance of the Labour Party's emergence as a product of the position of workers within the existing capitalist framework is perhaps clearer by contrast to the position of an ideologically committed Socialist party representing opposition to capitalism itself, and seeking support from the labour movement on that basis. Such a party would largely initiate policy in the form of a 'broad assault' (rather than instrumentalist sectionalism). It would, through it's own interventions, prompt and support workers struggling themselves to combat the system's injustices (rather than be embarrassed by such struggles, and seek to play them down as potentially electorally damaging). Such a party would attempt to build and extend its support in the nation via such 'local to central' means (rather than outlaw them as did the Labour Party and 'Poplarism'). It would seek to recruit working class members who may well be trade unionists, but these members would have to be *won* to *Socialism* and support the party on that basis (rather than their support being assumed via structural incorporation into the project). Similarly, such a basis of recruitment would undermine rather than reinforce sectionalism.

The abandonment of a local to central, bottom-up strategy to power in favour of the traditionalist mode of capturing the centre, therefore represents one more element in the party's constitutionalization. There was nevertheless the widespread belief inside and outside of the party at the time of it's election in 1945, that it's aim was to achieve the Socialist transformation of Britain. Since I have argued that the Labour Party's conception of Socialism and of its achievement was quantitative, elitist and bureaucratic, it is unsurprizing that bureaucratic management characterizes this period of British government. But the period establishes not bureaucratic Socialism, but rather bureaucratic welfare capitalism. This is not in itself a controversial conclusion. However, posing the question as to what accounts for it reproduces both the question of the changed orthodoxy and the norm of the pluralist/Liberal - Marxist dichotomy regarding its explanation. As I have attempted thus far to go beyond the analytical limitations of such approaches, building upon the foregoing analysis we will now turn our attention to the 1945-50 Labour Government.

As Beer says, the Labour government had initially maintained much of the wartime methods of central economic planning, since they were compatible with it's concept of Socialism. In the first year the emphasis was on physical planning; a system of production and allocation controls and licensing, price controls and rationing. These physical controls were used in conjunction with a series of quantitative programmes, or economic 'budgets'. The main emphasis here was on the 'manpower budget' (sic). As Attlee explained to the House in February 1946, the intention of the government was to concentrate on 'manpower rather than finance - our human resources rather than our financial resources' (Beer, 1982, p. 192). Thus by 'direction' or 'encouragement' labour was to be concentrated where it was most needed and most effectively utilized.

Economic management was however very complex and difficult in the immediate post-war economy, and particularly so in regard to the transition from war to peacetime production. During 1947 inflationary pressures mounted, and against this background the government was persuaded, between 1947 and 1950, to reverse it's emphasis. It thus virtually abandoned (what we might more appropriately today call) the 'labour-power budget' approach in favour of one led by the financial budget. Beer explains:

> The sequence in which this (disinflationary) analysis arose and spread through the political community seems to have been: academic economists; then economic journalists; then Members of Parliament, especially the Opposition; and finally the Government (Beer, 1984, p. 195).

This shift in 'means' (methods of quantitative planning) - led by those who were primarily concerned with more efficiently managing the existing capitalist economy - was the first step in undermining the admittedly somewhat woolly Socialist vision of the future held by the government. Being a change in *methods* whilst overtly maintaining the (rhetoric of the) Socialist *goal*, the implications of the shift in emphasis were less noticeable.

Some did notice the change of direction however, and opposed it. The 'Keep Left' group was most directly critical of the government's foreign policy orientation, but it also advocated more direct, rather than indirect planning, including giving power to the planners to override the autonomy of government departments. In addition they called for the nationalization of 'every industry which has a hold over our economy or which cannot be made efficient in private hands' (Beer, 1982, p. 197). Their manifesto, 'Keep Left', published in April 1947, argued that:

> present difficulties are not the result of socialist planning; they are the result of not enough boldness and urgency, and too much tenderness for vested interests. You can't make socialist omelettes without breaking capitalist eggs (from Foote, 1986, p. 269).

The group were also unhappy about the initial dilution and then the actual dropping of 'workers' control' from Labour's project, particularly in regard to the nationalized industries.

'Keep Left' was however far too small to be very influential, and, (although gradually rather than in a dramatic or overt manner), the switch in policy orientation continued. Thus, by it's last years, the Attlee goverment had:

> more and more ... turned away from direct control by public administration and toward indirect control by manipulation of the market. From physical planning it turned to economic management. This approach to planning is quite compatible with private ownership, competition and profit-seeking. Indeed it depends upon a general pursuit of economic self-interest. From the viewpoint of economic planning, in consequence, it makes public ownership superfluous and the whole Socialist conception of the co-operative economy sustained by the public service motive irrelevant (Beer, 1982, pp. 199-200).

Hence Beer suggests that 'practical problems' had led to this change of direction. What is neglected in this analysis however, is first that practical problems would undoubtably arise whether from the requirements of revitalizing capitalism or undertaking a Socialist transformation. Secondly, Beer fails to make clear that the *solutions* adopted by the government were those appropriate to the former case (just as those suggested by the 'Keep Left ' group were more appropriate to the latter). This is not quite the same thing as making clear - as he does - that the *result* of the adoption of those particular solutions was to favour capitalism rather than Socialism. The government did have to be *persuaded* towards one orientation and away from the other.

Seizing upon the solutions involving the least disruption and seemingly the best prospect for short term benefit *is* 'practical' and *is* sensible from the point of view of *government* (ie government as an *end* rather than a *means*). The 'Keep Left' solutions, requiring the instigation of machinery to override the autonomy of government departments, were thereby contentious and disruptive in terms of the British constitution and established governmental conventions [9]. Direct central planning and 'doctrinaire' nationalization would be similarly antagonistic to the political and governmental norms in this country. Neither would these disruptive alternatives offer much prospect of a short-term improvement in prevailing conditions. On the contrary, things would be almost certain to get worse before they got better. Even more certain is that the business and professional sectors in economy and society would resist these more 'extreme' measures. Beer thus plays down the political content of the shift in favour of the idea of a natural and practical reorientation in response to changed conditions. Miliband on the other hand plays up the political content in terms of this demonstrating what happens to Socialist governments attempting to operate in bourgeois systems. Whilst each has a powerful case providing a backdrop, the ambiguity of the Socialist goal is I believe crucial.

In this respect the earlier mentioned anomaly regarding the confusion and conflation of Labourism and Socialism is to the fore. In the Labourist perspective, being in the forefront of the struggle to combat the rigours of capitalism, defending the interests of labour against those of capital, the unions were clearly a leading progressive force. However, given the ambiguities in the party's conception of Socialism, the static and defensive nature of such a role, and it's inappropriateness to any strategy for Socialist transition, was never properly considered. Consequently, the traditional role of the trades unions, rather than being favourable to - or even compatible with - Socialist change, was in fact found to be an obstacle. This can be illustrated in relation to the Attlee Government's initial policy orientation. As Beer puts it:

> A system of physical planning that expresses its objectives in quantitative programs must be able to include manpower (sic) in those programs, especially the manpower needed in industries of critical importance to the economy at any particular time. If these manpower programs cannot be carried out, some more relaxed method of planning will have to be adopted. In Britain between 1947 and 1950, the attitude of the unions obliged the planners gradually to move to this conclusion (Beer, 1982, p. 200).

The success of a labour-power budget approach therefore depended upon either the continuation of wartime methods of compulsory direction of labour to where it was most needed, or a less direct means of achieving the same end. A government-set wages policy to so encourage and reward the movement of labour would be a good example of the latter.

However, neither one of these approaches is compatible with the traditional 'free collective bargaining' role of the trades unions. This certainly *resulted* in 'practical problems' for the government, but was *caused* by the weakness of the Labour Party's theoretical basis. The two things come together in the unions' unwillingness to set aside the advantages of a for-once strong bargaining position provided by the post-war labour shortage. Whilst their economic organization offered immediate gains in the shape of better pay and conditions, the abstract (and suspiciously familiar-sounding 'jam tomorrow') promise of a Socialist new dawn of the future, was unattractive. If a government-set wages policy was thus ruled out, the continuation of compulsory directive methods - with connotations of 'totalitarianism' - would enliven Churchill's spectre of a 'Gestapo'; the Conservative Opposition would certainly have eagerly seized such an opportunity to discredit the Labour Government.

With the government thus unable to follow it's favoured course, and with the increasing pressure for a solution to the worsening economic situation, the road away from 'Socialist Commonwealth' towards the social-democratic 'Welfare State' becomes the easier to appreciate. As previously said though, the shift in policy does not seem to have been particularly adversely received. The Labour Party rank-and-file in general remained supportive of the government, and, given that it never lost a by-election between 1945-50, the level of support for the government in the country can be assumed to have held up well. It is however very unlikely that the significance of the policy change was appreciated by many party members or electors.

A broad consensus of opinion sees the Attlee Government as having simply 'run out of steam', but this view is tempered by Ball, who says for example:

> the argument that Labour had completed its reform programme and was
> intellectually exhausted lacks conviction. The programme endorsed by
> the Labour Party Conference in June 1949, *Labour Believes in Britain*,
> provided a number of nationalization proposals to implement. The tiny
> Labour majority in the House of Commons after the 1950 general
> election was not the only reason for the failure to act on this
> programme; the Labour government of 1950-51 deliberately chose not
> to attempt any implementation (Ball, 1987, p. 166).

Though basically correct in my view this does perhaps overstate the case. That is, whilst there *was* a growing divergence between the PLP (majority) and the wider party over appropriate policy; whilst the Socialist perspective *had* been consciously abandoned or at least so 'redefined' in the PLP as to be at odds with the old orthodoxy still characterizing the extra-parliamentary party; it was also true that: a major reform programme *had* been carried through between 1945-50; the government *had* been weakened by the deaths of Bevin and Cripps; the major rearmament programme necessitated by the outbreak of the Korean War in 1950 *had* seen the resignations of Bevan, Wilson and Freeman from the government over the consequent NHS economies; and, despite polling over 1.25 million *more* votes than in 1945, the government's overall majority *had* been reduced to only five by the 1950 General Election.

All of the above plus the economic difficulties and the enforced austerity no doubt added to the loss of 'vision and zeal for change', as suggested by the quotation from Minkin (1980) cited earlier. No doubt the government became even more 'wary of antagonising the electorate' with 'extreme' policies (Minkin, 1980, p. 21). It is also true that Attlee was a remarkably conventional man and therefore well disposed to caution and the use of familiar means of implementation rather than instigating radical new ones. Similarly, as Morrison urged moderation and respectability as the way for Labour to win in 1945, so in 1950 he argued for 'consolidation' of that already achieved. Nevertheless, in my view it was again neither wholly the experience of governing within the parliamentary system nor the series of 'practical' 'realities' which account for the shift from Socialism to welfare capitalist social-democracy. Rather (with the mentioned shortcomings in the manner by which Socialism was conceptualized as the starting point), this particular outcome emerged out of the interaction between the two.

The shift in orientation is however clear, even in terms of what the Labour Manifestos of 1945 and 1950 say. In 1945 we find:

> The Labour Party is a Socialist Party and proud of it. Its ultimate
> purpose at home is the establishment of the Socialist Commonwealth of
> Great Britain ('Let Us Face The Future', in Craig 1975, p. 127).

The 1950 Manifesto on the other hand says that since 1945 under Labour, by 'hard work, good sense and self discipline', the people have 'laid the foundations of a future based upon free social democracy' ('Let Us Win Through Together', in Craig, 1975, p. 152). This abandonment of the party's ultimate end would come to also intensify the undermining of the previously accepted means.

Retreat from Socialist end undermines participatory means

If, at least with hindsight, the shift in orientation in the PLP was very significant, beyond its mentioned failure after the 1950 General Election to carry out 'official' policy, there was in fact little indication at this time that the party's means were also under question. The 1951 Manifesto had for example been drawn from 'Labour and the New Society', which had been passed by the 1950 Conference (if not without criticism). Similarly, Attlee had deliberately chosen late October for the General Election of 1951, which indicates a continuing regard for the role and authority of the Annual Conference. Likewise, lengthy debate over the Manifesto at the 1951 Conference confirms, in the main, the norm of its constituting a list of proposals that a Labour government would be expected to carry out during the lifetime of a new parliament. Orthodox procedures do therefore seem to have been maintained as the norm. This being so, even though the election saw the party turned out of government there were none of the recriminations of 1931.

Following Bevan's resignation over the prescription charges imposed upon 'his' National Health Service (he had been Minister of Health in the 1945 government), a focus for 'left opposition' to the party leadership - 'Bevanism' - was created. Again it was in foreign policy that this left alternative was clearest. Bevan took up the position of the old 'Keep Left' group in arguing for a 'third road' between Washington and Moscow. This position would get a boost with the emergence of the 'Non-Aligned Movement' under India's Nehru, Yugoslavia's Tito and Soekarno of Indonesia, although it never amounted to a real force for influence in the world. However, high profile disputes between the 'Bevanites' and the party leadership were not uncommon. In 1952 for example Bevan and 57 followers defied the party whips' instructions (to abstain) by voting against the Conservative government's rearmament programme. This led to the leadership moving against the Bevanites' 'party within a party'.

However, the 1952 Conference passed - with platform support - a resolution which called for the 'drawing up of a five year programme of policy and proposed legislation for submission to the electorate prior to the next election' (LPACR 1952, p. 91). The status of Labour Manifestos thus seemed confirmed. But the NEC's policy document presented to the 1953 Conference was at best a less than unequivocal response to the 1952 Conference decision. 'A Challenge To Britain' combined specific and detailed proposals for a single term of office with looser proposals - such as on public ownership - the completion of which would require more than one term. Arguably the nationalization proposals being in the 'non-immediate' category also evidenced the shift in policy orientation. There certainly was no general commitment to increasing state ownership, if the Conservative government's denationalization of steel and road transport had provided 'a well-gnawed bone which the leadership regularly threw back to the hungry activists, as a token of the leadership's belief in public ownership' (Miliband, 1973, p. 322). Similarly, although Crossman claimed this document to be the basis of the 1955 General Election Manifesto [10], more accurately, the Manifesto would seem to have been based upon a very selective reading of the document passed by Conference.

Meanwhile, the issue of German rearmament had produced more conflict with the Bevanites, and the party leadership only narrowly gained a majority on the issue at the 1954 Conference. Bevan resigned from the shadow cabinet over the issue, and the continuing conflict saw six PLP members expelled. In the following year, 1955:

> Bevan himself attacked Attlee on the floor of the House of Commons on the use of nuclear weapons after sixty-two MPs had abstained under the Conscience Clause. His punishment was expulsion by the PLP, and he only narrowly missed expulsion from the party (Ball, 1987, p. 168).

Some of the greatest disputes and animosities were rooted in Bevan's militant commitment to the working class and his consequent hatred of the Tories. There were notable ferocious exchanges between Bevan and certain ('lower than vermin') Conservative MPs, and such behaviour did nothing to endear Bevan to his more moderate party colleagues. Indeed, Bevan's 'cloth cap' Socialism was seemingly not too attractive to the masses in the boom conditions of the 1950s,

Adherence to the party's traditional procedures therefore does seem to become a little strained at this time, but the aftermath of the 1955 defeat has been noted as being 'the only post-war election defeat that didn't swing Labour to the left' (Williams, 1982, p. 193). It was thought that internal strife in the party, coupled with a decline in its level of organization, were largely to blame for the defeat. The NEC therefore set up a sub-committee to inquire into the state of party organization and report to the next Conference.

The party under Gaitskell

At the end of 1955 Attlee resigned the leadership of the Labour Party, and in the contest for the new leader (decided at that time by the PLP alone), Gaitskell was elected by 157 votes to Bevan's 70 and Morrison's 40. Whilst in terms of the ends envisaged for the party

Gaitskell was a 'revisionist', the retreat from the Socialist goal was already a fact. His leadership therefore had less impact on the instrumentalist nature of the party, and the balance between delegatory and representative intra-party democracy, than might be imagined. Nor did the short span of Gaitskell's leadership alter significantly the balance between the parliamentary leadership and the Party Conference. He fought only one General Election as Labour Party Leader, and the great controversies over nuclear disarmament and 'Clause 4' materialized after that election and had subsided before the next (by which time Gaitskell had in any case died).

If the Election Manifesto of 1955 had marked another victory over the left and a further consolidation of revisionism, this was all the more true of the adoption by the 1957 Conference of the policy document 'Industry and Society'. This proposed the renationalization of steel and road haulage but apart from that only vague references to the possibility of taking into public ownership industries which were failing the nation. In similar fashion to the way in which the 1955 Manifesto was said to be based upon the 1953 'Challenge to Britain' policy statement, the 1959 Manifesto 'was simply a diluted version of *Industry and Society* ' (Ball, 1987, p. 169). Thus the only election which the Labour Party fought with Gaitskell as leader was fought on a Manifesto which 'embodied (albeit in delicately worded phraseology) the programme ratified by Conference' (Minkin, 1980, p. 274). It has been alleged that Gaitskell rewrote all of the economic paragraphs of the Mainifesto (see eg Crossman, in Morgan [ed], 1981, p. 776), but there were no public arguments suggesting that Conference policy had been ignored either during or even immediately after the campaign.

The election result - the third consecutive defeat for Labour - did see a flurry of activity unleashed, but this was exclusively around policy itself rather than its derivation. Following the publication of *New Fabian Essays*, edited by Richard Crossman in 1952, and Anthony Crosland's *The Future of Socialism* in 1956, the revisionists had confirmed and consolidated their hold on the party. They argued essentially that many of Socialism's old battles had effectively been already won; the capitalism that the Labour Party of the 1920s and '30s had been so opposed to was no more.

With the 'managerial revolution' control had passed from the old style hard nosed capitalist to a new, professional managerial class. This separation of ownership and control, it was argued, had shifted the focus of concern away from ownership as an issue; in any case the old adage that 'you can't plan what you don't own' had been proven wrong during the War. Nationalization, which had always been a means to an end rather than an end in itself, was now therefore virtually irrelevant. As Keynesian economic management had removed the scourge of unemployment, the Welfare State had removed the insecurities and injustices of old style capitalism. Progressive taxation and public spending were now more appropriate means of furthering the old goals of equality and social justice. The existing balance between the public and private sectors was therefore about right, and pragmatism rather than 'dogma' should guide any future adjustments.

Given the above, and that the Labour Party was perceived as the party of the working class, it was hidebound by its image. At a time when the rising living standards of the post-war boom had undermined class identification, let alone class solidarity - many 'objectively' working class people did not *see themselves* as such at all - this 'cloth cap' image was said to be the reason for Labour's electoral defeats. Hence, in November 1959 Gaitskell launched an attempt to formalize such a revision of the party's mission and thereby change its image, via removal of Clause 4 part (IV) of the Party Constitution. However, a ground swell of rank-and-file opposition to this latest leadership move was taken up widely within all sections of the party to ensure the defeat of the attempt. But what was defeated was the attempt at *formalizing* the revisionism already *de facto* in place, there was no move back towards the old Socialist orthodoxy.

Apart from the Clause 4 controversy, the most notable incident of Gaitskell's leadership followed the 1960 Conference's decision favouring unilateral nuclear disarmament, and thereby running contrary to the policy of the PLP. In his Conference speech Gaitskell proclaimed his determination to 'fight, fight and fight again', to mobilize opinion against this decision so as 'to save the party we love'. This certainly indicates Gaitskell's belief that this Conference decision was wrong and his and the policy of the PLP was correct; thus the 'responsible' policy must be defended. Rather than acting simply as the party's 'mouthpiece' - or resigning if he felt unable to do so - Gaitskell repudiated this decision, disassociating himself and the PLP from it. This, arguably, set a new precedent. But in an interview in 1959 Gaitskell put the view that Conference determined the great issues of principle, and agreed that a properly passed resolution in favour of unilateral nuclear disarmament would bind a Labour government (Williams, 1982, p. 193). His determination to fight to *change* Conference policy, rather than simply ignoring it and asserting the policy of the parliamantary leadership, reinforces this view.

It should be remembered that the unilateralist position never obtained the two-thirds majority at Conference which would have required its automatic inclusion in an election manifesto. Pelling indeed considers Gaitskell's 'fight, fight and fight again' speech justified since there had never been a 'real' but only a short-lived 'technical' majority behind unilateralism (Pelling, 1982, p. 126). The fact that the very next year the decision was reversed and the Conference thus swung back behing the PLP's policy tends to support this view. In any case speculation as to what might have happened if the unilateralist position had been confirmed or strengthened is pointless, as it *can* only be *speculation*. Certainly Gaitskell gave no clear indication that he was willing to defy a two-thirds majority of Conference, his differences with Conference were short-lived, and were resolved, as they had arisen, via Conference decisions.

It can therefore be said that up until 1959, although the revisionism of policy objectives begun in 1947 had intensified and had established a new Social-Democratic (or old labourist) rationale, the party's instrumentalism and participatory principles were generally maintained. Manifestos were generally agreed to have been drawn from Conference policy, and to represent a binding contract with the electorate. Despite instances of Labour leaders having had personal disagreements with certain Conference policies, when it came to the Manifesto the Conference position was generally the dominant one. Likewise, even if at times party procedures were not followed to the letter, while the PLP were seen to be attempting to carry out 'official' policy, criticism from the wider party tended to be muted. However, the party under Gaitskell never attained office, and therefore the representational theory and practice associated with the parliamentary arena was never fully legitimized. The full potential for the increasing 'moderation' of policy to lead to the undermining of participatory assumptions and practices was thus not realized under Gaitskell. Harold Wilson's accession to the leadership did however see significant further moves in the direction of parliamentary elitism.

The Wilson era

In 1962 Harold Wilson had chaired the Labour Party Conference. At the 1963 Conference he was party leader. This Conference was in fact relatively non-controversial, and the Manifesto for the General Election which followed in 1964 was rather tame, with few specific commitments. But after 'thirteen years of Tory misrule' (Wilson) the party was more concerned to get the Conservatives out than anything else. After the election victory this mood was reflected in the self-congratulatory 1964 Party Conference. However, in his speech to Conference Wilson said:

> In the next General Election I want the Party to say that we believe in the public ownership of the means of production, distribution and exchange, not merely as a means of achieving economic efficiency, but as a way of getting rid of the windfall state and of preventing people from building up fortunes out of this system (LPACR, 1964, p. 118).

Thus with unilateralism a dead letter following the test-ban treaty, and Wilson seemingly embracing Clause 4, the two issues which had so recently opened a rift between Conference and the PLP seemed buried.

In forming his government Wilson, like Attlee before him, paid no attention to 'Provision 7' of 1933. But with a majority of only four meaning a new election could not be far off, between 1964 and that new election of 1966 the party did not have great expectations of the government, and was in general little disposed to criticize it. There were exceptions however. Foreign policy again provided a focus for criticism, this time because of the government's support for increasing American intervention in Vietnam. The government's proposals to enforce advance notification of wage claims as part of its incomes policy - itself running counter to free collective bargaining - also ran into opposition. Likewise, the U-turn represented by the government's proposals to limit (black) immigration spawned considerable opposition. The government line nevertheless won substantial majorities on all three issues at the 1965 Party Conference.

It is however now clear that even at this early stage Wilson was diverging fundamentally from the kind of consultative and co-operative procedures expected of a Labour leader. He had for example decided on a March 1966 election by the end of 1965 (Wilson, 1974, pp. 261-2), and organized a joint meeting of the NEC and cabinet for Sunday February 6 1966. Wilson had said nothing - even to his closest colleagues - about his intention to call an election. He had therefore consulted no-one, and he did not in fact dissolve parliament until the beginning of March. The meeting on February 6 was therefore clearly not a Clause V meeting as such, but its outcome seems to have been quite premeditated. As Crossman records in his diary:

> The net effect ... was a vote of confidence in the Government ... (which will) enable Harold Wilson and George Brown, as Chairman of the Home Affairs Committee, to say to the Executive, 'you've had it chums. We've given you your chance to complain, a whole day. You did nothing at all about it'. When the meeting was over it was clear that writing the election manifesto this time would be child's play (Howard [ed], 1979, p. 161).

Wilson had therefore deliberately set out to outmanoeuvre the NEC, which, in his own words, had become 'restive about the increasing remoteness to them of their own government' (Wilson, 1974, p. 262).

The eventual Clause V meeting seems, perhaps surprizingly, to have been relatively uncontentious, the main area of dispute being over incomes and prices policy. The inclusion in the Manifesto of a statutory incomes policy was quite in order however, since the policy had been endorsed by Conference. This period nevertheless marks the beginning of some changing attitudes within both the NEC and the PLP, a process that would reopen old divisions, since the two bodies changed attitudes in opposite directions.

The 1966 General Election campaign proved to be something of a Harold Wilson Labour one-man-band, but it saw no proclamation of Clause 4 in line with Wilson's speech to the 1964 Conference. In fact no new policies of any significance were offered to the electorate, 'although several of the old ones had been abandoned or considerably modified' (Pelling, 1982, p. 137). If much of the party were disappointed with the nature of the campaign and the content of the Manifesto, the election result - an overall Labour majority of 98 - provided a tremendous boost to morale. One result of this was to similarly boost the expectations held by the party as a whole of the new government. In a very real sense then, the new government was on trial.

It soon became apparent however, that the 1964-66 period, far from being an excusable lapse, had in fact been merely a foretaste of government behaviour which would become more and more unpalatable to the extra-parliamentary party. Between 1966-70, government policy increasingly diverged from that of Conference, and from the Manifesto upon which the government had been elected. The government became independent of Conference to a degree entirely unprecedented, and relations between the parliamentary leadership and the extra-parliamentary party reached a new low. Government policy was repudiated time and again at successive Conferences. But Wilson simply ignored such criticism. Worse, he infuriated much of the wider party by his habit in media interviews of making a virtue out of defying the Conference.

Wilson had overwhelming support however within a PLP now predominantly middle class/professional in social composition. The NEC on the other hand 'slowly shed the role of public apologist for Labour Government policy and took on a new, more active, role as the government of the party'; custodian of Conference policy (Pelling, 1982, pp. 140-43). Thus, whilst the Conference itself was only a once-a-year embarrassment for Wilson and his government, the NEC had now become a potential source of constant criticism for as long as government policy diverged from that of Conference. This too was unprecedented. The NEC had been critical of the PLP whilst the party was in Opposition - between 1931-33 for example - but never before whilst the party was in government.

As we have seen, Attlee had bowed to Conference even when he had questioned the wisdom of its policy. Likewise, Gaitskell acknowledged the Conference as the supreme policy making body of the party. Wilson however simply chose to ignore Conference when he disagreed with its policies. It would seem therefore that Wilson fell victim to the 'MacDonald syndrome'; going over to the idea of the 'independent' Prime Minister derived from the concept of 'responsible' government. At the 1966 Conference for example, facing opposition to the powers of compulsion within the Prices and Incomes Act (to freeze pay), Wilson made it clear that he had no intention of changing his mind, saying 'At the end of the day, the Government must take the final decision in the interests of the nation as a whole' (Pelling, 1982, p. 141).

The 1968 Conference passed, by a five to one majority (Pelling, 1982, p. 143), a similar resolution condemning the government's retention of legal powers over wages, with a similar (lack of) response. Worse was to come. A White Paper early in 1969, 'In Place Of Strife', floated proposals to set industrial relations in a formal legal framework including tough sanctions. This prompted immediate, furious and determined opposition. A special Trades Union Congress voted for and organized total opposition in the form of mass demonstrations, pickets and lobbies of important party meetings and of leading personalities. The revolt was even well supported within the PLP, going far beyond the usual small left-wing constituency. In fact such was the breadth and depth of opposition that Wilson and Barbara Castle, the Employment Secretary, were forced to drop the proposals. Giving way in the face of *parliamentary* opposition is consistent with 'responsible government' of course; it would be irresponsible for the Prime Minister to threaten the authority and prestige - even the survival perhaps - of the government, in the face of such *legitimate* opposition. In any case, by the 1969 Conference the party was distincly unhappy with the leadership, and demanding an end to its go-it-alone style.

Though the 1969 Conference approved the document 'Agenda For A Generation' as the basis for the 1970 Manifesto, there were angry scenes and harsh words in the discussion on government policies. The enthusiasm and expectation among the rank-and-file which had been apparent after the 1966 election had given way to frustration and anger at the failure of the government to act upon its 'agreed' programme. By-election swings against the party attested to Labour's unpopularity in the country, and most party members felt that although *they* were feeling the brunt of this loss of favour, it was the government rather than the party that was responsible. Unhappiness within the party over the government would soon be. matched by that over the 1970 General Election campaign however.

To an extent even greater than that of 1966, Wilson in the 1970 campaign played down the issues of principle between the parties. Instead, he laid the emphasis on the choice between himself and the Conservative leader, Edward Heath, and on the government's record against adverse conditions. The Election Manifesto, with a picture of Wilson on the cover and entitled 'Now Britain's Strong Let's Make It Great To Live In', was rather 'cautious, complacent and of uninspiring generality' (Minkin, 1980, p. 314). It seems that the more positive proposals favoured by the NEC were sacrificed in favour of Wilson's favoured approach. Thus, for the first time, where government and party policy diverged, such as on Vietnam for example, it was the *government* view rather than that of Conference that was the dominant one. Under pressure of time and Wilson's insistence, the NEC agreed to the Manifesto in the hope that all would come right in the end. The main thing, whatever disagreements there may be, was of course to get a new Labour government. It is nevertheless clear that in drawing ever closer to Conservative/Liberal norms, the Labour Party's parliamentary leadership had usurped the policy making sovereignty of the Annual Conference.

Labour in fact lost the General Election of 1970, the Conservatives emerging with an overall majority of 30. The Conference which followed in the wake of this election defeat saw an outraged backlash against the leadership; delegates clearly furious about the party's staid Manifesto. In the debate on the party programme for example, a successful National Union of Public Employees (NUPE) resolution called for the party to 're-establish a clearly defined sense of Socialist purpose', and instructed the NEC:

> to present to next year's Annual Conference a programme designed to, (a) secure greater equality in the distribution of wealth and income, (b) extend social ownership, and (c) develop industrial democracy and the role of the Trades Union Movement (LPACR 1970, p. 167).

These three specific points had been among those either left out of the 1970 Manifesto completely or unrecognizably diluted. Despite the debate supposedly being about future policy, speaker after speaker used the opportunity to condemn the previous government, which was said to have: 'sunk to the depths', allowing 'expediency to take the place of principle'; 'far from controlling the economy, our leaders in 1964 and onwards were controlled by the economy' (see eg LPACR 1970, pp. 168-78).

A second important resolution was passed during the general debate on the 1970 election, it read:

> This Conference believes that the Parliamentary Labour Party leaders, whether in Government or Opposition, should reflect the views and aspirations of the Labour and Trades Union Movement, by framing their policies on Annual Conference decisions. While appreciating that

the Parliamentary Labour Party must deal with matters arising in Parliament which have not been the subject of Annual Conference decision, it deplores the Parliamentary Labour Party's refusal to act on Conference decisions (LPACR 1970, p. 180).

This is virtually an amalgam of Clause V of the Party Constitution and the 1933 'Provision 7', and thus another condemnation of Labour government 'independence' and formal reiteration of the 'official' position. The weak Manifesto and go-it-alone style of Wilson and the leadership were again often referred to in this debate, in the context of that government's failure to carry out Conference policy. Despite Wilson himself replying to the debate and trying to get the resolution remitted, and then rejected, it was in fact passed by 3,085, 000 to 2, 801, 000 votes. Following this a whole range of committees and sub-committees were set up to formulate a detailed policy statement, the result of which was 'Labour's Programme For Britain 1973'. The 1973 Report of the Labour Party's Home Policy Committee states that 54 different policy groups were involved in the formulation of this document, which attests to the swing back to participatory assumptions and practices in the party.

There is little doubt that the wide policy making procedures which had produced the 1973 Party Programme made it much more difficult for the parliamentary leadership to ignore Conference policy in writing the Manifesto for the 1974 General Election. That Manifesto, 'Let Us Work Together - Labour's Way Out Of The Crisis', although short, and vague in places, was much firmer and more radical than the 1970 document. The idea of a 'National Enterprize Board', a major plank of the '73 programme was included, as was the pledge to 'bring about a fundamental shift in the balance of power and wealth in favour of working people and their families' (p. 10). A wealth tax and a capital transfer tax were included, as well as the nationalization of development land and mineral rights. It also promised the repeal of the Conservative government's Industrial Relations Act, and the renegotiation of Britain's terms of entry to the EEC.

However, the production of this Manifesto saw the emergence of another precedent: the leader's 'veto'. The NEC had intended to include a commitment to the nationalization of 25 of the top 100 companies. Wilson however refused to accept such a specific commitment, and in the final document it was replaced by a much vaguer pledge to 'substantially extend public enterprize' (p. 10). There is of course no basis in the Labour Party Constitution for such a veto by the party leader, so although in some areas the party had swung back behind its participatory and instrumentalist norms, elitist leadership had also made further gains.

The commitment to repeal the Industrial Relations Act showed solidarity with the unions, which had responded to the Conservatives' attempts to put industrial relations in a legal context in a manner similar to their response to Wilson and Castle's 'In Place Of Strife'. But as that attempt from the Labour government had divided the labour movement, so the attempt by the Tories to do the same kind of thing greatly aided in reunifying the Labour Party and the wider movement in their opposition to it. This, with the greater participation in the drawing up of the Party Programme and the more satisfactory Manifesto, boosted party morale. Hence (despite continuing division over the EEC), there was a widespread feeling that it was all going to be different this time.

The 1974-79 Labour government

Although Labour 'won' the 1974 General Election, the result was a disappointment in that it seemed like 1964 all over again, except worse. Labour had a majority of only four over the Conservatives, and with fourteen Liberals and twenty-three 'Others' in the new House, it was clear that a minority Labour government must soon be followed by another election. But with Tony Benn - champion of the left and of the Party Programme - given the Department of Industry, and Denis Healey dubbed by the press 'The Red Chancellor', it did indeed initially look as if things might be different this time, despite the problems. The unity of the election did not hold subsequently within the cabinet however, with Benn's calls for action regarding nationalization countered by those of Roy Jenkins and Reg Prentice for 'moderation' [11]. By the end of the Session the government had been defeated some twenty times (Pelling, 1982, p. 163), not to mention committee defeats. Thus Wilson called a new election for 10 October 1974.

The Labour Manifesto for this, the second General Election in seven months, was largely a re-emphasis of the February document, but promised in addition an Employment Protection Act to extend the rights of workers in industry, and a Christmas Bonus for pensioners. The key problem was the EEC; the left wanting a definite date for a referendum and the right wanting the issue fudged (see Wilson, 1979, pp. 52-53; Castle, 1980, pp. 154-55). Matters were not helped when, the day before the Clause V meeting, the 'Sunday Observer' published an article which claimed that Wilson had already vetted and diluted the Labour Manifesto to his satisfaction.

The issue of the EEC was resolved by an agreement to include in the Manifesto a pledge to 'give the British people the final say' on whether the renegotiated terms should be accepted or rejected ('Britain Will Win With Labour', in Craig, 1975, p. 465). Public ownership proposals remained vague, but on the eve of an election the left on the NEC did not wish to protest too loudly for fear of a damaging public split. It did appear that Labour were destined for a substantial majority, with opinion polls published the day before the Clause V meeting showing a ten point lead over the Conservatives (see Butler and Cavanagh, 1975, pp. 190-91) - whose Manifesto had just been 'leaked'! But in fact Labour gained an overall majority of only three. After its fall in 1979 the government's defenders countered the charge that it had failed to honour the Manifesto by emphasizing this tiny majority. However, Pelling, no left-wing biographer of the Labour Party, argues that this 'was in theory exiguous but in practice adequate, as the other parties rarely co-operated in opposition' (Pelling, 1982, p. 164). This possibly *underestimates* the difficulties, but serves to counterbalance the view that the government was straight-jacketed and unable even to attempt to carry out the Manifesto.

The government had in fact been in office only just over a year before resolutions poured in to the 1975 Conference calling for it to keep to the Manifesto commitments. Foremost among such resolutions were ones on 'Defence' and 'Industrial Policy', thereby identifying two areas of divergence between government and party (see LPACR 1975, pp. 215 and 319). There was also a direct debate on the 'Party Manifesto' organized around a composite resolution derived from 16 motions to Conference on the Manifesto, plus others mentioning it. This resolution read:

> This Conference calls upon the Labour Government to honour the 1974 Manifesto. The Party must reassure its workers who have devoted much time and energy to the cause of Socialism. Conference stresses upon the Government the disastrous results to it and the Labour Movement as a whole that any retreat from the Socialist policies upon which it was elected would bring about, particularly with regard to its policy on the public ownership of industry. Conference agrees to resist reductions in public expenditure in keeping with the 1974 Manifesto proposals (LPACR 1975, p. 311).

Speaker after speaker evidenced passionate support for this resolution, arguing fervently that 'keeping faith with the Manifesto' was central to the party's principles, as was the maintenance of significant power in the party outside of parliament [12]. The coming constitutional campaign to provide for a more representative and accountable party leadership can, in effect, be seen as beginning here. But at this time the left was significantly weakened by the EEC referendum defeat. After the referendum Wilson removed Benn from the Department of Industry, and another left winger, Judith Hart, also lost her place in the government. Likewise Eric Heffer was 'asked to resign', after breaking Wilson's guidelines for the EEC debate. At a time when the vast majority of the Labour Party and trades union movement were *against* continued EEC membership, Wilson's guidelines had required opponents of the *cabinet* majority *in favour*, to abstain from campaigning inside the House (though free to do so 'in the country'). In terms of British governmental principles this was of course quite in order, but it was equally clearly at odds with Labour Party principles. In fact a kind of mini-1931 situation emerged, with Wilson and the majority of the Labour cabinet joining the majority of the Tories and Liberals in supporting the EEC, despite the opposition of a special Labour Party Conference and the bulk of the trades union movement.

The struggles between left and right (or possibly as accurately characterized as between Labour Party and Labour Government), continued and intensified. The 1976 Conference debate over the 60,000 word 'Labour's Programme 1976' was highly charged. This was a radical programme outlining plans for the extension of public ownership, the abolition of the House of Lords, further powers for local authorities, a national housing plan and much else besides. In opening the debate Tony Benn stressed both the participatory nature of the party's policy making and the status of the programme, saying:

> subject to any amendments made by resolutions, it will become the official Party Programme from which we shall draw our next election manifesto (LPACR 1976, p. 157).

Benn then referred to the 1945 Manifesto and, by implication at least, criticized the failure of the current government to emulate the instrumentalism of Attlee's time. The 1945 Manifesto, he said:

> was an attack on capitalism ... an advocacy for Socialism. But it united the Labour Party and ... won massive public supprt. Why? Because we said what we wanted. We meant what we said. We did what we said we would do. We left that Manifesto inscribed in Acts of Parliament that stand today (LPACR 1976, p. 158).

If, as we have seen, those 'Acts of Parliament' did not in fact properly reflect the initial Socialist aspirations of the Attlee government, the point is clear; Labour governments should carry out Labour programmes and not make up their own policy as they go along.

In line with this sentiment the NEC brought forward a proposal to amend the Party Constitution to the effect that the NEC 'When a Labour Government is in office ... confer with its representatives prior to the formulation of legislative proposals for the next Parliamentary Session' (LPACR 1976, p. 212). This in fact derived from a resolution to the 1975 Conference which had been remitted to the NEC. This resolution had called upon the NEC to 'invite the leadership of the Parliamentary Labour Party to discuss with them ways of ensuring that the views of the Party, as expressed by the Annual Conference, are heeded by our Parliamentary colleagues' (LPACR 1975, p. 11). Outraged at the government's doing the opposite in 1975 to the Manifesto commitment on Defence [13], the NEC now was determined to so re-emphasize and strengthen the links between Manifesto and government, as the links between the wider party and the making of policy had earlier been strengthened.

There was at the 1976 Conference a range of feeling from unease to outright fury about the government's failure to follow through to the end this progression from wide party participation in initial policy formulation, to 'official' Conference policy, to programme, to Manifesto, to legislation. Clearly if the last stage of this instrumentalist rationale is omitted the whole process becomes an academic exercise, resulting in destructive feelings of betrayal. 'We knew it would be a battle', said one delegate, referring to the task of carrying out the Manifesto after the election victory, But:

> What I and many others want to know is when will the battle start?
> When will the howls of anguish be heard? When will the pips begin to
> squeak? (LPACR 1976, p 164), [14]

Following Wilson's unexpected retirement to the back-benches, Jim Callaghan had won the PLP election for new party leader, and he and Denis Healey headed the leadership's reply to this criticism at the 1976 Conference. Their defence did not challenge outright or overtly the instrumentalist assumptions upon which the Labour Party was founded. Indeed, Callaghan's speech as leader for example began with the assertion that the Manifesto *was* being carried out, listing several items which had been translated into legislation, but with a stress on 'the crisis' and the government's problems. However, he then proceeded - without actually acknowledging it - to put forward an analysis of the economic situation completely at odds with that underlying Labour's programmes of 1973 and '76. In short, Callaghan's analysis and economic prescriptions were straightforwardly applicable to capitalist recovery, whereas Labour's programmes were addressed to altering the balance of the 'mixed economy' and moving society towards Socialist change. Most significantly however, Callaghan concluded with a perfect Liberal/Conservative justification of the role of government in relation to party, and in particular, the Labour Party NEC, saying:

> I do not want to retreat behind the stock defence that 'the government must govern', if that becomes a polite way of telling the party to go to hell. But the NEC must remember that ... (whereas) they are responsible for their statements and their resolutions ... the government is accountable for its actions ... in a parliamentary democracy to Parliament. Parliamentary candidates who offer themselves to the electorate on the basis that *they are willing to suspend their judgement in favour of extra-parliamentary bodies* whoever they may be, will receive short shrift from the electorate (LPACR 1976, p. 193, my emphasis).

Thus Callaghan repudiates the whole prior history of the Labour Party, in impuning and rejecting the instrumentalist assumptions upon which it was founded. Within the above Liberal/Conservative view of government is the implication that attempts at participatory/popular accountable democracy are ill-conceived and futile. From being a means to an end determined by the wider party, the PLP is now seen as the end itself, with the extra-parliamentary party the means to their election and little else. Of course, as said, nobody actually said this to Conference. In fact Denis Healey was shouted down from the floor and invited to 'resign' in response to his own speech in similar vein, without even hinting explicitly at such a heresy.

Beyond the actual non-implementation of the Manifesto, party members were outraged by the perceived failure of the government to even *attempt* to do so ('when will the battle start?'). Labour's economic policy as laid out in the 1974 Manifesto was thus seen as having been surrendered even without a fight. The suspicion that at least some of the leadership had never intended to implement such policies was fuelled by such 'government policy must be made by government' (or simply 'government must govern') replies by the leadership. Such was the climate in the party in 1976.

As we have seen, participatory processes had produced a body of quite detailed policy [15]. Such policy as had been carried by two-thirds majority on a card vote at Conference was included, as was proper, in the 1976 'Labour's Programme For Britain'. Subsequently two further documents were produced on the same basis: the 1977 'Campaign Document' and a 1978 Joint Statement by the NEC, TUC and government called 'Into The 1980s'. In the process of producing the next Manifesto the NEC were keen to avoid any last-minute scramble which might follow a late announcement of a new election and result in vague content. To these ends it began in 1977, particularly through the party's Home Policy Committee, to work upon a new and clear programme. In July 1978 the Home Policy Committee resolved that the new Manifesto:

> should be seen primarily as a programme of action, clear and unambiguous, for the next Government; and this consideration should determine the length and nature of the Manifesto (Bish, in Coates [ed], 1979, p. 190).

At an NEC meeting in September 1978 Callaghan proposed setting up a joint NEC/Cabinet working group to discuss policy, which seems to have been making 'considerable progress' (Bish, p. 195 in Coates [ed], 1979). However, following the government defeat in the Commons and the announcement of a General Election, the Prime Minister's office presented its own draft manifesto to the party's Research Secretary. In the view of the latter this was 'appalling':

> not only did it ignore entire chapters of party policy it overturned and ignored many of the agreements which had been laboriously hammered out within the NEC/Cabinet group (Bish, p. 197 in Coates [ed], 1979).

In response the Research Department quickly produced its own draft manifesto based on decisions of the NEC/Cabinet group, and set up a drafting committee. But Callaghan insisted that his document be used as the basic text, and, in direct contradiction to the Home Policy Committee's view, that the Manifesto should be short and contain few commitments.

At the Clause V meeting on April 6 1979 the NEC were shown the draft for the first time - on the day it was to be published! There were some amendments made, but on three key issues Callaghan, the Prime Minister, effectively used a veto over their inclusion. These issues were the abolition of the House of Lords, mandatory planning agreements, and the nationalization of the construction industry. The veto was backed by Callaghan's twice repeated threat to resign the party leadership - on the eve of an election - if abolition of the Lords for example were included in the Manifesto (Butler and Cavanagh, 1974, p. 149).

The tame and dull nature of the Manifesto which thereby emerged is confirmed by the media reaction to it; 'The Economist' for example called it 'as moderate as any on which the Labour Party has campaigned during its 79 year history'. It was certainly an uninspiring document which made the Tories' Manifesto of 1979 look all the more radical. In the aftermath of Labour's election defeat the abuse of power which had led to the poor Manifesto came to light. The omission of even the penultimate stage in the instrumentalist progression, that is, the Party Programme's failure to reach the Manifesto let alone the Manifesto reaching the statute book, was the 'last straw' for many Labour activists. It prompted action to amend the Party Constitution in relation to the procedure for producing the Manifesto, as well as giving a significant boost to an existing campaign in the party to widen the franchise for the election of the party leader, and for mandatory reselection of the party's MPs.

The Constitutional changes 1979-81

The main organizing force pushing for Constitutional changes to re-emphasize the party's participatory and popular accountable intra-party democracy was the 'Campaign for Labour Party Demcracy' (CLPD). In every leaflet and newsletter from this organization its support for the instrumentalist orthodoxy was clear. An early 1979 newsletter argues for example that the changes proposed 'would create the direct accountability to Conference which is needed if the party is to ensure that an Election Manifesto is produced based on Conference decisions' (CLPD Newsletter No. 15, p. 3). The elitist representative view also had its organizing force, the 'Campaign for Labour Victory' (CLV). Set up in 1977 to counter the CLPD, the CLV marshalled support for the leadership position, issuing 'briefing notes' to Conference for example. One such document, issued prior to the 1979 Conference, decries the 'Proposals before Conference' from CLPD, which it says would 'effectively take away the PLP's right to an equal say in drawing up the Party's election manifesto'. It continues: 'Wouldn't it be a ludicrous spectacle for the Party leadership and a prospective Prime Minister to be expected to fight an election on a manifesto over which they had no control?' (CLV Briefing No. 12).

Clearly then the CLV thought it right for the leadership to be able to control the Manifesto, and thereby only be committed to policy with which they agreed. By this line of reasoning the leadership should therefore be free to ignore the Party Programme if they disagreed with it, which would make Conference a mere appendage of the party rather than its supreme organ. Given that this was exactly the complaint of the CLPD the two bodies clearly represented the two poles of the argument. However, in relation to the CLV statement above, the PLP was in fact in no danger of losing its 'right' to the role suggested in relation to the Manifesto, the reason being that it did not and had never had such a right.

It was the 'Parliamentary Committee' (shadow cabinet) or Labour cabinet which had had such an 'equal say' with the NEC. Indeed, MPs and ex-MPs speaking at the 1979 Conference had all agreed on this, whatever their position on Constitutional change.

The period 1979-81 saw these opposing positions fought out at every level and within every section of the party. At last though, the issues were resolved, or at least the Constitutional position was resolved. Mandatory reselection, by which Labour MPs' 'independence' was to be curbed via their having to account for their actions in facing alternative party candidates, was accepted in 1979, and confirmed at the 1980 Conference. The principle of widening the franchise for the election of the party leader beyond the PLP, thereby making the leader more representative of and accountable to the party as a whole, was also accepted by the 1980 Conference. A Special Conference at Wembley in 1981 was convened to decide on the details of such an electoral college. It accepted a 40/30/30 per cent split between trades unions, constituency parties and PLP respectively.

Just after the 1980 Conference Callaghan had resigned the leadership, to be replaced by Michael Foot. Immediately after the Wembley Special Conference leading right wingers and CLV figureheads formed the 'Council for Social Democracy', and in March the 'Social Democratic Party' (SDP) was founded. Thirteen Labour MPs - and most of the CLV organizers - immediately defected to the new party. At the 1981 Conference however, following Foot's speech as leader in which he repudiated the 'leader's veto' - 'There is no such thing in the Constitution of the Labour Party, and I have no wish to exercise any such thing' - Conference, eventually, voted not to change the procedure as laid down for producing the Manifesto.

However, with the SDP knowing that in order for it to become a force in British politics it must replace the Labour Party in the two party system, it used every media opportunity to propagate a perception of the Labour Party having lurched to the left. The media were not slow to take up such a campaign, particularly given the adoption of two 'left wing' proposals for Constitutional change and the third forstalled only by the accession of a new 'left wing' leader. Again there is a parallel with 1931, in that, as MacDonald and Snowden et al had then engaged in vilification of the Labour Party, the SDP leaders now did so characterizing the Labour Party as extreme beyond redemption. This was exacerbated during the 1983 election campaign by Callaghan, the ex-leader of the party, publicly repudiating the party's defence policy. 'Callaghan's revenge' was of course seized upon by the media, and many party members consider this to have been decisive in building and reinforcing the impression of an inexorably leftward moving but confused and self-contradictory party. The effects of Callaghan's intervention are probably greatly exaggerated, although it certainly did damage Labour's campaign. Callaghan's actions here might also be contrasted to those of his left-wing critics in 1979, who waited until after the election was over before making any public criticism of the Manifesto and the campaign.

After the 1983 defeat Neil Kinnock was elected to lead the party, and under his leadership 'unity' became the key word. Although formerly known as a left winger in the party (but then, so was Wilson!), Kinnock steadfastly turned the party back towards 'responsibility'. In the Gaitskell and CLV vein, Kinnock set out to ensure that what he did not want in the 1987 Manifesto would not appear there - compensation for the NUM for example (following their protracted strike 1984-85). This might be said to indicate his regard for the Manifesto, as Gaitskell's determination to change Conference policy showed his recognition of the importance of the Annual Conference. However, after what was by common consent a good campaign, Labour lost the 1987 election, which seemed to send Kinnock further down the road to 'responsibility'. He continually tried to lower people's expectations of a new Labour government for example, asserting that Labour would only spend 'what the country could afford'. Consistent with this was a determined tight rein on pledges and promises made by shadow ministers. Finally, in good Wilsonian style, the decision of the 1991 Conference that defence spending should be cut back to the European average, was immediately repudiated by Kinnock; such decisions would be taken by the government not the Party Conference.

Kinnock thus clearly played the leadership role in the Liberal/Conservative manner; attempting to demonstrate for example a similar toughness to that of Mrs Thatcher. He certainly attempted, and successfully so for the most part, to 'lead' opinion in the party rather than simply represent it. The 1991 Labour Party Conference evidenced the unselfconscious embracing of such an elitist leadership style, with no effort spared to elevate the stature of shadow cabinet spokespersons and minimize the role of the rank-and-file. It really would seem then that never has there been a period of a more thoroughly constitutionalized Labour Party, as much a guarantor of the British Constitution as the Conservatives themselves. Yet despite it all, and another generally agreed good campaign by Labour, the party was again defeated in the 1992 General Election.

Conclusion

As this detailed examination of the development of the Labour Party has shown, a definite trend is discernable in a movement from the dominance of a participatory and 'instrumentalist' rationale, with a 'delegatory' sense of representation, to that of an elite 'leadership' rationale allied to traditionalist 'responsibility'. This trend was neither accidental nor arbitrary [16], and, like the post-war retreat from the party's Socialist goal, cannot be reduced either to a natural 'maturity' via necessary accommodations with 'practical realities', nor the inevitabilities of working within 'bourgeois' political strictures. Rather, there are several variables which need to be taken into account in seeking such an explanation. These variables are not mutually exclusive [17] and should be regarded as analytical 'ideal types'. As such I believe they provide the most adequate means of understanding and explaining the Labour Party's 'constitutionalization'.

The first such variable concerns the mentioned differing environments, or 'cultural contexts', of the labour movement and parliamentary politics. These have had decisive effects in terms of the participatory and elitist views which have been in evidence in the Labour Party since its foundation. That is, the labour movement has sustained its own participatory instrumentalism and undermined the 'alien' ideas of PLP autonomy and the leadership principle dominant in the parliamentary context, and, more saliently, vice versa.

The second variable concerns the relevance, performance and prestige of a given sector of the party at a given historical juncture. For example, in general the progressively greater importance and prestige of the PLP would tend to give more weight to the ideas and practices associated with its environment, namely the elitist leadership rationale. Conversely, following a poor (electoral) performace or in situations of an overtly 'industrial' nature, or where the 'political wing' is seemingly impotent, the elitist 'product' of its environment will be devalued in favour of the participatory instrumentalism more 'appropriate' to the now dominant context.

The third variable concerns the socio-economic background against which the other two must be seen, and to which they will be closely related. For example, a confident, enthusiastic, united working class and labour movement, against an economic backdrop of full employment and rising expectations, will provide different dynamics and effects to that of a dispirited, demoralized and divided movement against a background of rising unemployment and recent defeats. Various combinations of such factors can combine to have a decisive effect on the outcome of events in a given set of circumstances. Nothing is inevitable through 'reading off' such combinations however. For example, even though against a background of rising prosperity and the apparent irrelevency of the old Socialist commitment, Gaitskell failed in the attempt to remove Clause 4 from the Party Constitution. On the other hand despite this failure to formalize the party's revisionism, it was nevertheless an established fact. Similarly, whatever was the case *within* the party, during this period the party was out of office.

To illustrate the explanatory utility of these variables, let us briefly review the major developments in the party's history.

Against the background of socio-economic conditions not favourable to the interests of labour, but with the constitutional recognition that such interests were among those legitimately deserving of representation, the Labour Party/LRC was founded as the independent parliamentary representative of the trades union and labour movement. Although both participatory/delegatory and elitist/representative views were present in the party at its inception, given the above, it was the former which was at first dominant. Long before any Socialist commitment - or commitment indeed to any form of programme - the tiny PLP was clearly regarded by and used as the 'instrument' of the labour movement and individual unions; the rationale of the parliamentary representation of the interests of labour was the pursuit of ends determined by the wider movement and not by the parliamentary representatives.

The primary concern of the early Labour Party was thus with defending the interests of labour. With a fundamental shift in the background circumstances - provided primarily by the outbreak of war - the aspirations and ambitions of the party's leaders grew. Coupled with the rise of Collectivism dealt with in Chapter Three, this changed significantly the party's fortunes. It is within this context that the adoption by the party of its Socialist Constitution in 1918 and its subsequent successful replacement of the Liberals in the British two party system should be seen. Initially though, the participatory and instrumentalist practices remained dominant.

However, a combination of formal institutional pressures with contingent and conjunctural factors led to the reversal of this norm. Among the former category, the emergence of the Labour Party as the official Opposition both raised the importance and prestige of the PLP vis-à-vis the wider party and, because a 'leader' of the Opposition was required, instituted within the PLP the leadership principle. A contingent factor was the particular choice of MacDonald as leader. Had Henderson for example been selected instead, there is reason to believe things would not have followed the same path. Of course this can only be speculation, but Henderson was dedicated 'to the principle of Conference sovereignty and strict obedience to the programme' whilst MacDonald never was. Where MacDonald was totally seduced by the elitism of traditional British governmental norms, Henderson was 'living proof that a devotion to Parliamentarianism and a commitment to intra-Party democracy were by no means impossible to reconcile' (Minkin, 1980, pp. 14-15).

However, in the event, the combination of this raised prestige of the PLP and leadership and the concomitant increased effects of the parliamentary environment, had their effects. In general, the raised influence of elitist/representative views encouraged both the claims for PLP autonomy and the rapid development of the leadership principle within it. This, through the patronage of party leaders enshrined within British governmental practice, created a hierarchy in the PLP whereby Labour Members looked up to the leadership for approval (and advancement) rather than 'down' to their Constituency Labour Party. A conjunction between this particular stage of development and another contingent factor now intervened. There having been no firm 'instructions' to the PLP on the matter, when Labour became the largest party in parliament but without an overall majority, the decision as to whether to form a minority government was taken within the leadership 'inner circle'. The consequent rejection of a 'maximalist' strategy in favour of the minimalist 'responsible government' approach so marked in the British political tradition, would shape crucially future strategy.

So powerful was the parliamentary cultural context upon the Labour leader that when subsequently at the head of another minority Labour government, he allowed himself to become detached entirely from the labour movement context. He was drawn completely into the Liberal/Conservative constitutionalist mould, thereby committing the 1931 'treachery'. But equally, so great was the commitment to participatory/accountable instrumentalism in the rest of the party that it held together virtually intact after expelling MacDonald. The 'convalescence' period which followed saw the trades union movement (via its leadership) take charge of the party once again, its participatory/accountable nature being thus re-emphasized and strengthened. In its solidaristic isolation the party recovered surprizingly quickly, and re-equipped itself the better to challenge for government again. The resulting increased size of the PLP, with another fundamental shift in background circumstances provided by the outbreak of war again, saw the importance and prestige of the PLP further enhanced. Correspondingly, elitist/representative views also became more influential, though not so as to replace the participatory/accountable orthodoxy.

The post-war Labour landslide, with a confident, enthusiastic labour movement, a Collectivist seachange in public opinion and the embracing of Keynesianism within the societal elites, put the old Labour orthodoxy to the test. Great advances were made in improving the conditions of life for ordinary people, but a gradual retreat from the Socialist goal was nevertheless undertaken. 'Institutionalized political culture' had a profound influence upon this outcome. We have seen how the elitist parliamentary context undermined the organizational means of the Labour Party, and no less so were the ends. In order to maintain the original Socialist perspective the kind of approach advanced by the 'Keep Left' group - for a central planning agency with the authority to override the autonomy of all other government departments - would have needed to be adopted. Such a strategy was undoubtably greatly inhibited by its being in conflict with established British governmental norms. Maintaining the integrity of traditional British government therefore meant abandoning the Socialist goal. In this sense the Socialist goal was defeated by the 'bourgeois' political system, but such was not inevitable and therefore this in itself is insufficient an explanation.

It is also true that similar considerations to those above were crucial in relation to the government's handling of the various 'practical problems' of the time, which also greatly influenced the change of direction. But some important influences derive from nothing more than chance - the incredibly severe winter of 1947 for example did untold damage to the government economically and politically. More saliently, a central problem was located in Labour's 'quantitative' conception of Socialism. This was itself quite susceptible to being so undermined, and the theoretical weaknesses - indeed internal contradictions - of the envisaged means of achieving the Socialist goal were no less important. In turn, these things need to be borne in mind when considering the again notable element of 'feint hearts' at the top when the background circumstances deteriorated, as does the availability of the less extreme Keynesian alternative. These things together offer a far more persuasive explanation for the movement from 'Socisalist Commonwealth' to 'Welfare State' than any attempt to reduce it to a single dynamic.

The lack of willingness to override the traditional institutions and conventions of British government nevertheless does suggest that the parliamentarians in the Labour Party had become more attached to the 'means' of the old orthodoxy than its ends. In turn this again suggests the power of the parliamentary context to seduce Labour's 'representatives' and subvert the party's goals. With the new background circumstances of prolonged economic boom, the moderation of party policy objectives continued; the old means increasingly coming to be thought as irrelevant as the old ends. As progressive taxation and high public spending replaced nationalization as the policy rationale of Labour governments, so any specific goal became less clear; the party competing with the Conservatives on the basis of its being able to do a better job in government. Government thus became an end rather than a means, and an end seen more and more as the simple setting of priorities; the art of balance and compromize to achieve equity, plus the 'fine tuning' of the economy. In this way 'consensus politics' emerged; the PLP having moved far more in line with Liberal/Conservative concepts, principles and practices [18]. This not only further strengthened the parliamentary context but continued its move to the right, since previously PLP autonomy was justified in terms of *achieving* the party's goals, not setting them.

With renewed economic crisis in the 1960s, and with the encumbent Conservative government flirting with 'planning' via the setting up of the National Economic Development Council, the Labour Party in its 'official' (ie Conference) policy perspective moved to the left. The successes and failures of the Attlee Government were re-examined, and in proposing a Department of Economic Affairs as a central planning agency the party seemed to be taking the 'Keep Left' route of the 1940s. On the whole though, the PLP and the parliamentary leadership did not much like the new strategies emerging via the Labour Party Conference. Each 'cultural context' therefore has its own analysis of the crisis and prescription for its resolution - but only the parliamentary party is in a position to act, independently, on its own view. In abandoning the Party Programme however, the party leadership breaks the sacred instrumentalism of the party.

As the crisis deepened in the 1970s, the ideological differences in the party deepened similarly. The repeat of the abandonment of the Party Programme demonstrated, as did the words and actions of the Wilson/Callaghan leadership, that the Labour government was as 'independent' and 'responsible' as any Conservative government had ever been. Extra-parliamentary backlashes mount throughout the latter half of the '70s, emerging after the loss of the 1979 election as a Constitutional Crusade. Despite the 'success' of the crusade though (as despite the 'failure' of Gaitskell's attempt to remove Clause 4), nothing much changes. The party under Kinnock today is as moderate and 'responsible' in Opposition as any previous Labour *government*.

The Labour Party is thus thoroughly constitutionalized; from initially representing a threat to the British Constitution it has come to be one of its major guarantors. There are some important implications here for the contemporary matter of Freedom of Information Vs official secrecy. We have seen that official secrecy is often misperceived as an aberration in British government, but is in fact completely consistent with the elitist norms of the British Constitution. We have also seen that Freedom of Information is underpinned by participatory assumptions. In the following chapter we will see many parallels between the Labour Party experience and the manner by which the modern Campaign for Freedom of Information has also been constitutionalized. We will also take up the point that 'Thatcherism' has been seen as an aberration, as a departure from British governmental norms. This is in fact only true of post-war norms however, which were themselves aberrant in terms of traditional British government. 'Thatcherism' is therefore more accurately seen as the *reassertion* of the British political tradition, and we will see how this project of deep radical reform is *aided* by its *compatibility* with British governmental norms.

Notes

1. It needs to be borne in mind that there has been a fundamental shift in the meaning of 'Social Democratic' today, as opposed to towards the end of the nineteenth century. The term was originally applied to movements derived from revolutionary Marxism, Lenin eg speaking of the Social Democratic movement of which the Bolshevik Party was a part. Today, on the other hand, it is a term applied to the moderately left of centre, progressive constitutionalist parties of Europe and Scandinavia.

2. Lenin for example argued that without the proper ideological guidance the working class would not move beyond 'trade union consciousness': the recognition of their interests as workers within the capitalist framework and that collective action was necessary to further those interests. In order to achieve Socialism, what was necessary, said Lenin, was the development of 'revolutionary consciousness': the recognition by the workers that their true interests required the overthrow of the capitalist system itself, and their commitment to class action to that end (Lenin, *What Is To Be Done* ?, 1902). The argument that I am making is that, in the above context, the sectionalism of the British trades union movement seems even to detract from 'trade union consciousness'.

3. Miliband says eg in his 'Introduction' to *Parliamentary Socialism* (1973):

> The main purpose of this book is to analyze *the consequences which this approach to politics* (ie not straying 'from the narrow path of parliamentary politics') *has had* for the Labour Party and the Labour movement from the time the Labour Party came into existence (my emphases, Miliband, 1973, p. 13).

4. Beer does not mention the Russian Revolution as an influence of the Labour Party's adoption of Socialism, but he is very much in a minority here. Most other writers on this period concede some influence, and some consider it to be quite significant.

5. Marx was involved with the 'First International' (The International Workingmen's Association 1864-1876) which split over the dispute between Marxists and Anarchists. The 'Second International' (1889-1914) was, in the eyes of Lenin and other revolutionaries, completely discredited given that most of its member parties supported their own national cause (rather than their avowed Socialist internationalism) with the outbreak of the First World War. After the Bolshevik Revolution Lenin considered that a 'Third International' was essential, in order that the workers of the west learn the lessons from a successful revolution in Russia. With the change of name from Bolshevik to 'Communist Party' in

1918, the 'Third' or 'Communist' International (Comintern) was set up in March 1919. It was officially dissolved in 1939, with the signing of the Nazi-Soviet Pact. After his exile from the Soviet Union for his opposition to Stalin and the system growing up under Stalin, Trotsky founded the 'Fourth International' in 1929, to perpetuate the 'genuine' version of Bolshevism/Marxism-Leninism.

6. Miliband (1972) eg is a study in restrained venom:

> Given the fact that Britain was in 1931 one of the richest countries in the world, and blessed with one of the richest ruling classes in the world, it is surely amazing that there were actually found rational men to argue that the saving of a few million pounds a year on the miserable pittance allowed to unemployed men and women and their children was the essential condition of British solvency; even less credible that two men (ie MacDonald and Snowden), exalted by the Labour movement and owing what they were to the faithful support of millions of working men and women, should have been the main actors in this obscene charade (Miliband, 1972, p.185, parenthesized insert is mine).

7. As Miliband, again, puts it:

> What had earlier been deemed the end of civilization, to be avoided by the economy cuts and a 'National' Government, was now accepted as the inevitable command of common sense, and ... 'hardly a leaf stirred' (Miliband, 1972, p. 185).

8. The elitism of the Labour Party's conception of Socialism is evident within it's article of Socialist faith, namely Clause IV (part 4) of the Party Constitution, which begins: 'to secure *for* the workers by hand *or* by brain the full fruits of their industry ...' (my emphases). Thus, rather than (as Marx eg would have it), the *self* emancipation of the working class, Socialism is seen as something *to be done for the workers*. The implication is the acceptance that the working class is incapable of its own emancipation and therefore it is something to be done *on their behalf* by a special group in society, broadly, the Labour Party, but more specifically, by a Labour *government*. Given that the Labour Party (increasingly) accepted the basic nature of the British political and governmental system, and saw a *Labour* government as being different in that it would follow different *policies*, this leads to the idea of Socialism as policy rather than system,

and thus ignores the extent to which policy - content - is inevitably conditioned by the operational context - form - within which it is to be implemented. Similarly, by emphasizing 'workers by hand *or* by brain' this article again accepts the 'bourgeois' assumption of a status hierarchy based upon merit; those working *by brain* are deemed worth more than those working *by hand* since the brains of those working by hand are thereby clearly inferior. The class argument is therefore lost; in such a conception the extent to which it is the restricted educational and other opportunities of most working class people which tend to consign them to work 'by hand' rather than 'brain' is ignored. The presence of such attitudes in the key clause of the Labour Party's claim to be a Socialist party does therefore in my view evidence an elitist conception of Socialism.

9. This was a problem which would recur in that, the National Economic Development Council (NEDC) set up by the Conservatives in 1963, the Department of Economic Affairs (DEA) set up by Labour in 1964, and the National Enterprize Board (NEB) under the last Labour Government, each suffered from their being subordinated to the Treasury, and the resultant inability to override such departmental autonomy.

10. Richard Crossman, who wrote the 1955 Election Manifesto, claimed that it was 'merely "Challenge To Britain" properly written' (Crossman, in Morgan [ed], 1981, p. 420).

11. Jenkins had always been on the right of the party, but after the 1970 defeat Prentice had complained about the 'drift to the right' of the previous Labour government, which had been 'Not Socialist Enough' (the title of Prentice's article in *Political Quarterly,* Vol. 41, No. 2, April/June). Thus from being a left-wing critic of the 1970 government Prentice became a 'moderate' in 1974, and eventually joined the Conservative Party in October 1977.

12. The mover of the resolution referred to saying eg:

> This Party began outside Parliament. Keir Hardie was a worker and a
> Socialist long before he became our first MP. Conference should stress
> today, by voting for this motion and the spirit contained in it, that a
> significant degree of power in the Labour Party should always remain
> outside Parliament (LPACR 1975, p 312).

13. The February 1974 Manifesto had called (p. 14) for reductions in defence expenditure. A resolution on 'Defence' to the 1974 Conference had been remitted to the NEC following Ian Mikado's statement, for the NEC, that a White Paper was due shortly which would detail how this commitment was to be acted upon (LPACR 1974, p. 300). When the White Paper was published however, it announced *increases* in expenditure. The NEC sent an

angry letter to the government (see LPACR 1975, p. 30), and Mikado claimed he had been 'conned' by the government over the whole matter (LPACR 1975, p. 232). Thus it was the in 1975 the NEC accepted a resolution slamming the government for failing to implement the Manifesto commitments on defence cuts. The resolution was passed.

14. The last question is a reference to Denis Healey's pre-election promise to 'squeeze the rich until the pips squeak'.

15. The summary of events here is largely taken from an article, ('Drafting the Manifesto') by Geoff Bish, Secretary of the party's Research Department at this time. This article is included (pp. 187-206) among a number of other essays on the failure of the 1974-79 Labour Government, in a work edited by K Coates entitled *What Went Wrong* (1979). The account given by Bish is confirmed and amplified in Butler and Cavanagh's *The British General Election of February 1974* (1974).

16. Nor is it complete, since in the Constituency Labour Parties and union branches affiliated to them the participatory/ accountable theory and practice is still dominant.

17. That is, it is possible of course for a Labour MP to uphold the participatory /accountable theory and practice - although most who do come from a trade union background - and there are also CLP members upholding the elitist/representative norms of belief and practice. Similarly there are and have always been (elitist) parliamentary Socialists and (participatory) extra-parliamentary labourists in the party.

18. Most accurately 'consensus politics' involved a shift to the left by the Conservatives on economic and industrial policy as well as a shift to the right by Labour on these constitutional matters.

PART III
Uniting Contemporary and Historical Analyses

5 Full circle: from the contemporary to the historical and back

Introduction

We saw in Chapter One that official secrecy is often misperceived as an aberration in British Liberal-Democracy, but is in fact completely consistent with the elitist norms of the British Constitution. The derivation of those elitist norms, and their results and consequences were examined and considered at length in Chapters Two, Three and Four. From the opening chapter we also saw that Freedom of Information (FOI) is underpinned by the same kind of participatory assumptions as those of Radicalism from the seventeenth to the twentieth century in this country. Chapter Two details how Radicalism was marginalized and defeated, as Chapter Four shows how the twentieth century Labour Party was constitutionalized; from initially representing a challenge to the nature of British government, or a threat to the British Constitution, it has come to be one of its major guarantors. We will see initially in this chapter how the Campaign for FOI has been similarly constitutionalized. It too set out to alter the elitist and Executive dominated nature of British government but has come instead to accept the necessity of compatibility with the conventions and practices of the system it set out to change [1].

The parallels in these developments are important. They indicate that the durability of the elitist British political system derives not from inherent merit, but rather, from a capacity for self-defence against contrary, participatory challenges which amounts to effective self-perpetuation. Radicalism, the Labour Party and the Campaign for FOI each represented a participatory challenge to elitist British government, but each of those challenges was blunted, marginalized and overcome by these means. The present chapter will begin by highlighting some of these parallels between the case of the Labour Party and the manner by which the modern Campaign for FOI has also been constitutionalized. We will see that the very meaning of FOI has indeed been (reluctantly) surrendered by the Campaign; effectively, control of the legislative process has allowed the government to define both FOI and the areas of its appropriateness.

Having established this parallel in what happens to radical projects contrary to the elitist nature of British government, we will turn to one entirely consistent with it: we will consider 'Thatcherism'. Interestingly 'Thatcherism' too has been seen as an aberration, as a departure from British governmental norms. However, this is in fact only true of post-war norms, which were themselves aberrant in terms of traditional British government. 'Thatcherism' is therefore more accurately seen as the *reassertion* of the British political tradition, and, reinforcing the importance of the relationship between institutions and the theory underpinning them, we will see how *this* project of deep radical reform is *aided* by its *compatibility* with British governmental norms.

The modern Campaign for Freedom of Information

As indicated in Chapter One, the origins of FOI campaigning in this country go back perhaps thirty years, but individuals and groups sharing a common position on this single issue did not come together formally until quite recently. 'The 1984 Campaign for Freedom of Information' (the Orwellian '1984' being dropped after that year), was thus a far more professional organization than had ever existed before. Under a specific constitution, it quickly managed to unite a broad coalition primarily to further parliamentary bills. More broadly, the aim was to create a movement which would make the demand for FOI irresistible. If in this the Campaign seems clearly to have been unsuccessful, it has not been completely without succcess. In charting the successes and failures of the Campaign, the distinctions made in Chapter One between 'freedom of information' and 'open government', and between High Politics and Low Politics, require reiteration.

'Freedom of information' is, I have argued, an appropriate term to refer to access to information held by government departments and public authorities which has a strong bearing on individuals' personal or civil freedom; it is official information with the emphasis on the *information*. 'Open government', on the other hand, I suggested was a more appropriate term to refer to information pertaining to the processes of government itself, particularly in regard to policy and decision making; this is official information with the emphasis upon the *official* (ie, relating to 'office'). Related to these initial distinctions are those between 'High' and 'Low' politics. High Politics has traditionally referred to areas such as: national defence; foreign policy; the balance of payments; defence of the pound sterling (exchange rate policy); public expenditure levels; monetary and fiscal policy. Conversely, the administration and management of local affairs - the organization and presentation of the 'particular insterests' - is regarded as Low Politics.

As we have seen, the British political tradition upholds governmental independence and initiative, that the 'national interest' be identified and followed, and British government has jealously guarded its prerogatives in regard to High Politics concerns. However, central government has usually been willing to allow relative autonomy to local authorities in regard to Low Politics (see for example Bulpitt, 1983). In terms of these distinctions, the experience of the modern Campaign for FOI suggests that the government has been willing to allow 'freedom of information' in regard to Low Politics, whilst steadfastly resisting 'open government' in High Politics. Indeed, the replacement in 1989 of the 'catch-all' Section Two of the 1911 Official Secrets Act goes beyond defence of the status quo and, by common consent, represents a further tightening up of official secrecy. We will consider this when we look at the 'Thatcherite' period, for now, let us turn to look at the progress of the Campaign for FOI.

Government hostility

In a letter, immediately after the launch of the modern Campaign, Mrs Thatcher's attitude was made clear:

> Under our constitution, ministers are accountable to parliament for ...
> the provision of information. A statutory   right of public access would
> ... transfer ultimate decisions to the courts .... Ministers' accountability
> to parliament would (therefore) be reduced, and parliament itself
> diminished. ... I firmly believe that major constitutional changes such
> as your campaign is proposing are inappropriate and unnecessary (see
> also note 7, Chapter One).

Beyond this, Mrs Thatcher refused to talk - or allow her ministers to talk - to the Campaign. Further, she ordered the cabinet Office to instruct civil servants not to enter into any such discussions. Such an unfavourable climate of government hostility provided the context for the Campaign's abandonment of the aim of access to ministerial advice and information. As is clear from Chapter One, this had been a key demand in the 1970s, and was quite explicit in the Freud bill. But in the attempts to achieve compatibility between principles of FOI and traditional Constitutional practice, elements of 'open government' were even then being filtered out. This key demand was therefore an explicit *exclusion* in the model bill published by the Campaign for publicity purposes.

In fact, the very idea of a Freud-like single FOI Act was set aside in favour of a new piecemeal strategy aimed at gaining a 'toehold', which would subsequently facilitate extension of the FOI principle. That is, such short term activity, though certainly valuable in itself, was also seen as important in a longer term 'climate changing' project. Thus the Campaign put its energies behind a number of limited and specific bills, initially in the areas of local government, personal files and environmental pollution. However, given the 'strong government' tradition shown in Chapters Two, Three and Four, which justifies the Executive dominance of the British governmental system, only the Private Members Bill procedure offered a means for the Campaign to further their aims. Yet as Marsh and Read (1988) show, in fact this procedure too is dominated by government. Indeed, without government time a bill will go nowhere, and since 1979 government has been less willing to grant time to 'genuine' Private Members Bills, as opposed to those which are in all but name, government bills. That is, government has made increasing use of the procedure to facilitate minor legislation it favours. This will be elaborated and contextualized in the section on 'Thatcherism' which closes the present chapter.

It is this necessity for government support which, even with the Campaign's new strategy of furthering limited bills, has given government, rather than the Campaign, the opportunity to define what FOI will mean, and where it is appropriate. To illustrate this point, let us consider the progress of some of these limited bills.

The Local Government Bill

The first legislative success for FOI was with the Local Government (Access to information) Act 1985. This bill began with the launch of the Community Rights Project (CRP) in December 1983, just one month before that of the Campaign for FOI itself. The progress of the bill was engineered by a joint and combined effort by both organizations, but the early work was undertaken by the CRP. It drew up the draft bill and actively promoted it in the regions. In Birmingham, Manchester, Leeds, Newcastle, Bristol and Glasgow, the national launches of the CRP and the Campaign for FOI were repeated, and appeals were made to the local authorities for support. Indeed local authorities were urged to take the initiative by amending their standing orders and thereby change their practices immediately, without waiting for legislation.

This relatively passive approach was supplemented by deeper, more aggressive activity however. CRP researchers spent some time making up a list of documents that councils, under *existing* legislation were required to make available to the public. Requests to see these documents were then made at Town Halls all over the country. Although it had of course been expected that some documents would be unavailable at some councils - providing opportunities for more publicity work - the actual results of this exercise were staggering. Out of sixty-one councils visited, not one was found to be complying fully with its legal obligations! On the basis of this a report 'Illegality In Your Town Hall', was published, helping to raise the profile of Town Hall secrecy, and thereby the issue of FOI. Similar spot-checks prompted by the results of this activity, for example, by 'The South Wales Argus', 'The Watford Observer', 'The Bromley Times' and Radio Sussex, all returned similar results. Thus, by the beginning of 1985 support for the proposed bill had been considerably broadened, which seems to have been influential in getting it adopted under the Private Members Bill procedure.

The bill itself required that sub-committees be open to the public, and amended the Public Bodies (Admissions to Meetings) Act 1960, which had allowed secrecy for such non-specific reasons as 'confidentiality' and the 'public interest'. In addition, minutes of council meetings and sub-committee meetings were to be publicly available, as well as those of committees with powers of recommendation, although minutes of any confidential part of a meeting were to be published in such a way as to preserve that confidentiality. Reports discussed at meetings were also to be publicly available to electors three days before the next meeting. However, the most controversial aspect of the bill was Clause Four, whereby, after the agenda had been published but before the actual meeting took place, internal research data, background papers to reports, interim reports and other matters relating to an item on the public part of the agenda of a council, council committee or sub-committee meeting, were to be available for public inspection. Finally, councils would be required to publish a summary of the public's right of access to information (see Current Law Statutes Annotated, 1985); rights being of little value unless people are aware of them.

As mentioned, this bill was one of the initial priorities of the Campaign for FOI, and the original plan was for it to be introduced into the Commons under the Ten Minute Rule procedure by Conservative Robin Squire, Labour's Allan Roberts or Liberal Simon Hughes. Indeed Hughes did introduce the bill in this way, and thus it received its First Reading, but inevitably it lapsed for lack of parliamentary time. However, at the end of 1984 Robin Squire came third in the Private Members ballot, and announced that he would be adopting the bill. Following this announcement, Mr Squire, with Des Wilson and Ron Bailey of the CRP, met with William Waldegrave, the minister, and Department of the

Environment officials. The three were told that there would be no government opposition to the bill's Second Reading, and sure enough, it went through this stage on 1 February 1985.

In a fairly long parliamentary debate, William Waldegrave, for the government, in fact 'welcomed' the bill, but said that there would have to be further consideration of Clause Four. In addition he suggested that the Secretary of State should be given power to amend the schedule from time to time, to allow changes 'as a result of experience'. He concluded:

> To make the bill practical and acceptable, the Committee will have to tighten up the drafting and deal with some of the points of principle that have been raised. If that can be done, there is no reason why a satisfactory Act should not reach the Statute Book (Hansard 1984-5, HC Vol. 72, col. 580).

The fact that the Campaign accepted the necessity to 'deal with' certain 'points of principle' in order to provide a 'satisfactory' Act is significant, as will subsequently be shown. However, the bill's progress was in fact relatively smooth and swift for a Private Members Bill; it passed through all stages to come into force on 1 April 1986. Thus a major priority for the Campaign for FOI had been achieved within eighteen months of its launch. In reaction to this success Des Wilson commented: 'We should acknowledge that DoE ministers, notably William Waldegrave, chose to support the bill, when they could easily have sunk it' (*Secrets* [2], No. 6, p. 8). Maurice Frankel also acknowledges the Campaign's dependency upon government support, saying 'A bill like that ... only goes through, at the end of the day, with government support. You can't get a Private Members Bill, at least on this type of issue ... passed without government support'. Frankel also confirmed the Campaign's longer term strategy however, in going on to say that by giving that support: '...the government really puts its signature to the basic freedom of information principle' (Interview, May 1989). A 'minimalist' (Ramsay MacDonald-like) strategy of moderation and responsibility thus seemed to be able to pay dividends, however, that had also seemed to be the case for the first Labour government. We must continue to examine the Campaign's progress elewhere to see if Frankel's point is borne out.

The Access to Personal Files Bill

The Access to Personal Files Bill was drawn up early in 1984, as a measure designed to provide the right of access by individuals to files held on themselves. An individual would also have the right to have inaccurate information corrected and incomplete information supplemented. Safeguards were to be provided against information from files held by one body being passed on to another without the subject's permission. The main areas covered by the bill were in relation to education, health, housing, social work and pensions and benefits.

The Campaign propagated the bill via three main justifications. Firstly, it would end the anomaly which would be created by the Data Protection Bill (then passing through parliament), giving these rights and safeguards in relation to computerized files but not to old fashioned paper ones. Secondly, it argued that more effective and efficient decision making would result. As the Campaign newspaper put it:

> Public authorities ... provide an enormous range of services and benefits to those whom they judge need or are entitled to them; a decision based on wrong information can have devastating effects on those involved. At present members of the public ... (are prevented) from taking part in the making of the decisions... (Yet) Education, health care (and) social work services ... require active consent and participation. Teachers, doctors and social workers all increasingly stress that they can only be fully effective if there is an atmosphere of trust and shared co operation between them and those they seek to help. Secret record-keeping inevitably invites suspicion and works against the development of a co-operative relationship (Frankel, 'Our right to see our own files', *Secrets*, No. 2, p. 8).

The participatory and popular accountable view underpinning FOI is very clear in the above.

However, thirdly, the measures contained in the bill were propounded in terms of the injustice and potential harm to individuals which could result from the keeping of inaccurate records. Factual errors, misheard remarks, incorrectly transcribed notes, even subjective and ill-founded comment are all able to find their way into individuals' files, and safeguards against the worst effects of these need to be taken, before harmful decisions result. Further, the Campaign pointed to the iniquity whereby individuals may not know what was in 'their' file whilst such were accessible to a considerable number of 'professionals' of one type or another. The bill would seek to reverse this.

Maurice Frankel, who had undertaken much of the early work on the draft of the bill, set up consultations with professional bodies; with the aim of furthering the bill's aims. There were some promising results: the National Council for Voluntary Organizations supported the proposed new rights in its book entitled 'Client's Rights'; the Department of the Environment took up consultations with interested parties in relation to access to housing files; the British Association of Social Workers was about to publish a draft scheme for access to files; the Community Rights Project published a report showing that a number of authorities had taken the lead even without legislation.

With some encouragement then, the Campaign announced a 'big push' for the bill which it hoped would see its adoption following the Private Members ballot in the Autumn of 1985. An all-party Westminster 'team' was set up to campaign for the measure in both Houses; a special report ('I want to know what's in my file'), was published to coincide with a major publicity drive; fringe meetings were organized at all of the party conferences; and a major conference was set up, chaired by Sir Patrick Nairn (Permanent Secretary at the DHSS 1975-81). Yet despite all of this the Campaign failed to secure support for the bill among highly placed Members in the ballot. The work continued however, and the Campaign were delighted when Archy Kirkwood adopted the bill following the ballot in 1986.

The bill in fact had an unopposed Second Reading on 20 February 1987, and went into committee on 25 March. As was the case with the Local Government Bill, the government made it clear that a price would have to be paid for it to become law. The then Home Office Minister, David Waddington, said the bill would not be allowed to proceed unless its original scope was restricted to deal with local authority education, housing and social work records. This was reluctantly accepted by the Campaign and an amended bill was substituted. In addition, the new much shorter bill made provision - again in similar fashion to the Local Government Bill - for future governmental imput, in that it left details of exemptions and procedures to be spelled out by the minister in later regulations. It was on this basis that it became law just before the General Election of 1987 (see Current Law Statutes Annotated 1987).

Further bills

A spirited but unsuccessful rearguard action had been fought by the Campaign to keep medical records in the above bill. However, with further success in the Private Members ballot Archy Kirkwood subsequently introduced the Access to Medical Reports Bill. This would mean that: in addition to where an individual's medical records were held on computer, which would facilitate access via the Data Protection Act 1984; and in addition to where a GP's letter to a social worker or council housing department must be able to be seen by the subject, under the Access to Personal Files Act 1987; an individual would be entitled to a copy of a GP's report on their health required by an insurance company or employer. This further concession was in fact passed on 8 July 1988.

Building upon this success, the Campaign's cumulative strategy then saw the Access to Health Records Bill adopted as a Private Members Bill by Campaign supporter Doug Henderson. This bill represented virtually the remainder of the provisions which had been included in the original Access to Personal Files Bill, and it was twice blocked in its early stages. It did however finally gain a Second Reading, and, after amendments in committee, it too went through its remaining stages with government support. It thus became the Access to Health Records Act 1990, and came into force in November 1991. However, although the government gave an undertaking to make them available (that is, at its discretion), part of the 'price' for government support was the removal from the Act itself of medical records for social security purposes supplied by the DSS's regional medical service. Further, in the original bill patients would have had to have been informed of any information being withheld under any exemption. This provision too was dropped at the government's insistence.

A further success for the Campaign was gained with the Environment and Safety Information Bill. This was adopted as a Private Members Bill and introduced by Campaign supporter Chris Smith. It required the authorities who enforce four major safety, fire and environmental laws to set up public registers with details of the enforcement notices they have served. With the amendment once again that the minister be established as final arbiter in cases of dispute as to what should be disclosed in such a notice, this bill was passed on 8 July 1988, the same day as the Access to Medical Reports Bill (see Current Law Statutes Annotated 1988).

Bases for success and failure

This brief analysis of the bills successfully introduced by the Campaign raises three key points. First, it is clear that the Private Members Bill procedure is the only legislative avenue open to the Campaign to further its parliamentary aims. At best this is something of a hit and miss affair, if the Campaign has enjoyed good fortune on the whole. Secondly, and more importantly, whatever the outcome of the Private Members ballots, without government support for a bill the chances of legislative success are virtually nil. This reflects clearly the imbalance between Executive and legislature in Britain, an imbalance underpinned by this country's elitist political tradition, which the Campaign initially set out to challenge. But it is long recognized that 'governments discriminate against radical pressure groups in favour of liberal or conservative groups whose views imply no fundamental critique of the existing economic and political order' (Ryan, 1978, p. 1). Further, as has been demonstrated in the current work, the nature of the institutions and conventions of a political and governmental system itself provides severe constraints upon reforming projects underpinned by contrary assumptions.

The Campaign therefore sought to compromize, to make its demands - at least in the short term - essentially compatible with the governmental status quo. It thus pursued the limited bills strategy, both to demonstrate its 'responsibility' and in the hope that thereby the climate might become more favourable. There is a paradox in that at the very time that this strategy was adopted, in general the climate worsened. The Tisdal and Ponting cases, the increased use of injunctions to prevent publications and broadcasts, and the new Official Secrets Act will all be considered in the following section on 'Thatcherism'. The third and crucial point is however that the outcome of this strategy adopted by the Campaign is that success is now effectively dependent upon the government's willingness to reform itself.

This conclusion begs the question as to why a dominant Executive would take on board legislation that it did not like. Or, to put it slightly differently, what would be the cost demanded, in terms of the meaning of FOI, as the price of government support ?

In general terms of course the answer lies in the acceptance of a process of constitutionalization such as we have seen to have transformed the Labour Party. In terms of the particulars dealt with here, much will be dependent upon a number of strategic considerations: the importance of the issue to the Executive; the circumstances under which it entered the arena; the principles involved; and the resources available to each side. It must certainly be the case however that the outcome will be conditioned crucially by the conflict being fought out on the government's terrain.

The limited FOI bills considered here can generally be considered to be on the periphery of governmental concerns. Those dealing with access to medical and other personal files and environmental safety information are most accurately described as 'freedom of information bills', for the most part very much on the periphery of British politics. The Local Government Bill was also predominantly of a 'freedom of information' nature, and peripheral to central government concerns except, as will shortly be better illustrated, where there was an important interface with High Politics and 'open government' concerns. As we would expect from the foregoing, it was in relation to these that government insisted upon changes. Indeed, it was in anticipation of such a governmental attitude that the Campaign excluded from its 'full' bill the initial demand for access to the information and advice given to ministers. Maurice Frankel is quite clear about the rationale behind this, saying:

> we don't think there is any chance of obtaining ... legislation in the short or medium term if we go for policy advice ... That's the first pragmatic thing, as a political judgement that rules it out (Interview, March 1986).

Yet despite the Campaign limiting its demands to 'freedom of information' rather than including 'open government', it has still had some difficulty in persuading government to give parliamentary time to Private Members Bills it has sponsored. The depth of support often apparent behind the modern Campaign, its sheer persistence and the perseverance of its parliamentary supporters, are all admirable, but not the reason why government has found it an interest group difficult to ignore. Much more important as regards the success the Campaign has had with limited bills, are certain strategic advantages which have been seized upon by the Campaign and pressed home.

In the debate over the Local Government (Access to Information) Bill for example, Robin Squire quoted the following words:

> Publicity is the greatest and most effective check against arbitrary action. This is one of the fundamental rights of the subject. Further, publicity stimulates the interest of local persons in local government This is also very important. The paramount function of this House is to safeguard civil liberties, rather than to think that administrative convenience should take priority in law (Hansard 1984-5, HC Vol. 72, col. 520).

These were in fact *Margaret Thatcher's* words when, as a new Member, she introduced a Private Members Bill championing the cause of local government FOI in 1960! Clearly here the Campaign had a valuable propaganda weapon to encourage government support. This is particularly so since the Campaign were able to argue that the new bill was necessary partly because of the bureaucratic manoeuvering through which Mrs Thatcher's bill (which increased access to full council and council sub-committee meetings), was being evaded. Taken in conjunction with the government's general intention to see greater accountability at local government level, and their determination to prevent local government from thwarting central government's High Politics intentions, this tipped the balance in favour of government finding time for this bill.

As indicated earlier, in the case of the Access to Personal Files Bill, a significant aid was accorded by the passing of the Data Protection Act 1984. This Act had been received by the Campaign with mixed feelings, James Michael points out for example that 'it was passed for commercial resasons rather than out of a governmental interest in protecting privacy'. Michael elaborates:

> There was widespread concern that other countries might use their data protection laws to cut off business with British data processors. To avoid this the Council of Europe ... Data Protection Convention ... (established) minimum standards for processing personal information by computers. The British Data Protection Act is designed to meet the bare minimum standards of the Convention so that the United Kingdom can join the club (Michael, 'Data Protection Act creates precedent for the right to know', *Secrets*, No. 3, p. 2).

However, this Act created the anomaly whereby information stored in old fashioned manual, as opposed to computer files, was exempt from such safeguards. The Council of Europe Data Protection Convention gave encouragement to member countries to establish similar rights for manual files, and several other countries proceeded to do so. Hence a natural opportunity arose for the introduction of the Access to Personal Files Bill. The Campaign were able to argue that this was in line with policy to which government was already committed and to point to the European Data Convention's recommendations.

The Data Protection Convention also made provision for exemptions on grounds of 'national security' however, and, unsurprizingly from what we know of 'the story so far', the British Data Protection Act takes full advantage of this:

> If a cabinet minister certifies that personal information is processed for purposes of national security, then that processing is completely outside of the Act (Michael, *Secrets* No. 3, p. 2).

It seems then that the elitist concepts underpinning official secrecy survive in the Data Protection Act, and, therefore, we should not be surprized to find that the same is true of any supplementary legislation.

A similar tactical advantage also aided the case of the Environment and Safety Information Bill, with the Campaign presented with a propaganda weapon by the government itself. The Bill was introduced by Chris Smith MP, but was twice blocked by the government on Second Reading. However, in correspondence between Maurice Frankel and the minister, Mr Patrick Nicholls, the latter said emphatically that the government did not object to the aims of the bill (if he doubted its ability to achieve them). Subsequently, a government whip, who was named by the Speaker and reported in Hansard, *did* stand up and object to the bill. This tactical mistake by government meant they were embarrassed into supporting the bill (Frankel, interview, May 1989).

So in each case the Campaign had some strategic advantage it could exploit to maximize the chances of governmental support. However, equally, there was a price to be paid by the Campaign for that support. As we have seen, *ministerial* decisions will determine the outcome where a dispute arises under the provisions of the Environment and Safety Information Act. Similarly, ministerial initiative is incorporated into the Data Protection Act from which the severely limited version of the original Access to Personal Files Act (and the supplementary Acts seeking to make up the original 'shortfall'), derived. In addition, in the case of the Local Government (Access to Information) Act, Maurice Frankel admits that:

> There are some obvious changes ... (from the bill to the final Act). One of the main ... costs of government not opposing it ... was an additional exempt category of restrictive information, which was basically confidential information as applied under an obligation of maintaining confidence by government. The government has basically said any information which it passes to a local authority is not subject to the Act. It just has to say 'In Confidence' on the top of the document and its automatically restricted (Interview, March 1986).

So where 'freedom of information' crosses the boundary towards 'open government' and Low Politics meet High Politics, government acts swiftly and firmly to maintain the distinctions and thereby, its traditional prerogatives. Hence it is government, rather than the Campaign or the courts, which is able to define what FOI will mean.

However, in the light of its strategy of building upon limited gains, the Campaign accepted this concession in order to establish and later hope to extend the principle of FOI. Des Wilson for example, echoing the view of Maurice Frankel indicated earlier, argued that with the Local Government Act the government had now implicitly accepted the principle of FOI:

> This in turn makes continued obstinacy on freedom of information at national level even more unacceptable. Ministers cannot have it both ways. They cannot say that they believe in the maximum possible freedom of information at local level, and at the same time continue to perpetuate excessive secrecy at national level... the government's position ... has become hopelessly inconsistent and untenable.

Wilson continues by arguing that the government is in fact unduly suspicious of FOI. He bemoans their rash over-reaction to the Campaign from the outset. If they would take another look at what the Campaign stood for today they would surely be surprized:

> Surprized by how much common ground they would find. Surprized by the answers we have found ... to any practical problems. Surprized by the advantages that exist for governors as well as for the governed. Surprized even by the political advantages of a more constructive approach (Wilson, *Secrets*, No. 5, p. 8).

Let us consider first the idea that with the Local Government Act the FOI principle was established, and that government must act consistently: it cannot follow one set of principles in central government whilst setting another for local government. The Campaign pushed this argument hard, but to no avail; government was simply unmoved. Indeed the contemporary Conservative government has been willing to activate participatory democracy in other fields. The Trade Union Act 1984 for example, embodies clearly such popular participatory and accountable democratic principles as being appropriate for the running of trades unions (see for example, Makie, 1984). This view of democracy is clearly at odds with the principles by which central government deals with High Politics; the steadfast maintenance of government's chosen policies - despite possible widespread unpopularity - being seen as a virtue, 'responsible government'. In this view, even if such policies are opposed by a wide range of 'particular' interests which, collectively, make up a majority, government is still entitled to maintain its policies; being retrospectively accountable for its performance at periodic General Elections.

The contrast between 'participatory' and elitist 'leadership' democracy is certainly clearly in evidence here, with government seemingly finding no difficulty in maintaining such an 'inconsistency'. Given that, like trades union interests, local interests too are regarded in the traditional doctrines as 'particular' interests, it is easier to understand how the Campaign's attempt to extend their legislative success by highlighting the inconsistency between local and central governmental principles has not taken them beyond 'freedom of information'.

The second strand of Wilson's argument holds that government actually has nothing to fear from the Campaign, and Wilson goes so far as to allude to political advantages deriving to the government from freedom of information. The fact that such an argument could be made by a leading member of the Campaign indicates how far it has moved from the original principles of 'open government'. Even so, such an appeal is unlikely to impress government, given the differing principles by which the particular and national interests are to be dealt with in its, the traditional, viewpoint.

As I have argued thus far, and will attempt to further elaborate subsequently in looking at 'Thatcherism', it is my contention that official secrecy is entirely consistent with the central theoretical underpinnings of British government, we should therefore not be surprized at governmental reluctance to embrace reform. However, the substance of the analysis undertaken here suggests that though understandable, the government's hostility to the current demands of the Campaign for FOI is unjustified. The principles of a 'Westminster' model of government are not irreconcilable with a statutory right of access to official information with clear exclusions, such as is represented by the Campaign's 'constitutionalized' model bill. Indeed, Australia, Canada and New Zealand have all managed this change without even the repeal of their existing official secrecy legislation (only in New Zealand was the Official Secrets Act even amended). Further, eight or nine years of experience in these countries now demonstrates that not only is their capacity to protect genuine government secrets unimpaired, but on the whole, the problems warned against by FOI's detractors have not materialized (see for example Hazell, 1989). Further, in these countries:

> ... ministers remain fully accountable. When policy papers are disclosed, the press and public are not interested in the identity of the author, but in the response of the minister. Accountability continues to rest where it always has, on ministers (Hazell, 1989, p. 197).

The government's opposition to change on the grounds that it would undermine parliamentary accountability - the substance of Mrs Thatcher's argument for example - therefore seems spurious. Indeed:

> Most of the information released through FOI is of no interest to
> ministers or Parliament: it is generally either personal information, or
> technical or commercial information which is of interest only to the
> requester. In so far as the information is of wider interest and gives rise
> to questions being asked in Parliament, ministerial accountability may
> be *strengthened* [my emphasis] because parliamentary scrutiny is
> increased. But what the minister is accountable for is the action (or
> inaction) revealed by the information, and not the provision of the
> information itself. Under FOI, ministers lose some of their discretion in
> relation to the provision of information; but their accountablity for the
> underlying activity or decision remains unchanged (Hazell, 1989, p.
> 198).

It is my contention that it is in fact this increased effectiveness of parliamentary
accountability, rather than its undermining, which government actually wishes to resist;
government does not *want* to be effectively held to account. The present means of
parliamentary accountability are certainly at best ineffective, being no less dominated by
government than the legislative process itself. This point is reinforced by the ample
evidence that ministerial and cabinet reponsibility are in any case more myth than reality
these days. With regard to the former, nobody really believes that a minister can oversee all
that goes on in a modern government department. More importantly, even when a minister
is found clearly to be at fault - Prior in the case of the Maze breakout for example -
resignation rarely follows. Similarly, there have been any number of incidents in recent
years, some of the more memorable ones being in relation to Westlands, John Moore and
the NHS, Lawson-Thatcher over monetary policy, and various divisions over Europe,
which demonstrate that cabinet responsibility is at best now a limited concept.

It would therefore seem that genuine and more effective accountability is what the
government seeks to resist. So despite the filtering out of 'open government' elements, the
achievement of a FOI Act such as is represented by the Campaign's model bill and exists
already in Canada, Australia and New Zealand, would be a tremendous advance, not just
for FOI but also in terms of the broader constitutional norms. The gains already made by
the Campaign in this country are significant, and demonstrate that 'freedom of information'
is compatible with the existing context of British government. The problems are thus
practical rather than genuinely constitutional. Though the underlying principle is one of
participatory democracy, this does not conflict with British governmental principles on

peripheral and Low Politics matters, since these concern the organization and presentation of 'particular' interests, whereas central government is concerned with High Politics and the national interest. The gradual, cumulative approach by which the Campaign have been operating is therefore likely to continue, falteringly, to bear fruit in this delimited area.

Unlike elsewhere however, the highly restrictive revised British Official Secrets Act (1989) would have to be repealed or radically amended before a general right of public access to information could be established in this country. The present government's ability to reinforce and even extend official secrecy where it suits them, and to control the definition of FOI where such is thought appropriate, is a measure of the extent of British Executive dominance. This brings us to the second concern of this chapter, in that 'Thatcherism' has represented the intensification of this characteristic of the British system, and therefore the reassertion of the British political tradition. We therefore now turn to look at how a radical political project can be *aided* by its *consistency* with the nature of the British political system.

'Thatcherism' and the British political tradition

Just as in Chapter One I argued that 'condemnatory' works on official secrecy often - mistakenly - see it as an aberration, it is common (even orthodox), to characterize the post-1979 period as one of a 'Thatcherite revolution' marking a decisive break from the past. Indeed a recent review of approaches to 'Thatcherism' (see Douglas, 1989), exempts only Bulpitt (1986) from what might be called the 'Thatcherite exceptionalism' thesis. However, since Bulpitt highlights continuity between 'Thatcherite' and previous Conservative 'statecraft' [3], Douglas criticizes Bulpitt's approach for paying too little attention to policy. This would seem a reasonable point. More striking however, is a common failure (see also eg Graham and Prosser, 1989) to place the analysis of 'statecraft' in the context of a broader discussion of the British political tradition and the nature of British democracy. Thus, whilst in some respects 'there is a greater similarity between ... Mrs Thatcher and ... Churchill and Macmillan than is often suggested' (Bulpitt, 1989, p. 39), Graham and Prosser (1989) are equally entitled to point to the institutional realignments within state structures and institutions. Examined in the context mentioned as generally neglected however, it is quite possible that although Mrs Thatcher undoubtably changed some key relationships within British politics, in so doing she in fact reasserted the norms of the British political tradition. This will be the basis of the argument propounded here.

In this sense then, 'Thatcherism' did not represent a break with the past, but a return to pre-war norms; it was the post-war era which represented an uncharacteristic 'responsive' rather than 'responsible' nature of British government [4]. Mrs Thatcher's emphasis on strong, decisive leadership, her rejection of consultation, her preference for 'Prime Ministerial' rather than cabinet government [5], along with a number of other features of her governmental style which will be considered here, fit very well with the elitist, top-down view of democracy which underpins the traditional institutions and processes of British government. Thus 'Thatcherism' was both underpinned by, and reinforced, the dominant concepts of political representation and good government found in the British political tradition.

However. this general argument that changes made under Mrs Thatcher provided a realignment with the British political tradition should not be taken to imply that such changes have been (unambiguously) successful in achieving the results intended. As will be shown for example, the determined attempt to change the relationship between central and local government has been far from totally successful. Nor is it the case that *all* the changes made have intensified or confirmed the British political tradition. The establishment of the new Parliamentary Select Committee System in 1979, which, as will be shown, had the potential to strengthen the legislature against the dominant British Executive, might be cited here.

Having established what will and what will not be argued here (and having entered a plea for greater sophistication in the approach to the study of 'Thatcherism'), the rest of the chapter will parallel the approach taken in regard to the development of the modern Campaign for Freedom of Information. That is, the changes made in a number of important institutions and processes of British government under Mrs Thatcher, will be related to the traditional nature of British government and the British political tradition. In this respect, particular reference will also be made to the distinction (made first in Chapter One and then above, in relation to the modern Campaign for FOI) between 'High Politics' and 'Low Politics'. We looked at this distinction in relation to policy areas above, but some elaboration in relation to institutions and processes is required before going on.

We might thus further characterize High Politics as the politics of the centre: Whitehall politics. It therefore encompasses institutions such as the cabinet, cabinet Committees and Government Departments, and the relationships with the civil service within and between these institutions. This is particularly important where such relationships might affect the popular perception of the government's competence and thereby their chances of re-election. By contrast, Low Politics can be said to be the politics of the peripheries. It thus encompasses the institutions of the peripheries, for example local authorities and interest groups, and processes governing the relationship between these and local, 'particular' interests and the electorate. Obviously, 'peripheral' institutions are involved with those of the centre, and given the British tradition of 'centre autonomy', High Politics can, in some policy instances, incorporate them. The relationship between central and local government for example, or between central government and organized interest groups, may become High Politics concerns inasmuch as they might affect central government policy or popular perceptions of the centre's governing competence. However, relations between peripheral institutions and their members and electorates are always within the realm of Low Politics. The High Politics - Low Politics distinction (Bulpitt, 1986) is important here again since I will argue that since 1979 there has been a significant centralization of power in the realm of High Politics but at the same time an emphasis on increased participation in the realm of Low Politics.

The following examination will therefore focus upon: the relationships between central and local government; Executive and Legislature; government and interest groups; and Prime Minister and cabinet.

Inter-governmental relations

If a government is to provide strong, decisive leadership in the manner emphasized in the British political tradition, political power will almost inevitably be concentrated at the centre. There is little doubt that in Britain power has been so concentrated. We have traced the British tradition of Executive dominance in earlier chapters, and of course territorially, Britain's is a unitary political system; attempts to devolve power, whether to Stormont, Cardiff or Edinburgh, having been unsuccessful [6]. However, we have also had a system of local government in this country giving local authorities more autonomy and authority than many of their European counterparts. In addition, there has been a traditional relationship between national and local government perhaps best characterized as an exchange relationship; central government controlled the legal rules and to a large extent the purse strings, but was dependent upon local government to deliver the services (Rhodes, 1988). Given that each side had resources important to the other, Rhodes and others thus view the relationship as one based upon bargaining; outcomes were most often negotiated settlements.

It is not surprising that this arrangement held little attraction for Mrs Thatcher and contemporary 'New Right' Conservatives, since they were concerned to re-establish government authority in general and their governing competence in particular. In their view (autonomous) local authorities were a significant constraint upon the government's ability to rule. In addition, given their key aim of cutting government expenditure and public borrowing, the local authorities - and particularly their finances - were an obvious target.

The legal position of British local government has been transformed since 1979; Benyon (1989) has calculated that fifty pieces of Conservative legislation affecting local government had been introduced by March 1989. In fact, as Rhodes argues, what dominated the period up to 1987 was:

> the search by central government for more effective instruments of control over the expenditure of sub-central government, in accordance with the overall economic strategies of monetarism and reduction of the public sector (Budge, et al, 1988, p. 127).

In the first two terms of 'Thatcherite' government two major attempts to control local government expenditure were made. First the system of allocating central grants to localities was changed; indeed this took seven different forms in the five financial years between 1979 and 1983 (Rhodes, 1991). The tradition of Executive dominance and centre autonomy certainly made it easier to mount these attempts; they were nevertheless unsuccessful in their primary aim. That is, the government had wanted to cut local current expenditure, but despite central government's contribution to current local expenditure (through the block grant system) being reduced from sixty-one percent to fifty-three percent between 1979-80 and 1982-83, it was local **capital** expenditure (on building projects, roads or sewers) which was in fact cut. Local **current** expenditure in fact **rose** (by nine percent); the exact opposite of what the government had hoped to achieve.

The centre progressively abandoned consultation and bargaining as guiding principles governing its relations with local government and moved towards direction. But a considerable number of local authorities, by no means all Labour controlled, increased their rates in order to compensate for the reduced income from the centre; their expenditure thus inevitably exceeded central government targets. In addition, litigation became a major feature of inter-governmental relations. The government responded with the Rates Act 1984; 'rate-capping' restricting local authorities' ability to attempt to maintain local services by increased rates. The legislation reflected ministerial prerogative in good British traditional governmental manner; rather than by firm set criteria, the Secretary of State for the Environment could *choose* the local authorities to be rate-capped. He did have to give a reason for such decisions, but invariably it was claimed (seemingly regardless of local conditions and circumstances) that those to be rate-capped were 'high spending authorities'. Given that ultimately a local authority could not levy a rate greater than that allowed by the Secretary of State, this represents a major contribution to increased centralization of power in the British political system. However, again the effect was not that intended; rate-capping brought about little reduction in local expenditure. Relatively few authorities were actually rate-capped: 18 in 1984, and 12, including two selected again, in 1985. At the same time rate-capping led, indirectly, to increased spending, since, as Rhodes puts it:

> High spending local authorities, worried that they might be future candidates for rate-capping, levied rates to increase their resources to ensure that they were cut back from the highest feasible level with money in the bank. Even 'moderates' found they had increased their rates to cope with the additional functions inherited from the abolition of the GLC and the MCCs (Budge, et al, 1988, pp. 131-132).

The attempt to control expenditure can be said to have culminated with the 1988 Local Government Finance Act. This saw non-domestic rates replaced by the centrally set Universal Business Rate, and the property based domestic rates completely replaced by the individually based Community Charge or 'Poll Tax' (the Rate Support Grant being replaced by a Revenue Support Grant). The Act also allowed, as a reserve measure, the same kind of 'capping' as had applied to the domestic rate. Increased government control over local authority income and expenditure was thereby further facilitated; indeed, it has been calculated that about 75 percent of local authority expenditure came under the control of central government as a result (see eg Travers, 1989). The Poll Tax was however introduced in terms of the primary aim being to increase local authority accountability to their electors. More will be said of this subsequently, but it can be mentioned here that this evidences the earlier mentioned dichotomy between the tendency for increasing centralization in High Politics areas and the willingness of the government to facilitate increased participation in Low Politics matters. The reality of 'charge capping' however makes it clear where the government's first priority lay. Indeed, as Travers points out:

> in the long term, the introduction of the new system of local government finance, with only a quarter of revenue income raised from a locally determined tax, and with capital spending under greater central control, must weaken the financial base of local authorities (Travers, 1989, p. 28).

Stewart and Stoker (1989) argue that by its third term the government had broadened its concerns about local government beyond the necessity of public expenditure restraint 'to a more broad-ranging attempt to restructure local government' (p. 2). They point out many aspects of this restructuring, notably:

> local government has been fragmented with some delivery, regulatory and strategic responsibilities removed from them; there has been an increased commitment to competition in relation to tendering, and choice in relation to schools and housing; greater emphasis has been placed on the relationship between receiving and paying for a service which has led to higher rents and charges; producer interests, particularly public sector trade unions and professional groups, have been challenged and their influence checked; there has been a growing commitment to more 'business like' management in local government; and we have witnessed an increased emphasis on holding local authorities accountable to central government through the use of contracts (Stewart and Stoker, 1989, pp. 2-4, see also Bulpitt, 1990).

This would seem to reflect accurately the recent general trends in relation to local authority practice and inter-governmental relations. Nor does the government's decision to scrap the Poll Tax and replace it with the 'Council Tax' seem to represent a step back from present levels of centralization (although no further increase in the trend is represented either). It would therefore seem, as Rhodes argues, that it would be 'foolhardy to deny that the thrust of the post-1984 reforms is centralising'. However, this is neither to say that all the changes have been designed merely to strengthen the centre, nor, as Rhodes also points out, should we 'overestimate the capacity of the centre to realise its objectives' via these means (Rhodes, 1988, p. 252).

It is nevertheless evident both that there has been a significant centralization of power which in large part has strengthened the authority of central government, and that such a development sits easily with the British political tradition and the basic nature of British government. Bulpitt, commenting on the post-1979 changes argues for instance:

> For the first time there is a clear and direct connection between what the Conservatives want from national politics and their views on central-local relations and the role of local authorities... *This is another attempt*

to get central-local relations back to the 1930s, when the two levels of government knew their respective places. Local government becomes, once again, limited government, respectable and prudent within its own confines and respectful to the central government. Neville Chamberlain would have liked this particular tune (Bulpitt, 1990, my emphasis).

It is clear then that as a result of the Thatcher governments' policy orientation towards cutting public borrowing and spending, inter-governmental relations entered the realm of High Politics. It is equally clear that in this area a centralizing trend can be identified, although the extent to which outcomes have matched the governments' aims is questionable. The emphasis on central control has however abated somewhat since 1987, with accountability rather than cuts becoming the watchword. As indicated earlier, the government was quick to emphasize that the Poll Tax was designed to ensure that all electors should pay towards the costs of the services they use. The Green Paper argued similarly that it would 'make local services more accountable to their electors' by ensuring 'that the local electors know what the costs of their local services are, so that armed with this knowledge they can influence the spending decisions of the council through the ballot box' ('Paying for Local Government', 1986, pp. 9 and vii).

The Poll Tax was of course deeply unpopular in the country and with the Opposition parties, yet the government was able to implement it regardless; the elitist and centralized British political system certainly aided the implementation of this major reform. The fact that a popular vote for the Conservatives of 42.3 percent in the 1987 General Election turned into a 100 seat majority provides clear initial evidence for this. Mrs Thatcher also certainly exercised 'Prime Ministerial power' to further the Poll Tax option, the unenthusiastic Patrick Jenkin was for example removed as Environment Secretary and replaced by Thatcher loyalist Kenneth Baker. Thatcher simply set aside objections that the tax would be inefficient to collect and was unrelated to ability to pay, and it seems that although most departmental ministers had attended many and various 'briefings', no full cabinet meeting discussed the matter before publication of the Green Paper. Indeed, despite its inclusion in the 1987 manifesto, it seems the Poll Tax for England and Wales, as opposed to its prior introduction in Scotland, was *never* discussed in full cabinet.

Subsequent executions of Prime Ministerial power would also result in a more radical introduction of the Poll Tax than had originally been envisaged. The Green Paper says in the Foreword for example: 'It would not be realistic to seek to overturn the present arrangements, however justifiable the case for doing so, in one step'. Subsequently, it continues:

> People need time to adjust ... It is reasonable to expect domestic rates
> to be phased out completely *within ten years* of the introduction of
> the new system (my emphasis).

Indeed the Green Paper suggests that in the first year of the proposed 'phasing-in', new contributors would need to find only £50, the same figure by which existing rate payers would see their rates reduced.

Yet this gradual, cumulative approach was transformed following further cabinet changes involving the removal of others cool to the idea of the Poll Tax (and alive to the possible consequences of its poor management). Michael Heseltine, who had preferred to avoid the whole subject of rates reform, resigned from the government around the time of the Green Paper. Shortly afterwards Leon Brittan, who had offered some resistance on civil liberties grounds, ingloriously left the cabinet. The then Chancellor, Nigel Lawson - and indeed the Treasury - did not consider the Poll Tax to be right even in its gradualist form. But Lawson too would soon leave the cabinet, following the public row with Thatcher over her economics advisor, Sir Alan Walters. Kenneth Baker, author of the 'softly softly' line of the Green Paper, had been moved to Education and replaced by the Poll Tax's staunchest supporter, Nicholas Ridley. With some relish Ridley proceeded to argue in cabinet for the straightforward and simultaneous replacement of the rates with the Poll Tax. The remaining resistance was broken down following former Scottish MP Gerry Malone's passionate speech at the 1988 Conservative Party Conference in favour of the Ridley-Thatcher line. The Conference rose and cheered enthusiastically, and from that moment 'phasing-in' was dead.

The eventual outcome of this decision - the debacle represented by the retreat from the Poll Tax - saw the local accountability argument buried. But it should be said that the emphasis upon accountability stretched far beyond the field of local government finance. The Educational Reform Act (1988) for example allows parents greater input into the running of their childrens' schools and allows the schools to opt out of local Education Authority control. It gives governors responsibilities for school budgets and the appointment and dismissal of staff. Also, the Local Government and Housing Act (1989) prevents councils subsidizing rents, in order, it is argued, that this change will reinforce the link between receiving and paying for a service. Such changes are notable, but three points are crucial. First, as before, it is doubtful if the changes will achieve the government's ends in any simple way (see eg Rhodes, 1991). Secondly, and more importantly, it is the accountability of the local authority to its electors/'customers' which is emphasized, as quite distinct from the 'responsiveness' of central government to local government or the electorate in general. Such accountability as is represented is therefore solidly within the area of Low Politics. Thirdly, the accountability argument is in any case abandoned where it directly affects inter-governmental relations; since this has become a High Politics area. As Rhodes argues:

> In theory poll tax clarifies the link between services and paying for them, encouraging electors to remove profligate Labour councils from office. However, in case electors either fail to spot the link between services and poll tax bills or, in an aberrant moment, vote for high levels of expenditure, the paternalistic government will step in and remedy the oversight by setting the poll tax at the "correct" level. Accountability is the objective of the poll tax, provided electors do not vote for increased expenditure (Rhodes, 1991).

Thus the dichotomy between central government's insistence upon defending its prerogatives in High Politics whilst accepting greater popular participation in Low Politics is again clear.

Executive - legislature relations

We have seen that the dominance of the Executive over the legislature rests, to a large extent, upon the persistence of a two party system and strong party discipline. Such dominance is of course clearly associated with the emphasis in the British political tradition upon strong decisive leadership and 'responsible' government; which would surely be undermined by a legislature able to effectively question or even overturn government legislation. Executive dominance has therefore been a key feature of British politics, particularly in this century, and has indeed become one of the central pillars of British government. It thus pre-existed Mrs Thatcher and continues despite her political demise. Nevertheless, it is a feature of British government that seemingly intensified, at least to some degree, during Mrs Thatcher's governmental terms. As always however, developments here do not suggest any simple, unidimensional change, but we will first examine some moves signifying greater Executive dominance.

In regard to government control over the timetable of bills in Standing Committee, with a small number of big and contentious bills - though most are not of this type - the

Opposition's only feasible tactic is to play for time. That is, they attempt to slow down business in committee so that the smallest number of clauses are discussed in the greatest number of sittings. Governments of recent years have tended to respond with an allocation of time, or 'guillotine' motion, which lays down time limits for the completion of the remaining stages of the bill. This means that many, if not most, important bills are eventually passed with little or no careful scrutiny of many of their clauses.

The First Report of the Select Committee on Procedure (an all-party committee of back-benchers) in the 1977/8 Session, proposed that Special Standing Committees be established which would take evidence from interested parties on bills *prior* to their consideration in the adversarial setting of a normal Standing Committee (see Drewry, 1988, p. 130). This recommendation was accepted - on an experimental basis - by the then Labour government. Subsequently, in the 1984/5 Session, the Conservative government agreed that the new style committees should be enshrined in standing orders. However, they proved very reluctant to use the procedure; it was used only three times in the 1980/81 Session, and once each in the '81/82 and '83/84 Sessions. The 1984/5 Report of the Procedure Committee then recommended that a new Legislative Business Committee be established to specify in advance the timetable for the committee stage of any bill likely to require more than twenty-five hours in Standing Committee. This was rejected by both Government and Opposition front benches; an unholy alliance reflecting common support for (and their long-term common interest in) Executive dominance.

However, having established the norms in this respect, the Thatcher governments can be said to have exercised increased control over bills in Standing Committee. They have both made greater use of the guillotine and introduced it at an earlier stage of Standing Committee deliberations than did previous governments. This is well illustrated by for example the Dock Work Regulation Bill, a very politically contentious measure guillotined in the 1988/9 Session; its committee stage lasted a mere 25 hours, compared with a norm of 100 hours.

A similar picture emerges in relation to delegated legislation. Parliament has a long history of delegating to others, by statute, a limited power to legislate; Acts of Parliament now commonly delegate to the Executive the authority to legislate by statutory instrument. Indeed, in the last thirty years there have been approximately 2,000 statutory instruments made each year (see eg Bates, 1988, pp. 200-205 and Drewry, 1988, pp. 138-140). There is little doubt however that significant changes have occurred in relation to the use of the procedure. For example, fewer pieces of delegated legislation are now of a detailed technical nature, and therefore relatively uncontroversial as such, than was previously the case. Indeed, the contemporary Conservative government has 'taken powers to make delegated legislation to repeal primary legislation and to give it retrospective effect' (Bates, 1988, p. 200).

The intensification in such a trend is the more serious given the clear inadequacies in the relevant procedures for parliamentary scrutiny. Since 1973, a small proportion have been considered by the Standing Committee on Statutory Instruments; most recently about 90 to 100 statutory instruments have been considered in about 70 or 80 sittings of the Committee each year. This means that the House devotes about four or five hours per week to discussing statutory instruments; it would probably be *less*, but the government is required to make time available for certain of them to be discussed (see eg Bates, 1988, p. 200). So this area of procedure too indicates a clear growth of Executive dominance which, although having its origins in an earlier period, has been extended since 1979. However, the most salient point is well made by Drewry:

> The trouble with achieving worthwhile procedural reform is that almost
> anything designed to make legislative scrutiny more effective also
> makes ministers' lives harder (Drewry, 1988, p. 130).

Given that ministers do not want their lives made harder, and Executive dominance enables them to prevent it, ineffective parliamentary scrutiny and accountability follow.

The one procedure through which back-bench MPs can have a direct effect on legislation, indeed can initiate it, is the Private Members Bills procedure. Even here however, government has in fact always played a key role (see eg Marsh and Read, 1988, pp. 41-61); modern governments have effectively been able to control outcomes, and this has become all the clearer since 1979. Many bills are, in effect, government bills which a back-bencher introduces in order to ensure that it can be successfully piloted onto the statute book; government gets favourable legislation and the back-bencher valuable experience. Burton and Drewry make the general point well illustrated earlier in this chapter, by saying that in reality: 'a major determinant of the success or otherwise of any back-bench bill is the government's attitude towards it' (Burton and Drewry, 1981, p. 214). More specifically, the analysis of Marsh and Read also supports the conclusions of the earlier part of this chapter; contentious Private Members Bills can only succeed if they are given government time (and government time is only given at a price).

However, again, having established the norms in this regard, Marsh and Read (1988) also show clearly that the role of the government in this procedure has increased significantly since 1979. The contemporary Conservative government has been less willing to grant time than had previous governments, and more successful Private Members Bills than ever have been, in all but name, government bills. So despite its control of the vast majority of parliamentary time anyway, the government has still used Private Members time to get through minor legislation. It is therefore difficult not to agree with the conclusions of Marsh and Read, in that:

> Such bills may be useful but they are Government bills and their prevalence indicates once again the very restricted role that the legislature plays in the British system. At the same time this indicates why change is unlikely. Any major reform of the procedure would inevitably involve a shift in the balance of power, albeit a fairly minor one, in the relationship between the executive and the legislature. What is more the executive is well-suited by the present practice as it can achieve minor legislative change without using its own time. For both these reasons the executive is not likely to initiate, or welcome, any radical change. Equally, the very advocacy of major change almost inevitably reflects a view that the executive is too dominant in the British system, and probably more fundamentally, that the British political system is too elitist (Marsh and Read, 1988, p. 188).

There are however two areas in which, in recent years, the position of the Executive might be said to have been *weakened* in relation to the legislature. Firstly, the latest reform of the Parliamentary Select Committee system in the 1979/80 Session was designed, at least in part, to improve the legislature's ability to scrutinize government administration. Secondly, since 1970 at least, there has been a growth of 'dissent', and thus a weakening of party discipline; if, since 1979 such dissent has been less pronounced.

The latest reform of Select Committees, introduced by Norman St John Stevas as Leader of the House, was the third major reform of the system in 13 years. It was approved by parliament in June 1979 despite Mrs Thatcher being clearly less than a wholehearted supporter of the changes. Under the reform, most of the existing Select Committees were abolished, with the notable exception of the Public Accounts Committee. Twelve new Committees were established which broadly paralleled the major spending departments, to which were added two more, dealing with Scottish and Welsh affairs.

In regard to the effects of these changes (see eg Drewry [ed], 1985; Johnson, 1988 and Likierman, 1988, for a fuller discussion), it can be said at the outset that the *range* of scrutiny of the Executive has increased. Secondly, the new Committees have been able to obtain *more*, and *better quality* evidence from the departments, than was previously the case. Thirdly, they are taken *more seriously* by ministers and civil servants than in the past; their parallel presence to departments clearly ensures a greater *wariness*. Perhaps the clearest sense in which the new Committees have been appreciated is less related to scrutiny and accountability however. That is, they have provided back-benchers with the opportunity to specialize and develop expertise in particular policy areas. This allows ambitious MPs to demonstrate their potential for office, which in turn fits in well with the (traditionalist) assumption that parliamentary life should develop appropriate 'responsibility' among MPs; training and preparing the best to become ministers. There is in fact very considerable doubt as to whether any of the above represents *more effective* parliamentary scrutiny or accountability of the Executive. Even Johnson, a strong supporter of the new system, acknowledges for example:

> Notwithstanding great improvements they remain essentially critical
> bodies dependent solely on their powers of argument and persuasion
> (Johnson, 1988, p. 184).

Similarly, Drewry (1985), in a thorough analysis of the work of the new Committees, accepts that the best they can hope for is to accrue power drip by drip.

The fact is that in an Executive dominated system Select Committees can hold government to account only if government is willing to be held accountable. Parliament would need to transcend the 'Government Vs Opposition' norm in favour of (a more Liberal-Democratic) 'Legislature Vs Executive' standpoint - that is, it would need to develop a 'legislative view' transcending party discipline - in order to significantly change the nature of British Executive legislature relations. In the current context Select Committees are virtually impotent.

For example, the new Committees now usually produce unanimous Reports (rather than the party-split Majority and Minority Reports often seen in the past). Some of these unanimous Reports have been highly critical of government. But again the timetable for debate of these Reports is controlled by government, which is perfectly able to delay sensitive debates. Even where this is overcome however, the fact is that in the vote even members of the Committee rarely vote for the Committee/Report against their party line. For example, none of the Conservative MPs on the Transport Committee voted against the government's decision to increase the maximum permitted weight of heavy lorries in 1981, although the Committee had opposed this change. Similarly, despite the Treasury and Civil Service Committee's objections to the government's economic strategy in both its 1980 and 1981 Reports, only one Conservative member of the Committee, Richard Shepherd, even abstained in the vote on the government's handling of the economy on 13 December 1981. Again, though the Transport Committee opposed parts of the 1981 Transport Bill, including the government's plans for school transport, only one Conservative member of the Committee, Peter Fry, dissented in the vote. Indeed, in all the cases of dissent between 1979 and 1983, the proportion of dissenting Conservative Select Committee members was no greater than the overall proportion of dissenting Conservative MPs. There was of course no occasion upon which all the members of a Committee voted against the government on an issue - even where they had unanimously approved a Report which opposed government policy.

The case of Clive Ponting provides further evidence of the absence of a 'legislative view', and as to why significant change is unlikely. Ponting, a civil servant in the upper echelons, 'leaked' information to Tam Dalyell, a member of the Foreign Affairs Select Committee. The leaked information concerned the sinking of the Argentine cruiser, General Belgrano, during the Falklands War. For our purposes however, the most significant aspect of the affair was the reaction of the Chair of the Committee, Sir Anthony Kershaw, when *he* recieved the leaked documents. Although these documents made clear that both parliament in general, and the Committee itself had been deceived by the Ministry of Defence, there was no outraged determination to hold the government to account now that the means were available. Rather, Kershaw took the documents immediately to his party colleague and Minister of Defence, Michael Heseltine, so that a 'leak inquiry' could be initiated to find the 'culprit' who had provided the information! This action by the Chair of a body supposedly upholding government accountability amply illustrates the distorting effects on Committee activity of party allegiances (and of the Official Secrets Act). The sheer scale of the problem is also indicated by the failure of other Committee members to take public issue with the action of Kershaw, or even show any surprize at it.

The root of the problem is then that an elitist view of democracy legitimates Executive dominance in the eyes of *most MPs*, as well as all ministers; both views see Executive dominance as favourable to achieving effective government. As such, the Executive is able to determine - and therefore restrict - the power of the legislature. The most revealing evidence of this is provided by the civil service memorandum governing what civil servants can, and more crucially cannot, discuss with Select Committees. Specifically proscribed are: advice given to ministers; inter-departmental exchanges; discussions in cabinet Committee; advice given by law officers; and questions involving public controversy. The two-page memorandum in effect proscribes much of the information a Select Committee would require to properly assess government policy and administration. However, the memorandum itself had never been a matter of controversy and while certain Committees have questioned its consequences none have criticized its existence. This surely reflects accurately the dominance of the Executive and passivity of the legislature in Britain. The Thatcher style of government may have accentuated this, but it is a basic feature of British politics and government.

Philip Norton has charted the rise in dissent in British politics since 1970, paying particular attention to the number of government back-benchers voting against their party in whipped divisions on the floor of the House (see particularly Norton, 1978). Between 1970 and 1974 there were sixty-nine divisions in which more than ten MPs dissented; forty-one MPs (twelve percent) cast six or more dissenting votes and seventeen MPs dissented on twenty or more occasions. In fact one Conservative MP, (Enoch Powell) dissented 115 times. Dissent has always been more widespread in the Labour Party, but it rose to virtually epidemic proportions in the 1974-79 parliament. No less than forty-five percent of all whipped divisions in the 1978/79 Session saw some Labour MPs voting against the government. What is more, only sixty-two Labour MPs (nineteen percent of the total) cast no dissenting votes.

Although after Mrs Thatcher was elected Prime Minister in 1979 dissent was not as widespread as it had been under Edward Heath, it was still common, and on occasions spectacular. During the first term one or more MPs dissented on ten per cent of the votes, and there were sixteen occasions on which more than ten Conservative MPs defied their party whip; a total of 393 dissenting votes accruing over these sixteen divisions. The two most spectacular incidents concerned the Immigration Rules, with more than fifty back-bench MPs taking a harder line than their front-bench on the two occasions where there was a division. When the Conservatives were re-elected in 1983 dissent persisted. There were rebellions in 1984 on the Trade Union Bill (forty dissenters) and on the Local Government Bill (nineteen dissenters), and in 1985 on the Water Fluoridation Bill (forty-eight dissenters). In all these cases however the large government majority carried the day regardless.

The government was not so fortunate following a large rebellion over the siting of the third London airport in 1985 however. So many Conservatives objected to the Inspector's Report on the matter that the government whips, convinced that they were going to be defeated on an Adjournment vote, instructed Conservative MPs to abstain. In the end 70 back-bench Conservatives defied these instructions and voted with the Opposition against the Inspector's Report, which the government of course supported. However, the failure of the Shops Bill to get a Second Reading in 1986 was the government's biggest debacle. The government had hoped to extend hours for Sunday trading (see eg Read, 1988), but such 'liberalization' was opposed by a strong, if unusual, alliance between the churches, the trades unions, the National Chamber of Trade and the Co-operative Society. Many Conservative back-benchers believed that the bill would 'change the nature of Sundays', and many more were under considerable pressure from the constituencies. In the end no fewer than 72 Conservative MPs dissented, and the government thereby lost a bill which had been a significant element in the Queen's Speech.

There is no doubt then that dissent is much more frequent than it was before 1970. However, it very rarely has any effect on the fate of government legislation; the Shops Bill providing the, admittedly spectacular, exception which proves the rule. As Drewry points out, of the 165 'ordinary bills introduced during the second Thatcher administration only eight failed to reach the Statute Book, and four of these failed for technical reasons' (Drewry, 1988, p. 135). The government thus still dominates almost totally on the legislative front.

While the pattern is not totally straightforward, on balance it is clear that Executive dominance did increase after 1979, if there have also been developments which suggest a more effective legislature. As Drewry acknowledges:

> the real problem of legislative scrutiny ... is not procedural at all, it is constitutional. Parliament's role vis-a-vis the Executive is reactive and supportive; many parliamentarians, invoking constitutional dogma and democratic theory, feel that it should have a more active and meaningful role. But no amount of procedural tinkering can ever achieve that (Drewry, 1988, p. 131).

Relations between government and interest groups

From the outset Mrs Thatcher made it clear that she was determined that her government should stick 'resolutely' to objectives considered correct: 'It must be a conviction government' (Mrs Thatcher, *The Observer*, 25 February 1979). Equally clearly, the 'warrior' style (Crewe, 1988) of Mrs Thatcher's governments involved the rejection of the post-war norms of consultation and negotiation. Instead, 'particular' interests which might represent obstacles to the achievement of government objectives must be directly confronted. It is well known that Mrs Thatcher regarded the post-war consensus built upon a commitment to full employment, the mixed economy and a universalist welfare state as a damaging mistake. Those with a vested interest in such a set-up were therefore prime targets for 'Thatcherism'.

In fact, the process of compromize was seen as a bad thing in itself, leading, in the 'Thatcherite' view, to 'fudge', muddle and a failure to tackle difficult problems. But in addition, the particular compromizes embodied in the post-war consensus were viewed as having resulted in deleterious economic, social and political consequences. Too much 'responsiveness' by governments in the post-war era had led to a spiral of rising public demands upon, and expectations of, government. This in turn meant that government became ever more dependent upon non-governmental sources in the attempt to fulfill these expectations. Ultimately, this led to 'overload' and 'ungovernability' (see eg King, 1975, Beer, 1982).

In the 'Thatcherite' view therefore, governments must stop abdicating their proper responsibility in this way. Both aspects of the 'independent authority' of government - emphasized strongly in the British political system - must be reasserted. Government must govern, which means that it must do what it thinks is right; taking the tough decisions and implementing them, even despite unpopularity and opposition. At the same time, those reponsibilities regarded as inappropriate for government should be shed, in order that government is the better able to undertake its legitimate tasks. In effect, this is the rationale behind the 'free economy - strong state' dualism emphasized by a number of commentators on 'Thatcherism' (see particularly Gamble, 1988). Government needs to be strong to withstand the claims of the particular interests, but its role is to govern, not to intervene directly in the economy; 'the government of business is not the business of government'. Government knows best how to govern, governing should therefore be left to the government, the business community on the other hand knows best how to make profits, running the economy should therefore be left to the capitalists.

The last Labour government's Social Contract epitomized what Mrs Thatcher saw as the bad old days; with nothing illustrating this as well as the manner of its demise in the 'Winter of Discontent'. The 'bargained corporatism' (Crouch, 1979) which gave rise to the Social Contract, as well as its actual content, were each anathema to 'Thatcherites'. In their view, wage and price controls, interventionist economic and industrial policies and a voluntarist industrial relations approach, all restricted the operation of the free market. At the same time the social objectives of this period were also strongly opposed by Mrs Thatcher, because they were seen to encourage the very sort of 'dependency culture' which she wanted to see ended.

Thus 'government must govern' became just another way of saying Corporatism/Collectivism/Socialism - terms which Mrs Thatcher used seemingly interchangeably - must go. As indicated, this required 'a set of policies designed to produce a strong state and a government strong enough to resist the selfish claims of pressure groups' (Kavanagh, 1987, p. 9). The chief 'beneficiaries' of this strong, decisive leadership were to be the trades unions. As Mitchell (1987) shows, 'beer and sandwiches' at Downing Street became a thing of the past, and the government enacted cumulative legislation to restrict union activity (for a fuller discussion see Marsh, 1989, and especially Marsh, 1992).

The industrial relations issue was at the forefront of the 1979 Conservative Manifesto (not least because of the 'Winter of Discontent'). The 'softly softly' strategy favoured by Mrs Thatcher's first Secretary of State for Employment, Jim Prior, was not favoured by the 'Thatcherites', but it should be remembered that they were in a cabinet minority at this time. The Employment Act 1980 was thus far more limited than the Conservative right wing would have liked. It nevertheless curbed mass picketing and weakened the closed shop, and crucially, Prior's caution paid off; trade union reaction to the Act was muted (possibly because they had expected worse). The restrained reaction from the unions added to the government's confidence however, and as Mrs Thatcher began the process of marginalizing the 'wets', Prior was replaced as Employment Secretary by Norman Tebbit.

Tebbit's Employment Act 1982 narrowed the definition of a trade dispute, and thereby limited the immunities granted to trades unions in 1906 (see Chapter Three). Unions were now legally responsible for their members' actions and the consequences thereof. The position of a trade union was thus brought into line with that of individual trades unionists under the 1980 Act. Employers were able to claim through the courts for up to £250, 000 damages where - under the new definition - trade union action could no longer be said to have arisen out of a legitimate trade dispute. In addition, further restrictions on closed shops were brought in, narrowing the range of circumstances where a dismissal of a worker for non-trade union membership, by an employer upholding a closed shop agreement, might be deemed fair.

Initially wrong-footed by the moderation of the 1980 Act, and labouring under the impression that the government would soon U-turn or be replaced by a union-friendly new Labour Government, the TUC had thus far offered only token resistance. The unimpressive first 'Day of Action' seemed however to make it more difficult to organize firm resistance when it was deemed necessary in 1982. Following Labour's humiliating defeat in the 1983 General Election, concerted and effective resistance became all the more difficult to achieve: 'new realism' came to the fore. A number of cases during 1981-82 had seen unions faced with, and accepting, court injunctions, and following these came a whole series of defeats for unions which had shown a willingness to fight. Most traumatic of all such defeats was that of the miners strike 1984-85, which seemed to demonstrate that there really was no alternative to new realism.

Meanwhile, Tom King replaced Tebbit at the Department of Employment, and further legislation was enacted in the form of the Trade Union Act 1984. This required the election, by secret ballot, of trade union officers. Similar ballots were also required to be held before a strike could be called, and to legitimize trade union political funds. This legislation was therefore aimed both at the internal workings of trades unions and at their relationship with the Labour Party. Greater participation by members in the selection of leaders and officials would, it was argued, make those leaders and officials more representative of, and accountable to, ordinary trades unionists; the unions were to be 'given back to their members'. The argument for pre-strike and political fund ballots was essentially the same: greater participation would lead to more representative and accountable decisions on these matters. Again this shows the dichotomy between greater centralization and elitism in High Politics and 'devolution' with greater popular participation and accountability in Low Politics. In any case these further reforms went through with little trouble, and the Conservatives went on the win the 1987 General Election. Lord Young had replaced King at the Department of Employment in September 1985, and, in the wake of this third successive election victory, Norman Fowler became the new Employment Secretary.

The fourth stage in what the government itself called its 'step-by-step' approach followed, with the Employment Act 1988. This extended the rights conferred upon individual trades union members in the 1984 legislation, as well as strengthening those of non-union members in the now-emasculated closed shops. The 1984 Act had removed immunities where a strike was called without a ballot. Unions acting thus were thereby subject to harsh penalties. Nevertheless, the new Act went further still, providing for 'prior restraint'. That is, any individual union member may seek a court injunction preventing a union from calling upon such an individual to take industrial action prior to a ballot. Further, a union's ability to discipline members is curtailed: even if a union member has taken part in a ballot which decided upon a strike, but then continues to work in defiance of that collective decision, that member is protected from disciplinary action by the union as a result. This in fact goes far beyond making unions popularly accountable and epitomizes Mrs Thatcher's core philosophical attitude: the championing of the individual over the collective.

The legislation was certainly intended to strengthen the position of employers in relation to the unions, so as to preserve order and discipline and restrict the ability of the unions to act as an effective constraint on the operation of the market. As Marsh (1992) indicates however, such aims have met with limited success. In summary: the legislation is relatively little used; much on the shop-floor remains substantively the same; and wages have risen at a higher rate than prices. Nevertheless, the government has asserted itself in relation to the unions and this in itself has had the effect of a growing 'new realism' in the union movement.

It has not only been the unions which have been affected by the government's desire to purge the system of consultative norms and establish government independence however. An admittedly rather less determined attack was also opened upon a series of professional monopolies; opticians, solicitors, doctors and barristers. In addition, some attempt was made to control other potentially powerful economic interests, notably the farmers and even the brewers. It is again significant though, that in most cases and particularly in the first two terms of Conservative government, such attempts were less than successful. However, the government's overall strategy was clear; it wanted to re-establish governmental independence and authority. In this regard holding the 'particular' corporate and collective interests at bay, and rejecting the corporatist practices which were their corollary, was, as indicated earlier, accompanied by the positive reassertion of individualism. Hence Mrs Thatcher favoured an individual - state dichotomy in her attempts to wean the public away from collectivist and towards individualistic modes of thought and action. The reassertion of the individual and the attempt to break collectivist attitudes - to 'eradicate Socialism' - were therefore two sides of the same coin; each seeking to undermine the strength of the 'particular interests' and thereby ease government's own task as arbiter of the national interest.

Kavanagh (1987, p. 291) comments: 'One mark of a radical government is seen in its politicisation of hitherto non-political areas'. This can be seen to be true of 'Thatcherism'; perhaps as a kind of by-product of the attempts to free themselves from the constraints of pressure groups, the Thatcher governments had the effect of politicizing intermediary groups. Rhodes (1988, pp. 250-51, 321, 385-86) has documented this process for local government, but it is equally applicable to non-departmental public bodies. In this vein Dahrendorf (1985, p. 198) worries that it will be 'very difficult to get back to the old system' now that appointments at the BBC for example 'have been made in order to push it in a particular direction' (see also Walters, 1989). Moreover, this politicization should not be seen as random swings of the handbag but as deliberate and necessary steps in breaking 'the resistance of all special interests, including the new class of public sector professionals' (Gamble, 1988, p. 33), or in the restructuring of civil society 'around the Thatcherites' preferred agenda of the pursuit of possessive individualism' (Jessop et al, 1988, p. 177).

The process of centralization is thus clear in the area of High Politics. The determination to achieve greater governmental autonomy was coupled to an assertion of greater authority over the 'particular' interests (including any tendencies towards such among administration); greater autonomy and authority each tending towards such an increase in centralization. However, as we have also seen, there have been moves in Low Politics areas which have encouraged greater popular participation and accountability; the whole thrust of the Trade Union Act 1984 in particular being to 'give the unions back to their members'. A similar picture emerges in relation to local government. In relation to the organization and presentation of the 'particular' interests then, the government has been willing to use participatory arguments.   There is more to this than an odd paradox however. We should bear in mind that the government's High Politics aims are best served by preventing local or corporate elites from gaining too much power and freedom of action in their dealing with central government. A similar conclusion may be drawn in regard to the assertion of the individual over the collective. Mrs Thatcher's presentation of herself: 'to the working class as champion of the taxpayer against the Treasury, the worker against his (sic) trade union, the council tenant against the landlord, and the citizen against the state' (Jenkins, 1989, p. 53), represents an effective populist appeal made to the people (over the heads of their local or corporate 'leaderships'), and going beyond simply reinforcing individual as distinct from collectivist values. Just as the Campaign for Freedom of Information sought (unsuccessfully) to use this paradox in pointing out the apparently 'hopelessly inconsistent and untenable' (Wilson, *Secrets* No. 5, p. 8) hypocrisy of the government's position, others too have asked:

> Why should trade unions be given back to their members by the state, (when) political parties and parliament, the courts or employers (are) not 'given' in this manner to the various groups to which they are accountable? (Mackie, 1984, p. 92).

Mackie continues in incisive vein :

> It is clear that the present government has not chosen the trade unions as their example of the model democratic state which they would call on others to emulate, as indicated by government resistance to EEC proposals on the reform of industrial democracy. Rather they intended that the 1984 Act should lead to their preferred political and economic outcomes within the range of union activities. Achieving this change by extending 'democracy' has the double political advantage of an inherent appeal to the wider electorate at the same time as it inhibits trade union

opposition because it is equally a central part of the values of the union movements (Mackie, 1984, p. 92).

Again then, the emphasis on popular participation and accountability in the areas of Low Politics serves the purposes of central government in that it facilitates central control in the areas of High Politics.

The strengthening of prime-ministerial government

As least since Crossman (1963) and/or Mackintosh (1962), many students of British politics have argued that prime-ministerial government has replaced cabinet government. Following Walter Bagehot's distinctions of 1867, Crossman argued that the cabinet, as the Monarchy before it, had become part of the 'dignified' rather than the 'efficient' side of the governmental system. Mackintosh too saw as very significant the rise through the twentieth century - and particularly in the post-war era - of prime-ministerial power. In support of this general argument various developments are cited: the establishment of party government and the rise in party discipline; the emergence of a cabinet Secretariat providing something like a Prime Ministerial department; the unification of the hierarchically structured civil service effectively answerable to the Prime Minister; and the development of the cabinet Committee system under Prime Ministerial patronage and providing opportunities for an astute Prime Minister to manage the cabinet. In addition:

> Other students of government point to the concentrated media spotlight within which the modern premier works. Whatever he (sic) does is instant news and with clever media management - especially when playing the prestigious globe-trotting role of world leader - the PM can project an attractive, impressive and vote-winning image. The sheer pace of modern politics also delivers power to the premier: many things have to be decided quickly by small groups over which the PM can exert decisive control (Kavanagh, 1991).

In a system within which strong, decisive leadership is emphasized, we should not be surprised to find a centralization of power and authority. We have dealt at some length with this reality in previous chapters, here we are therefore concerned with the extent to which

Mrs Thatcher's terms in office can be said to have intensified such a concentration of power within the centre.

King (1986) presents the fullest academic analysis of Mrs Thatcher's style of governing to date (see also Burch, 1988, Doherty, 1988). He argues that she was an unusual Prime Minister both because she was in a minority in her own party and government and because she had a clear policy agenda. He suggests, at different points, that: she led in 'an unusually forthright, assertive manner' (p. 116); although she 'led from the front' nonetheless, as Prime Minister, she was a remarkably cautious politician' (p. 118); she was sensitive to power, respected it, and had an ability to weigh it (p. 112); she did not solve problems by creating new institutions but by finding the right person for the job. For Mrs Thatcher then, 'weighing people, like weighing power', was central to the way she governed (p. 123). She was: 'a highly self-conscious, self-projecting' politician (p. 128); she sought 'to command by appearing to be in command'; she was a good listener, 'a prodigious worker', a 'quick and eager learner'; and she made 'use of fear as a conscious weapon in her armoury of command' (pp. 128-131). In short, King concludes that Mrs Thatcher pushed 'out the frontiers of her authority' during her period in office (p. 137).

Mrs Thatcher's governmental style is important in regard to the current task, but as an approach to the understanding of 'Thatcherism' more generally, King's analysis is in my view far too narrow to be satisfactory. Such a stress upon Mrs Thatcher's individual personality ignores for example Vincent's plea that we should: 'Always allow for what would have happened anyway' (Vincent, 1989). Developing this point, Vincent continues for example:

> Had Mrs Thatcher never existed or her party not held office, the central questions of the 1980s would have been the same... Consider Mrs Thatcher's inheritance from Labour: the return of financial rectitude in 1976; the explicit rejection of orthodox Keynesianism by James Callaghan; the commitment to 3 per cent per annum growth in defence spending, the demise, beyond all hope of resurrection, of incomes policy in the 'winter of discontent' in 1978-9; and an ominously overpriced pound. ... the ending by Labour of the era of mass council house building, and the official adoption by Labour of the view that the state of education was a cause for concern. These were legacies. They left no room for manoeuvre. Many of the main decisions that shaped government in the 1980s had already been made under Labour (Vincent, 1989, p. 275).

Vincent therefore provides a valuable counterweight to King, if, as said, in regard to the (further) centralization of power and prime-ministerial government, the Thatcher governmental style is important. In this respect then King's more measured conclusion is surely correct. He writes, as indeed many have argued:

> the British constitution and the imperatives of party leadership in the
> British system mean that the office of prime minister evolves only
> slowly and that it is probably beyond the capacity of any one holder of
> the office to change it both radically and permanently (King, 1988, p.
> 136).

Yet at the same time Mrs Thatcher certainly maximized her authority within the constraints that operate in relation to the office of Prime Minister, and:

> one of the great strengths in the British office lies in the fact that the
> outer limits of its authority are so ill-defined. It is open to a determined
> prime minister to take more and more decisions and to defy other
> members of the cabinet to say that he or she has no right to take these
> decisions (King, 1988, p. 137).

It seems that this is exactly the course taken by Mrs Thatcher. For example, she made very good and effective use of cabinet reshuffles as a means both to promote Thatcher loyalists and isolate 'wets'. After her election victory in 1979, Mrs Thatcher had found herself at the head of a non-'Thatcherite' cabinet, and it stayed that way until at least 1981. She had been sure to appoint her supporters to the key economic departments however, and:

> During 1981 she gradually dismissed a number of dissenters from her
> cabinet, including Soames, Gilmour, Carlisle, and St John Stevas, and
> moved James Prior to the office of Northern Ireland. Later she
> dismissed Francis Pym ... and David Howell. She appointed
> newcomers like Parkinson, Brittan, King, Lord Young and Lawson,
> who were more supportive of her policies and owed their promotion to
> her (Kavanagh, 1991, p. 405).

It is also quite clear that Mrs Thatcher circumvented the cabinet, in two ways: first she held only about half the number of cabinet meetings held by her Labour predecessors (see eg Hennessy, 1986), and secondly, according to ex-Defence Minister John Knott for example, cabinet meetings were not so much where policy was decided as occasions when decisions reached elsewhere were formally endorsed (see eg Kavanagh, 1991, p. 405). In relation to these points Vincent is interesting, he argues that early on there were in fact two 'parallel Cabinets':

> one 'Thatcherite', running the economic ministries, and one Tory, running everything else. Since the two cancelled (each other) out, there was little point in seeking cabinet views, and accordingly they were not sought (Vincent, 1989, p. 284).

This may well have been the initial rationale behind Mrs Thatcher's style, she did seemingly come to make a virtue out of such a necessity however. It is well documented for example that such a bypassing of the cabinet intensified. Mrs Thatcher relied heavily 'upon her Policy Unit' and as the norm came to make decisions 'either in cabinet committees, bilateral meetings between herself and her advisers and the departmental minister, or high powered inter-departmental task forces of able Civil Servants reporting direct to No. 10' (Kavanagh, 1991, p. 406, see also Hennessy, 1986, p. 189).

Thus, Vincent's plea that her orientation towards (or rather, away from) the cabinet was a policy necessity rather than by choice or design seems rather flat. To bolster this argument Vincent nevertheless reminds us that Mrs Thatcher did not seek 'to build a White House. Indeed she rejected plans for a Prime Minister's department', and she also 'abolished the Think Tank'. These, says Vincent, were 'hardly the actions of a centralizer'. Again, Vincent asserts that Mrs Thatcher was merely interested in 'getting things done', and:

> The cabinet stopped things getting done. The long list of her defeats in cabinet is one reason why meetings of the full cabinet ... (were) kept to a minimum (Vincent, 1991, p. 188).

As I said, this is an interesting argument, but I think there is more within it to support the idea of Mrs Thatcher's centralizing tendencies than the contrary. If you are sufficiently politically committed to certain goals for example, it may well be justified to circumvent the cabinet when it proves to be an obstacle to the achievement of those goals; to argue that this does not represent a centralization of power is nonetheless crass in my view. Indeed, subsequently Vincent himself says 'For all her free market credentials, Mrs Thatcher is perhaps happier as a dirigiste'! He then goes on in this vein:

> She (was) the best manager the state industries ... ever had ... Somehow the command economy suit(ed) her... She ... not only manage(d) existing areas of state power, but ... also added to them. By means of the Manpower Services Commission ... she ... virtually nationalized youth - and ... outside the conventional Whitehall structure. For the first time the state ... accepted full reponsibility for the lives of all school-leavers. Quantitatively, this (was) the largest extension of the welfare state since the 1940s (Vincent, 1989, pp. 291-92).

Again then, Vincent seems actually to provide evidence for a centralizing ('dirigiste') Mrs Thatcher, despite what he has said earlier. In any case it is also clear that Mrs Thatcher established and maintained a level of Prime Ministerial 'supervision' over governmental departments far in excess of that of previous Prime Ministers. That is: 'in extending her surveillance of senior civil service appointments' and 'in making it clear to her colleagues that she expect(ed) to be consulted about virtually the whole range of ministerial activity' (King, 1986, p. 137), she further established a centralization of governmental power.

The (ab)use of Prime Ministerial prerogatives and the demise of cabinet government were of course bemoaned by Michael Heseltine on his resignation from the government on 9 January 1986. Heseltine, then Secretary of State for Defence, had walked out of a cabinet meeting as the culmination of a dispute over the future of the Westland Helicopter Company, and immediately charged Prime Minister Thatcher with unconstitutional behaviour. He asserted that he had been unable to defend properly the interests represented by his Department because Mrs Thatcher (favouring the pro-US position of Trade and Industry Secretary Leon Brittan), had curtailed proper discussion of the issue and had indeed prevented it from being raised at full cabinet. Heseltine's argument that government had become too centralized 'was taken up by a range of commentators':

> Sir John Hoskyns, once Mrs Thatcher's policy adviser, saw Whitehall and Westminster as an 'embattled culture' which could only be improved by serious attention to the machinery of government (Financial Times, 11 April 1986). Two books and a series of television documentaries by one of the most respected of Whitehall

commentators, Peter Hennessy, also ... came to similar conclusions (Gray and Jenkins, 1991).

But the very ambiguity of the 'outer limits' of Prime Ministerial authority made these charges of abuse and unconstitutional practices (epitomized by the Hitlerite Thatcher of TV's 'Spitting Image') impossible to substantiate. Again though, this is not evidence that a greater centralization of power did not take place, it indicates only that such could not be shown to be unconstitutional.

As has been found to be the case elsewhere, it should be mentioned that some contrary arguments can be advanced to challenge the view of Mrs Thatcher as a 'dirigiste' centralizer. Some have for example argued that - in one sense at least - Mrs Thatcher was a more responsive Prime Minister than previous ones. Such a view seems to underlie King's emphasis upon her 'people-orientated' approach to governing and to practical politics. Similarly King and others have pointed to an apparent abiding awareness within Mrs Thatcher of what others want. Indeed Norton has explained the fall in back-bench dissent during the period of Mrs Thatcher's governments, as compared with Heath's, in terms of Thatcher's communication skills in relation to her back-benchers (Norton, 1985). However, to recognize such skills and their effectiveness is not to agree that Mrs Thatcher was a responsive Prime Minister; 'listening' and acting in response to what one hears are not the same thing. I think both King and Norton would acknowledge that in so far as such behaviour formed part of Mrs Thatcher's style, it resulted from a series of strategic judgements, and the latter rather than the former determined Mrs Thatcher's policy responses. Thus she may have been a 'listening Prime Minister', she may even have given way on occasions when to persist would have led to defeat, but she was not a responsive Prime Minister; her 'concessions' resulted from tactical political judgements as to how best to achieve her ends (they were thus open to reversal as and when subsequent conditions would allow). In short, Mrs Thatcher was a Prime Minister who might have been designed for the elitist, top-down British political and governmental system.

Conclusion

This chapter first considered the constitutionalization of the Campaign for FOI, and showed parallels with the way that Radicalism and the Labour Party's Socialism - also contrary to the elitist nature of British government - were undermined and sanitized. Where the earlier chapters showed British Executive dominance to be underpinned by this country's elitist political tradition, in the present chapter the contemporary effects of this dominance were demonstrated. This was seen first in that government, rather than the Campaign for FOI, was enabled to determine the definition and applicability of FOI. This is particularly evident in relation to the Local Government (Access to Information) Act, but was clear throughout the consideration of the progress of parliamentary bills sponsored by the modern Campaign. The only legislative avenue open to the Campaign was the Private Members Bill procedure, and in both the earlier and latter parts of this chapter it has been shown that - without government support - there is virtually no chance of success via such a means. The Campaign can therefore be said to have been largely thwarted by the very imbalance between Executive - legislature relations that it set out to change. Thus the nature of the institutions and conventions of Britain's political and governmental system are shown to represent severe constraints upon reforming projects underpinned by contrary assumptions.

In the attempt to mitigate against these realities the Campaign sought to compromise, to make its demands - at least in the short term - essentially compatible with the governmental status quo. It thus pursued the limited bills strategy, both to demonstrate its 'responsibility' and in the hope that thereby the climate might become more favourable. In similar vein to the early Labour Party the Campaign thus sought to demonstrate its 'responsibility'. But as their strategy was similar to that of the Labour Party, so was the outcome: 'constitutionalization'. The only real progress made by the Campaign was in 'Low Politics' areas inconsequential to central government's 'High Politics' concerns.

The second part of the chapter turned to consider 'Thatcherism', as a radical governmental project compatible with the elitist nature of British government. Interestingly, like official secrecy, 'Thatcherism' too has been seen as an aberration, as a departure from British governmental norms. However, this was argued to be true only in relation to post-war norms, which were themselves aberrant in terms of traditional British government. 'Thatcherism' is therefore more accurately seen as the reassertion - or even an intensification - of the British political tradition. The chapter showed how this project of deep radical reform was in fact aided by its compatibility with British governmental norms, and how this compatibility enabled an even greater centralization of power and intensification of Executive dominance.

Some of the changes in the institutions and processes of British government having occurred since 1979 were identified, and a number of conclusions may be drawn. First, since Britain has always had a political and governmental system characterized by Executive dominance, there have been few moves towards greater domination of the legislature; long before Mrs Thatcher the British legislature had very limited power to constrain the Executive. Nevertheless, and secondly, there *have* been clear and significant attempts to further centralize power since 1979; this is particularly true in the areas of inter-governmental relations and government - interest group relations. Yet, thirdly, whilst the government has been able to introduce legislation, or take other action to centralize, it has not been able to ensure that its intentions have been (fully) realized. The area of inter-governmental relations again probably best illustrates both the attempts at further centralization and their incomplete success. Fouthly, although the centralization attempt is clear in the area of High Politics, government has been willing to allow - indeed has advocated and legislated for - greater participation in areas of Low Politics. Again, the historical and contemporary aspects of the present work come together most clearly in this regard when we consider the government's attitude to FOI.

The fifth and final conclusion that may be drawn, following from the above, is that Mrs Thatcher did not represent a break with the past, but rather she broke with the break from the past. As we have seen, the participatory strand of democratic thought has had little influence in terms of British governmental practice, except in the Collectivist and 'responsive' post-war period. The norms of this period are what Mrs Thatcher saw as 'corporatism' or 'creeping Socialism', and these were what she wanted to break with. Her determination that Britain's 'ungovernability' and government 'overload' must be ended, was the earliest definitive feature of 'Thatcherism'. To a large extent 'Thatcherite' policy, for example 'rolling back the state', embodied the idea that in order for government to do well what it *ought* to be doing it must shed the functions inappropriately accrued during the 'responsive' post-war era. Thus 'government must govern' equates with the reappropriation of proper 'responsible' British government. Mrs Thatcher's style of leadership was in fact an almost perfect embodiment of the Executive dominance and strong leadership which has characterized the British political tradition and is stressed within the British political system. It was perfectly consistent with the elitist top-down orientation which underpins the institutions and processes of British government. If not 'orthodox' this view is not unique, Johnson (1988), writing about parliament, has argued for example that:

> the governments headed by Mrs Thatcher since 1979 cannot be regarded as anything other than 'strong' in the traditional sense. They have been headed by a determined and even imperious party leader with a firmly, conservative view of the British parliamentary constitution. Her concern has been to pursue a wide range of substantive policy objectives, many of them involving radical economic and social change. To this end she has used the traditional institutions

in the traditional way, governing effectively and sometimes dramatically (Johnson, 1988, p. 165).

Thus, the watchword of the first Thatcher administration serves equally well to express the dominant elitist view of government and political representation in this country - 'There Is No Alternative'. Hence the triumph of elitism.

Notes

1. It should be mentioned here that many in the Campaign for FOI see the organization as still, if in the longer term, committed to achieving 'open government' and not just 'freedom of information'. When I questioned Maurice Frankel about this, having outlined to him the basis of the distinction, he said for example that in his view the latter aim was part of the strategy for achieving the former, more ambitious one:

> 'Freedom of information' is only a mechanism ... a bureaucratic legalistic procedure for obtaining information, the (ultimate) object is 'open government'. 'Freedom of information' is the only way (we can think of) of imposing this on a government that doesn't want it (interview with author, March 1986).

The Campaign's experience since Frankel spoke these words would however suggest that it is government that is continuing to be able to 'impose' their wishes upon the Campaign rather than vice versa. It is also true of course that many Labour Party members still see that party as 'ultimately' a vehicle for the transformation of Britain into a Socialist society. Only time will tell of course, but the weight of evidence seems to be against both of these propositions in themselves.

2. 'Secrets' is the Newspaper of the Campaign for Freedom of Information.

3. In relation to Mrs Thatcher's first government Bulpitt argues for example, that:

> ... this administration attempted to achieve a governing competence by reconstructing traditional Conservative concerns with centre autonomy in matters of 'high politics' (Bulpitt, 1986, p. 19).

4. It deserves mention here however, that the 'breaking of the post-war consensus by Mrs Thatcher' argument can itself be taken too far. Much of the material on the post-war consensus is far stronger on broad statements and grand generalizations than on detailed analysis. Indeed Bulpitt (effectively, if briefly) establishes this criticism, and Pimlott has developed a similar argument (see Pimlott, 1989). Also, whilst it is true that many elements of the post-war consensus have disappeared, it can also be demonstrated that processes leading to these changes were underway well before 1979, and owed as much (if not more) to structural economic changes as to political instigation (for an elaboration of such a position, see eg Marsh and Rhodes, 1992).

5. It should also be noted that I am not arguing that pre-war norms were 'Thatcherite' in terms of intra-governmental style; cabinet government rather than the 'prime-ministerial' variety can be said to characterize that period. My argument is that Mrs Thatcher reasserted and re-emphasized the 'responsible' rather than 'responsive' norms of the British political tradition, and that her style of intra-governmental relations was merely a consequence of taking that elitism and centralism to its logical conclusion.

6. As with other proposed constitutional changes such as an electoral system based upon proportional representation, a written constitution and bill of rights, it is indeed debatable as to what extent such a successful devolution would in fact effectively undermine traditional British government.

Conclusions

This work has sought to establish firstly something I feel is generally underappreciated: the narrow and elitist nature of the British political system. I have attempted not just to establish this however, but also to explain it, via the historical processes from which the British political system derived its specific character. I have therefore sought to emphasize the extent to which traditional British governmental practices are underpinned by (pre-democratic) elitist concepts of representation, and the notion of 'responsible' (rather than responsive) government. Further, I have sought to establish the capacity engendered within such a system for self-perpetuation and self-defence against challenges from a contrary, participatory direction. The reforms advocated by supporters of FOI in the contemporary period are underpinned by just such contrary ideas of democratic government. So too were the demands of Radicals of the eighteenth and nineteenth centuries, and the Labour Party of the early twentieth century. The main focus here has therefore been to study the conflict over such proposed reforms, and consider their outcomes.

In general, my method of analysis has highlighted the relationship between three distinct contexts: the institutional framework; its underlying theory and philosophy; and actual political practice. Through the identification of the 'negative/inhibitive' aspects of 'political culture' I have sought to make the failure of the historical challenges of Radicalism and the Labour Party more easily understandable. Equally, the contemporary durability of official secrecy in the face of the Campaign for FOI becomes more easily understood. My basic argument is therefore that any political project, policy proposal or constitutional reform at odds with the representational and governmental theories underpinning the traditional operation of British government, is thereby inhibited. The abandonment for example of the Labour Government and its 'unconventional' political programme by Ramsay MacDonald in 1931 - in favour of the 'Treasury othodoxy' - is thereby better understood; if some will no doubt prefer an explanation founded upon personal treachery. This general approach is however also amenable to a switch of emphasis; to how a radical political project *complimentary* to the elitist nature of British government is *facilitated*. Such a switch of emphasis is represented by considering the way in which 'Thatcherism' - reasserting the basic nature of British government - was aided by favourable rather than hostile ideological and institutional norms and practices.

As I outlined in the Introduction, any attempt to gain a proper understanding and explanation of such matters must take full account of both the theoretical complexities within a particular, micro issue (such as the challenge of FOI), and those within the macro nature of the British political system itself. But in addition, in certain instances, contingent and conjunctural aspects of the relationship between the two might be crucial, and this forms the intermediary level of analysis. For example, in relation to the successes and failures of the Campaign for FOI, the theoretical complexities of the (micro) issue were first analyzed; the distinction between 'freedom of information', and 'open government' demands was shown to be important. The non-differentiation of the two in the early FOI bills had led to government hostility and defeat, since the macro analysis shows the participatory concept of democracy underpinning FOI to be at odds with the elitist assumptions of the British political system. With the recognition of the compatibility of 'freedom of information' demands in 'Low Politics' areas, and the willingness of the Campaign to see 'open government' demands abandoned and 'High Politics' left to traditional British governmental norms, some success was achieved. However, understanding the actual mechanics of such successes required taking full account of the intermediate level of analysis. Here we saw that each successful bill had some specific - and different - advantages, though as a *class* of bills they all faced the same disadvantages.

Having begun with the emphasis on the contemporary and the micro, we then moved to the historical and the macro. The seemingly self-perpetuating 'Executive dominance' through which the participatory challenge of FOI was held at bay, was now shown to be an abiding feature of the British political tradition as a whole. The role of governmental office, whether performed by the Monarch alone, shared by Monarch and unreformed parliament, or exercised by an Executive drawn from the reformed parliament, showed a remarkable consistency despite the deep changes in the nature of British society over several centuries.

It was government's task to weigh the 'particular interests' in the search for policy in the interest of the whole nation: government and only government was arbiter of the 'national interest'. This consistency saw the tradition of strong, centralized, independent and initiatory government sustained. Indeed, British political and governmental conventions, including the nature of the Executive's accountability to parliament, the nature of parliamentary representation, and that of the electoral system, all reflect and support Executive dominance and the elitist tradition.

I have argued that the 'orthodox' pluralist/liberal approach to the analysis of the British political tradition fails to challenge - or even properly acknowledge - this 'top-down' elitist nature of British government. My critique has therefore taken a 'bottom-up' (popular participatory and accountable) perspective, and was most concerned with the challenges to the status quo from such a direction. It follows that, by contrast to the emphasis in the orthodox works upon for example the success of Liberalism, I was concerned with why Radicalism failed. It was in this context that the negative-inhibitive concept of political culture first emerged.

The inhibiting force of institutionalized political culture - the mutually supportive environment of theory and practice expressed in contemporary institutions and conventions of politics and government - becomes crucial in explaining the failure of a challenge to the existing order. This is a much broader concept of political culture than the 'passive-continuous' concept evident in the pluralist/liberal works, and valuable insights into the manner of the defeat of participatory challenges are gained via its consideration. Its role in inhibiting other than marginal change was clearly demonstrated in relation to Radicalism's defeat, but a number of contingent/conjunctural analytical factors were also identified. For example, Radical theory was shown to have been distinctly 'grey' in certain areas, lacking integration and internal consistency.

The relevance of the three analytical bases and the role of 'negative-inhibitive' political culture is perhaps most clearly brought out in the detailed consideration of the development of the Labour Party however. Here particular attention was paid to the process whereby the party's political and economic orthodoxies - initially representing a threat to the nature of British politics and government - came to be made compatible with traditional norms; the party was 'constitutionalized'. Again, flaws were shown within the Labour Party's political orthodoxy and its conception of Socialism. The confusion and conflation of 'labourism' and 'Socialism' was an important element in the emergence of key assumptions regarding the role and purpose of a Labour Government. Another crucial element was the gradual extension of the leadership principle within the party. Initially this was quite alien to labour movement traditions, but parliamentary convention and the 'constitutional realities' certainly aided its growth. Also some specific circumstances and conditions - which were neither inevitable nor derived straightforwardly from the context within which the Labour Party chose to operate - were shown to be important.

Thus (micro) analytical and theoretical weaknesses within the Radical and Labour projects, as well as the (macro) strength of the hostile institutionalized political culture, are each very important to the analysis here. Likewise, both in regard to the Labour Party's constitutionalization and subsequently in Collectivism's failure to transform the Liberal/Conservative institutional context, a number of contingent and conjunctural aspects at the intermediate level of analysis require consideration. Together, these account for the survival of the traditional institutional framework of British government, which is in turn important in relation to both the failure of Collectivism, and the subsequent return to a laissez-faire approach under Mrs Thatcher.

In regard to the failure of Collectivism, like the Labour Party's Socialism, it emerged within a Liberal/Conservative political consensus, and never transcended that basic institutional framework. The post-war consensus was nevertheless another challenge to the British political tradition, which was more successful than Radicalism or Socialism, and which certainly marked a break from previous norms. But it never amounted to more than a partial departure from the norms of the British political tradition, since the institutional framework within which it was operationalized remained appropriate to a laissez-faire economic and political individualist approach. The institutions and conventions of British government were therefore 'inappropriate' for a Collectivist approach. Some were aware of this inappropriateness, and sought to develop more appropriate means, as we saw when looking at the demands of the 'Keep Left' group of Labour MPs. But this challenge too was defeated, if by a new, Keynesian, orthodoxy.

Thus, as the Labour Party had adopted Socialism as 'policy' rather than as 'system', so Collectivism became the new 'responsive' norm of governmental practice: a new version of the 'national interest' emerged without disturbing the idea of it being government's prerogative to determine the 'national interest'. The failure of Collectivism requires a far more thoroughgoing economic analysis than has been offered here. But the inappropriateness of traditional British government to run such a system is certainly an important aspect of any such explanation; it was an institutional environment unfavourable to the concerns and needs of the post-war consensus. What is equally clear is that Collectivism's failure was in turn a key element in the rise of New Right thinking and the emergence of 'Thatcherism'.

In many important respects Mrs Thatcher's governmental style, as well as her philosophical orientation, represented a reassertion of the British political tradition; rejecting consultation and 'responsiveness', stressing instead strong decisive leadership and the independent authority of 'responsible' initiatory government. Thus Mrs Thatcher was able to bring about radical change (from post-war norms) with a minimum of institutional innovation. She was simply willing to utilize fully the opportunities presented within the basic framework of British government, to achieve her policy goals. The willingness to do this, as much as the policies themselves, marks 'Thatcherism' as a break with the post-war consensus. Mrs Thatcher's determination to overturn it has therefore been aided by the struggle being fought out on terrain favourable to such a project.

Given that we have seen that official secrecy fits happily with the underlying assumptions and established conventions of British government, the analysis of 'Thatcherism' as the reassertion of the British political tradition therefore aids the understanding of its recent significant tightening. Similarly, Executive dominance has been shown to be a definitive feature of British government, and 'Thatcherism' saw this trend intensified in areas beyond that of official secrecy; most notably in inter-governmental relations and in relations between central government and interest groups. Nor can it be said that the legislature's means of holding the Executive to account have improved. On the contrary as Robertson put it: 'ministerial responsibility has ceased to be effective' (Robertson, 1982, p. 34). The Fulton Report as long ago as 1966 virtually pronounced it dead in all but name, and the recommendations of the Franks Committee Report published in 1972 implicitly rejected its reality. Yet, as we have also seen:

> It is constitutional fictions like ministerial accountability and parliamentary sovereignty that are invariably paraded in opposition to proposals to increase citizens' legal freedoms (G Robertson, 1989, p. 130).

cabinet responsibility too has been shown to be at best a doctrine inconsistently applied and more usually employed to gag unhappy ministers and/or enforce centralized decision making even within the dominant Executive.

It is well known these days that parliamentary 'question time', whether for Prime Minister or as a supposed means of calling any other minister to account, has become largely meaningless. Leaving aside the huge restrictions on what kinds of questions can even be asked and the archaic procedures surrounding it, so many questions are 'plants' - serving no other function than to give the government opportunities to 'agree' that they are doing splendidly whereas the Opposition are simply awful - that the convention has fallen into disrepute. Even the reformed Parliamentary Select Committee System has been shown to be largely ineffective as a means of holding the dominant Executive to account. The *range* of scrutiny of the Executive has increased, the *amount* and *quality* of evidence that they are able to obtain has improved, they are taken *more seriously* by ministers and civil servants than in the past, but they seem not to have become *more effective* in their ability to scrutinize the Executive's decision making and hold it to account. I have in fact argued that the government's resistance to 'open government' in High Politics areas is based to a large extent upon the awareness that this would improve the effectiveness of parliamentary accountability; government does not want to be effectively held to account, and the present means of its 'accountability' have the advantage to it of being no less dominated by government that the legislative process itself.

In terms of Liberal-Democratic norms I would contend that Britain therefore stands out like the proverbial sore thumb. Rather than a system of proportional representation, we have the 'first-past-the-post' electoral system, because rather than the purpose of a General Election being to produce a representative legislature, it is to allocate the status of Government or Opposition to the contending parties. Having so determined this, rather than the separation of governmental powers, our Executive dominated system concentrates them; Government Vs Opposition rather than Legislature Vs Executive is therefore maintained as the definitive divison. This would be undermined by strong parliamentary accountability over the Executive, therefore such accountability is weak. Further, rather than popular sovereignty and the assumption that government's authority derives from the majority will, in Britain there is parliamentary sovereignty. In theory this is the rule of the people's *representatives*, which, given the dominant Burkean representational doctrine, is elitist in itself. But in effect, as we have seen, a British government is itself sovereign; it is its own authority. Consequently, in Britain government has traditionally defended individual 'freedoms', but has discretion as to the extent and the manner by which this should be done, in a way which would not be possible if there were a written constitution specifying citizens' 'rights', which government would be required to uphold and defend. Thus, rather than a citizens' 'right to know' backed by a Freedom of Information Act, there is the assumption that government, as arbiter of the 'national interest', has the right to release official information or not, as it sees fit.

The implementation of a Freedom of Information Act, proportional representation and a written constitution with a bill of rights would therefore change British government profoundly, but only to bring it more in line with Liberal-Democratic norms. The British government's hostility to closer political, economic and social integration within the EC can be seen therefore to be perfectly consistent with long-standing elitist political attitudes; the challenge now made from the external European dimension. Could it be that the interaction between internal and external forces for change may finally prove irresistible? It is my hope that it will, and my belief that Britain's future would be the brighter for it.

Bibliography

Almond, G. and Powell, G. (1966), *Comparative Politics*, Little, Brown, Boston.

Ashley, M. (1990), *The English Civil War*, Guild Publishing, Gloucester.

Ball, A. R. (1987), *British Political Parties: The Emergence of a Modern Party System*, Macmillan, London.

Barnes, T. (1980), *Open Up! Britain and Freedom of Information in the 1980s*, Fabian Society, London.

Bates, St. John, (1988), 'Scrutiny of Administration', in Ryle, M. and Richards, P. *The Commons Under Scrutiny*, Routledge, London.

Beer, S. (1982), *Modern British Politics*, Faber and Faber, London.

Beer, S. (1982), *Britain Against Itself*, Faber and Faber, London.

Benn, T. (1980), *Arguments For Socialism*, Penguin, Harmondsworth.

Benn, T. (1981), *Arguments For Democracy*, Cape, London.

Benyon, J. (1989), 'Ten Years of Thatcherism', *Social Studies Review*, Vol. 4, No. 5, pp. 170-178.

Birch, A. (1979), *Representative and Responsible Government*, George Allen and Unwin, London.

Birch, A. (1980), *The British System of Government*, George Allen and Unwin, London.

Branson, N. (1980), *Poplarism*, Lawrence and Wishart, London.

Bromhead, P. (1974), *Britain's Developing Constitution*, George Allen and Unwin, London.

Budge, I. et al, (1988), *The New British Political System*, Longmans, London.

Bulpitt, J. (1983), *Territory and Power in the United Kingdom*, Manchester University Press, Manchester.

Bulpitt, J. (1986), 'The Discipline of the New Democracy: Mrs Thatcher's Domestic Statecraft', *Political Studies*, Vol. 34, pp.19-39.

Burch, M. (1988), 'The British Cabinet: A Residual Executive', *Parliamentary Affairs*, Vol. 41, No. 1, pp. 34-48.

Burton, I. and Drewry, G. (1981), *Legislation and Public Policy*, Macmillan, London.

Butler, D. and Kavanagh, D. (1974), *The British General Election of February 1974*, Macmillan, London.

Chapman, R. and Hunt, M. (eds) (1987), *Open Government*, Croom Helm, London.

Claeys, G. (1989), *Thomas Paine: Social And Political Thought*, Unwin Hyman, London.

Coates, K. (ed), (1979), *What Went Wrong*, Spokesman, Nottingham.

Cockerell, M., Hennessy, P. and Walker, D. (1984), *Sources Close to the Prime Minister*, Macmillan, London.

Craig, F. W. S. (1975), *British General Election Manifestos 1900-1974*, Macmillan, London.

Crewe, I. (1988), 'Has the electorate become Thatcherite?', in Skidelsky, R. (ed), *Thatcherism*, Chatto and Windus, London.

Crouch, C. (1979), *The Politics of Industrial Relations*, Manchester University Press, Manchester.

Dahrendorf, R. (1985), *Law and Order*, Stevens, London.

Davies, A. (1981), *Reformed Select Committees: The First Year*, Outer Circle Policy Unit, London.

Dearlove, J. and Saunders, P. (1984), *Introduction to British Politics*, Polity Press, Cambridge.

Delbridge, R. and Smith, M. (eds) (1982), *Consuming Secrets: how official secrecy affects everyday life in Britain*, Burnett Books, London.

Doherty, M. (1988), 'Prime Ministerial Power and Ministerial Responsibility in the Thatcher Era', *Parliamentary Affairs*, Vol. 41, No. 1, pp. 49-67.

Douglas, J. (1989), 'The Changing Tide: Some Recent Studies of Thatcherism', *British Journal of Political Science*, Vol.19, part three, pp. 399-424.

Drewry, G. (1985), *The New Select Committees*, Oxford University Press, Oxford.

Drewry, G. (1988), 'Legislation', in Ryle, M. and Richards, P. (eds), *The Commons Under Scrutiny*, Routledge, London.

Eccleshall, R. et al, (1984), *Political Ideologies*, Hutchinson, London.

Englefield, (ed) (1984), *Commons Select Committees*, Longman, London.

Ensor, R. E. (1988), *England: 1870 - 1914*, Oxford University Press, Oxford.

Foote, G. (1986), *The Labour Party's Political Thought: A History*, Croom Helm, New Hampshire.

Gamble, A. (1988), *The Free Economy and the Strong State: The Politics of Thatcherism*, Macmillan, London.

Gilmour, I. (1977), *Inside Right: A Study of Conservatism*, Hutchinson, London.

Gray, A. and Jenkins, B.(1991), 'Administering Central Government', in Jones, B. et al., *Politics UK*, Philip Allan, London.

Greenleaf, W. H. (1983), *The British Political Tradition*, Vol. One: *The Rise of Collectivism*, Methuen, London.

Greenleaf, W. H. (1983), *The British Political Tradition*, Vol. Two: *The Ideological Heritage*, Methuen, London.

Hall, S. and Jacques, M. (eds), (1983), *The Politics of Thatcherism*, Lawrence and Wishart, London.

Hanson, A. and Walles, M. (1984), *Governing Britain*, Fontana/Collins, Glasgow.

Hennessy, P. (1988), *Routine punctuated by Orgies: The Central Policy Review Staff 1970-83*, University of Strathclyde Department of Politics, Glasgow.

Hewitt, P. (1982), *The Abuse of Power*, Martin Robertson, Oxford.

Hood Phillips, O. and Jackson, P. (1987), *Constitutional and Administrative Law*, Sweet and Maxwell, London.

Howard, A. (ed), (1979), *The Crossman Diaries 1964-70*, Hamish Hamilton and Jonathan Cape, London.

James, S. (1992), *British Cabinet Government*, Routledge, London.

Johnson, N. (1988), 'Departmental Select Committees', in Ryle, M. and Richards, P. *The Commons Under Scrutiny*, Routledge, London.

Kavanagh, D. (1972), *Political Culture*, Macmillan, London.

Kavanagh, D. (1987), *Thatcherism and British Politics*, Oxford University Press, Oxford.

Kellner, P. (1983), 'The lobby, official secrets and good government', *Parliamentary Affairs*, Vol. 36 (Summer '83), pp. 275-81.

King, A. (1975), 'Overload: Problems of Governing in the 1970s', *Political Studies*, Vol. 23, Number. two, pp. 284-296.

King, A. (1986), 'Margaret Thatcher: The Style of a Prime Minister', in King, A. (ed), *The British Prime Minister*, Macmillan, London.

Langan, M. and Schwarz, B. (1985), *Crises in the British State 1880 - 1930*, Hutchinson, London.

Leigh, D. (1980), *The Frontiers of Secrecy*, Junction Books, London.

Lichtheim, G. (1978), *A Short History Of Socialism*, Fontana/Collins, Glasgow.

Likierman, A. (1988), 'Information on Expenditure for Parliament: An Overview and Future Directions', *Parliamentary Affairs*, Vol. 41, Number. three, pp. 362-379.

Macintosh, J. P. (1962), *The British Cabinet,* Stevens, London.

Macintosh, J. P. (1970), *The Government and Politics of Britain,* Hutchinson, London.

MacKenzie, R. T. (1955), *British Political Parties,* Heinemann, London.

Mackie, K. (1984), 'Three faces of democracy and three missing persons; the Trade Union Act 1984', *Industrial Relations Journal,* Vol. 15, Number. 4, pp. 83-97.

Marsh, D. (1971), 'Political Socialisation: the implicit assumptions questioned', *British Journal of Political Science,* Vol. One, part three. pp. 453-61.

Marsh, D. (1989), 'British Trade Unions in a Cold Climate', *West European Politics,* Vol. 12, pp. 142-198.

Marsh, D. (1992), *The New Politics of British Trade Unionism: Union Power and the Thatcher Legacy,* Macmillan, London.

Marsh, D. and Read, M. (1988), *Private Members' Bills,* Cambridge University Press, Cambridge.

Marsh, D. and Rhodes, R. (1992), *Implementing Thatcherite Policies: Audit of an Era,* Open University Press, Milton Keynes.

May, A. and Rowan, K. (eds) (1982), *Inside Information,* Constable, London.

Michael, J. (1982), *The Politics of Secrecy,* NCCL, London.

Miliband, R. (1973), *Parliamentary Socialism,* Merlin Press, London.

Minkin, L. (1980), *The Labour Party Conference: A Study in the Politics of Intra-Party Democracy,* Manchester University Press, Manchester.

Mitchell, N. (1987), 'Changing Pressure Group Politics', *British Journal of Political Science,* Vol. 17, part four, pp. 509-517.

Morgan, J. (ed), (1981), *The Backbench Diaries of Richard Crossman,* Hamish Hamilton and Jonathan Cape, London.

Morton, A. (ed), (1975), *Freedom in Arms: a selection of Leveller writings,* Seven Seas Books, Berlin.

Norton, P. (1975), *Dissention in the House of Commons 1945-74,* Macmillan, London.

Norton, P. (1978), *Conservative Dissidents,* Temple Smith, London.

Norton, P. (1980), *Dissention in the House of Commons, 1974-79,* Clarendon Press, Oxford.

Norton, P. (1982), *The Constitution in Flux,* Martin Robertson, Oxford.

Norton, P. (1984), *The British Polity,* Longman, London.

Peden, G. C. (1988), *British Economic and Social Policy: Lloyd George to Margaret Thatcher,* Philip Allen, Oxford.

Pelling, H. (1982), *A Short History of the Labour Party,* Macmillan, London.

Pimlott, B. (1989), 'Is the Post-War Consensus a Myth?', *Contemporary Record*, Vol. 2, Number. 6, pp. 12-14.

Plumb, J. H. (1950), *England in the Eighteenth Century*, Penguin, Harmondsworth.

Ponting, C. (1985), *The Right To Know*, Sphere, London.

Ponting, C. (1986), *Whitehall: Tragedy and Farce*, Hamish Hamilton, London.

Ponting, C. (1989), *Secrecy in Britain*, Basil Blackwell Ltd, Oxford.

Punnett, R. (1976), *British Government & Politics*, Heinemann, London.

Read, M. (1988), 'The Shops Bill 1986', *Essex Papers in Politics and Government*, Number. 61, University of Essex, Essex.

Rhodes, R. (1988), *Beyond Westminster and Whitehall*, Allen and Unwin, London.

Rhodes, R. (1991), 'Now Nobody Understands the System: The Changing Face of Local Government', Mimeo, University of York.

Robertson, G. (1989), *Freedom, the Individual and the Law*, Penguin Books, Harmondsworth.

Robertson, K.G. (1982), *Public Secrets*, Macmillan, London.

Robinson, A. (1978), *Parliament and public spending*, Heinemann, London.

Rose, R. (1985), *Politics in England Today*, Faber, London.

Rose, R. (1989), *Politics in England: change and resistance*, Macmillan, London.

Travers, T. (1989), 'Community Charge and other Financial Changes', in Stewart, J. and Stoker, G. *The Future of Local Government*, Macmillan, London.

Vincent, J. (1989), 'The Thatcher Governments, 1979-87', in Hennessy, P. and Seldon, A. (eds), *Ruling Performance*, Basil Blackwell, Oxford.

Walkland, S. and Ryle, M. (1977), *The Commons in the '70s*, Martin Robertson, London.

Walters, P. (1989), 'The Crisis of Responsible Government: Mrs Thatcher and the BBC', *Parliamentary Affairs*, Vol. 42, No. three, pp. 380-398.

Watson, J. S. (1991), *The Reign of George III: 1760 - 1815*, Oxford University Press, Oxford.

Williams, F. (1950), *Fifty Years' March: The Rise of the Labour Party*, Odhams Press, London.

Williams, P. (1982), *Hugh Gaitskell*, Oxford Paperbacks, Oxford.

Wilson, H. (1974), *The Labour Government 1964-70*, Pelican, Harmondsworth.

Woodward, L. (1988), *The Age of Reform: 1815 - 1870*, Oxford University Press, Oxford.